T0374644

HISPANIC IMMIGRANT LITERATURE

JOE R. AND TERESA LOZANO LONG SERIES IN
LATIN AMERICAN AND LATINO ART AND CULTURE

HISPANIC IMMIGRANT LITERATURE

El Sueño del Retorno

BY NICOLÁS KANELLOS

UNIVERSITY OF TEXAS PRESS ⟡ *Austin*

All photos and illustrations are courtesy of Recovering the U.S. Hispanic Literary Heritage, University of Houston.

LIBRARY OF CONGRESS CATALOGING-IN-PUBLICATION DATA

Kanellos, Nicolás.
Hispanic immigrant literature : el sueño del retorno / by Nicolás Kanellos. — 1st ed.
    p.   cm. — (Joe R. and Teresa Lozano Long series in Latin American and Latino art and culture)
  Includes bibliographical references and index.
  ISBN 978-0-292-74394-6

  1. American literature—Hispanic American authors—History and criticism.   2. Immigrants' writings, American—History and criticism.   3. Hispanic Americans in literature.   4. Emigration and immigration in literature.   5. Immigrants in literature.   I. Title.
PS153.H56K35   2011
860.9'868073—dc22

First paperback printing, 2012   2011003822

FOR ALL THE IMMIGRANTS I GREW UP WITH AND
AS ALWAYS FOR MY LOVING WIFE, CRISTELIA,
AND MY BELOVED SON, MIGUEL JOSÉ.

CONTENTS

Introduction   1

CHAPTER 1. The Context of Hispanic Immigrant Literature   17

CHAPTER 2. An Overview of Hispanic Immigrant Print Culture   35

CHAPTER 3. The Dream of Return to the Homeland   52

CHAPTER 4. Nation and Narration   80

CHAPTER 5. Immigration and Gender: Female Perspectives   101

CHAPTER 6. Immigration and Gender: Male Perspectives   123

AFTERWORD. Life on the Supposed Hyphen   146

Notes   155

Bibliography   185

Index   195

HISPANIC IMMIGRANT LITERATURE

INTRODUCTION

IMMIGRATION HAS BEEN a basic reality of life for Latino communities in the United States since the nineteenth century. It has been not only a sociocultural reality but also a powerful determinant of the Latino or Hispanic vision of the world. The impact of successive generations of immigrants, originating principally in Mexico and the Caribbean but also in Spain and Central and South America, has left an indelible mark on the psyche of Hispanic minorities in the United States. Persistent immigration has also reinvigorated and even changed the cultural character of the Hispanic communities in this country. As Paul White has argued, "Migration, dislocation and ensuing marginality are some of the most important influences subverting long-standing beliefs in the linearity of progress and the stability of cultural identity, and that these have been determining influences on the inner conditions of contemporary humanity" (6). It is no wonder that one of the most important themes in Hispanic literature is immigration and that it has given rise to a specific type of literature while defining what it means to be Hispanic in the United States.

Like all themes that arise from the grass roots of society and permeate many aspects of daily life, the theme of the Hispanic immigrant in the grand Metropolis or the Colossus of the North first arises in the immigrant imaginary in oral lore as personal experience narratives and anecdotes and spreads with characteristic vernacular articulation to jokes, songs, and such popular theatrical forms as vaudeville. Long before literary works based on immigrant life appeared in books, Spanish-language newspapers began collecting and printing these jokes, anecdotes, and tales of misfortune of the greenhorns come to the Metropolis. It is not surprising that the first Hispanic novel of immigration, *Lucas Guevara*, by the Colombian writer Alirio Díaz Guerra, appeared in New York City in 1914, given that the city was one of the favored ports of entry of Hispanic immigrants at the beginning of the twentieth century. New York and other cities have continued to serve as bases for the launching of a continuous stream of immigrant literature in Spanish-language publication. Included among the many immigrant novels and plays that have appeared in the twentieth century are Conrado Espinosa's *El sol de Texas* (San Antonio, 1926, *Under the Texas Sun*); *Las aventuras de Don Chipote, o Cuando los pericos mamen* (*The Adventures of Don Chipote, or When Parrots Breast Feed*, Los Angeles, 1928) by Daniel Venegas; *La factoría* (published in 1925 in Guatemala, written in New York), by Gustavo Alemán Bolaños; *Trópico en Manhattan* (written in New York but published in San Juan, 1951), by Guillermo Cotto-Thorner; *La carreta* (The oxcart, debuted in New York in 1952, published in Río Piedras in 1961), by René Marqués; *El super* (New York, 1977), by Iván Acosta; *Odisea del Norte* (*Odyssey to the North*, written in Washington, D.C., and published in Houston, 1998), by Mario Bencastro; Roberto Quesada's *The Big Banana* (1998) and *Not through Miami* (2001) (both written in Spanish in New York but published in English in Houston); and Eduardo González Viaña's *El corrido de Dante* (2006, written in Oregon but published in English in Houston as *Dante's Ballad* [2007]). While most of these works were written by and deal with immigrants from nation-states abroad, Puerto Ricans were well on their way to producing an immigrant literature on the U.S. continent well before 1917, when U.S. citizenship was extended to them by Congress via the Jones Act—and, it might be said, they became internal migrants, not immigrants. Nevertheless, Puerto Rican authors in New York continued to live in communities dominated by other Hispanic immigrants, published works in newspapers and magazines targeted at Spanish-speaking immigrants of all nationalities, and projected an immigrant identity in their printed and oral literatures, until their community became the predominant Hispanic population in New York and surroundings beginning during the Second World War and fought for its rights as U.S. citizens;[1] from then on, the popular as well as the written culture began to adopt the characteristics of a native literature that eventually would produce the English-dominant Nuyorican writing of the 1960s and 1970s (see chapter 1).

All of the works cited above are tales about greenhorn immigrants who come to the big city to improve their lives—that is, to seek their fortunes in the land of opportunity—but who in the end become disillusioned by what the authors or their narrators see as the ills of

American society: oppression of the working class, racial discrimination, the underworld and the underclass culture, and a capitalism that erodes Hispanic identity and values, including family, religion, machismo, language, and culture. In this way, Spanish-language immigrant literature opposes and deconstructs the myth of the American Dream, as opposed to the reinforcement and celebration of the American Dream that usually appears in the English-language ethnic autobiography written by the children of immigrants, for example, Julia Alvarez, Oscar Hijuelos, Esmeralda Santiago, and Victor Villaseñor. In fact, Spanish-language immigrant novels are written by the immigrants themselves, not by their children, and their texts thereby take on additional historical authenticity. In contrast to these are the stories re-created from inherited family sagas or remembered from the time the authors themselves came to the United States as young children and became acculturated in the Metropolis.

Lucas Guevara initiates the ethos and structure that will be repeated in many of the works cited above:

1. A naive Hispanic immigrant filled with high expectations
   and fascinated by the advanced technology and progress of the
   Metropolis ultimately becomes disillusioned with the United
   States.
2. The greenhorn, not knowing sophisticated city ways, becomes the
   victim of numerous abuses by the authorities, petty criminals, and
   hucksters as well as by the bosses and foremen where he works.
3. The narrators reject the materialism and supposed superiority of
   the Metropolis and embrace essentialist Latino cultural values and
   identity, a reversal which eventually leads them to return to their
   homelands.[2] Those who remain in the Metropolis, as in *Lucas
   Guevara* and *La carreta*, will either die—poetic justice for their
   betrayal of national values and ideals—or, having been corrupted
   and transformed by the materialist, corrupt culture of the United
   States, will cease to exist as representatives of their nation. In *El sol
   de Texas*, for example, those who remain are compared negatively
   with the true Mexicans who return to the *patria*.
4. Often the plot of immigrant novels and plays is a vehicle for
   occasionally biting criticism of Metropolitan culture: the lack
   of ethical standards, the prevalence of racial discrimination, the
   rampant sense of superiority to Latinos and their culture, and
   a hypocrisy endemic among Anglos. The Metropolis is seen as

Babylon or Sodom and Gomorrah, and Anglos are the corruptors of Latino innocence. Their money perverts everything. The technological marvels of their advanced civilization destroy humanism, dignity, and respect. They consider the Hispanic immigrant as nothing more than a beast of burden, or *camello* (camel), on whose back the technological marvels are built. The immigrants compare themselves to the slaves of Babylon, Egypt, and the Old South. Their foremen are slave drivers.

5. Cultural nationalism prevails in these works, and it tends to protect and preserve the Catholic religion, the Spanish language, and Hispanic customs threatened with assimilation. At times, however, the severest criticism is reserved for Latinos who have adopted Anglo-American cultural ways and consequently are seen as cultural traitors. They are denigrated as *agringados* (gringoized), *renegados* (renegades), *pochos* (no longer Mexicans) and *pitiyanquis* (petit Yankees).

6. Frequently the American female comes to represent the Metropolis, its amoral sexuality and liberalism, its materialism and erotic attraction for Latino males, while Latinas often represent the immigrant's national values of family, religion, and culture, even the homeland. When Latinas become assimilated in these narratives, theirs is seen as the greatest betrayal of the nation.

Las aventuras de Don Chipote, o Cuando los pericos mamen (1928; *The Adventures of Don Chipote, or When Parrots Breast Feed*), by Daniel Venegas, perhaps one of the greatest novels of immigration despite its many formalistic flaws, seems to have risen from the rich wellsprings of oral tradition, where its basic plot, character types, and the argot of the "Chicanos," for whom it was written, already existed; all of these elements had made their way from the anecdotes and lived experience of *bracero* immigrants into the jokes, popular ballads (*corridos*), and vaudeville routines that became so popular in Mexican-American culture in the United States in the early twentieth century. The character types as well as their picturesque argot had developed in oral culture from the beginning of the twentieth century, if not before, and broke into print first in the local-color columns (*crónicas*) of Spanish-language newspapers published throughout the Southwest. In the weekly crónicas of such satirists as the Mexicans "Jorge Ulica" (Julio G. Arce), "Kaskabel" (Benjamín Padilla), "Loreley" (María Luisa Garza); the Cuban "Ofa" (Alberto O'Farrill); the Puerto Rican "Miquis

Tiquis" (Jesús Colón); "El Malcriado" (Daniel Venegas), who presented himself as a Chicano; and many others, the customs of Hispanic immigrants were habitually transformed into literary texts. The written literature of immigration in the Spanish language was not represented just by crónicas; hundreds of books of immigrant prose and poetry were also issued by publishing houses and newspapers. As in *Lucas Guevara*, Venegas's *Don Chipote* contrasts the United States with the homeland, which is presented as pristine and honest although unable to afford its native son the education and economic resources to sustain an adequate level of existence. The United States, while seen as the seat of great industrial and technological progress, is also a center of corruption, racism, and dehumanization, as in *Lucas Guevara*. Beyond mere local color in these novels is the depiction of the social environment in the United States, which unanimously is portrayed as corrupt and anti-Hispanic.

So far as the folk base of *Don Chipote* is concerned, there is a notable similarity between its plot, in which a character comes to the United States "to sweep the gold up from the streets," and that of several corridos, including *El lavaplatos* (The dishwasher). These two works coincide not only in the narrative structure of immigrating and working on the *traque* (railroad), but also in the attraction that the cinema and theater hold for their respective protagonists, their progressive disillusionment ("Adiós sueños de mi vida" [Good-bye, my life's dreams]), and their return to Mexico ("vuelvo a mi patria querida/más pobre de lo que vine" [I return to my beloved fatherland/poorer than when I left]). The message of *El lavaplatos* is just as unmistakable as that of *Don Chipote*: Mexicans should not come to the United States.

Qué arrepentido
qué arrepentido
estoy de haber venido.
* * * * * * * *

Aquél que no quiera creer
que lo que digo es verdad,
Si se quiere convencer
que se venga para acá.

[*How regretful*
how regretful
I am for having come.

* * * * * * * *

He who won't believe
that what I say is true,
is sure to be convinced
by coming straight here.]

The burlesque tone of *Don Chipote*, so characteristic of *El lavaplatos* as well as of the crónicas that Venegas wrote for his weekly satiric newspaper *El Malcriado* (The brat), serves to entertain the reader and soften the criticism of the socioeconomic and political realities on both sides of the border that forced the poor to leave their homeland and be exploited in the United States by slave drivers, *coyotes* (labor contractors), ladies of the night, and flappers, all of whom are personifications of the hostile, corrupt metropolitan environment. Venegas's tragicomic treatment of immigration was developed during years of writing and directing vaudeville reviews for the poorest classes of Mexican immigrants and of writing, illustrating, and publishing his weekly satirical tabloid. The author of *Lucas Guevara*, Díaz Guerra, on the other hand, was a medical doctor and a poet from his early, privileged days among the elite in Colombia. An intellectual and political activist, he found his way to New York as a political exile, expelled from both Colombia and Venezuela. He avoided the kind of grass-roots-based humor characteristic of Venegas, choosing to explore instead the mythic dimensions of exile and Babylonian captivity in New York. While Venegas chose *Don Quijote* as a metatext, Díaz Guerra found his inspiration in the Bible. In *Don Chipote*, the flappers (acculturated but Mexican, after all) represent acculturation and disloyalty to the homeland; in *Lucas Guevara*, the Eves are the American temptresses, personifications of iniquitous Yankee culture, who lure the protagonist into perdition and turning his back on Latin American religion and morality. While in *Don Chipote* social order is reestablished when Doña Chipota rescues her straying husband and brings him back to Mexico—for she represents the hearth and home and Mexican family and cultural values— Díaz Guerra's Hispanic Everyman cannot be rescued, for no salvation is possible after he has given himself over completely to Eve. Lucas commits suicide by jumping off the Brooklyn Bridge, a symbol at that time of Yankee technological and industrial prowess. Before plunging into the waters of the East River, however, his gaze falls upon the Statue of Liberty, the other representative of American culture, its freedoms and its welcome of immigrants. Díaz Guerra, however, reenvisions her as a monument to Libertinage, the totalizing feminine symbol of the United States.

Novels and plays of immigration are still being written today, and they employ formulas similar to those of the foundational works aimed at preserving the integrity of the immigrant psyche and culture. The genre will exist as long as Hispanics continue to come to the United States to better their economic circumstances and opportunities and as long as they struggle against changing their identities, the price to be paid for economic betterment.

HISPANIC IMMIGRANT LITERATURE DEFINED

Hispanic immigrant literature is the literature created orally or in written form by immigrants from the Hispanic world who have come to U.S. shores since the early nineteenth century. Among its characteristics are (1) predominantly using the language of the homeland; (2) serving a population united by that language, irrespective of national origin; and (3) solidifying and furthering national identity. The literature of immigration serves a population in transition from the land of origin to the United States by reflecting the reasons for emigrating, recording the trials and tribulations of immigration, and facilitating adjustment to the new society, all the while maintaining a link with the old society.

Unlike the literature of European immigrants to the United States, Hispanic immigrant literature generally does not support the myths of the American Dream and the melting pot, which hold that the immigrants came to find a better life and implicitly a better culture and that soon they or their descendants would become Americans, thereby obviating the need for a literature in the language of the old country. While Hispanic authors writing in English since the Second World War may have subscribed to these notions in order to get published or to achieve a broad readership, Hispanic immigrant literature in Spanish is not about assimilating or "melting" into a generalized American identity. In fact, the history of Hispanic groups in the United States has shown an unmeltable ethnicity, and, given that immigration from Spanish-speaking countries has been an almost steady flow from the founding of the United States to the present, there seems no end to the phenomenon at this juncture in history or in the foreseeable future.

In general, the literature of Hispanic immigration displays a double-gaze perspective: forever comparing the past and the present, the homeland and the new country, and seeing the resolution of these conflicting points of reference only when the author, characters, or the audience (or all three) can return to the patria. The literature of immigration reinforces the culture of the homeland while facilitating the accommodation to the new land. While fervently nationalistic, this literature seeks to represent and protect the rights of immigrants by protesting discrimination, human rights abuses, and racism. As much of this literature arises from or is pitched to the working class, it adopts the working-class and rural dialects of the immigrants. As mentioned above, among the predominant themes in the literature of immigration are the description of the Metropolis, often in satirical or critical terms, as in the essays of José Martí, Francisco Gonzalo "Pachín" Marín, and Nicanor Bolet Peraza; the description of the trials and tribulations of immigrants, especially during their journey to the United States and, once there, in being subjected to exploitation as workers and to discrimination as foreigners and racial others, as in Venegas and Espinosa; the conflict between Anglo and Hispanic cultures, ubiquitous in this literature; and the expression of gender anxieties in nationalist reaction against assimilation into mainstream culture, as in the crónicas of Arce. Immigrant authors often cast their literary discourse within the framework of an imminent return to the homeland or a warning to those back home not to come to the United States and face the disillusionment their narrators and protagonists have already experienced. Authors' stance of writing in order to warn their compatriots, when in actuality they are speaking to the immigrant enclave or community in the United States, helps them establish common cause and solidarity with their audiences. Writers and readers alike are in effect rendering testimony to the uninitiated, the potential greenhorns destined to suffer like the protagonists of these immigrant genres. These formulae and recurring themes depend on the underlying premise of immigrant literature: the return to the patria, which necessitates the preservation of language and culture and loyalty to the homeland. Almost invariably the narratives of immigration end with the main characters returning to home soil; failure to do so results in death, the severest poetic justice, as in *Lucas Guevara* in 1914 and, almost half a century later, in *La carreta*. Because of the massive migrations of working-class Mexicans, Puerto Ricans, Dominicans, and Central Americans during the twentieth century, much of immigrant literature is to be found in oral expression, folk songs, vaudeville, and other working-class literary and artistic expression. The immigrants' song of uprootedness and longing for the homeland can be heard in the Puerto Rican *décima* (a song with

ten-line stanzas and a sonnet-like rhyme scheme) "Lamento de un jíbaro." But the ultimate disillusionment and disgrace for the immigrant
is deportation, as documented in the plaintive refrains of the corrido
"Los deportados." Quite often the setting for immigrant literature is
the workplace: for example, on the streets walked by the door-to-door
salesman in Wenceslao Gálvez's *Tampa: Impresiones de un emigrado*
(1897), in the factory of Alemán Bolaños's *La factoría* (1925), or under
the burning sun in the agricultural fields, as in Espinosa's *El sol de
Texas* (1927). Domestic settings are also frequent, as in Marqués's *La carreta* (1952) and Acosta's *El super* (1977), both of which depict the inter-
generational conflict splitting U.S.-acculturated children from their
immigrant parents.

In fact, culture conflict of all sorts typifies this work, and from this
conflict arise some of its most typical characters, such as the agringados, renegados, and pitiyanquis, who deny their own culture to
adopt American ways. But more than any other archetype of American
culture, the predominantly male authors have chosen the American
female to personify the eroticism, immorality, greed, and materialism
they perceive in American society. The amoral Eve in a Metropolis
identified as Sodom described by Díaz Guerra evolved into the flapper
of the 1920s in Colón, Venegas, and Arce; this enticing but treacherous Eve led unassuming Hispanic Adams into perdition. These authors
place the responsibility for preserving Hispanic customs and language
and for protecting identity in the hands of Hispanic women and subsequently levy severe criticism at those who adopt liberal American
customs or dare to behave like loose women themselves. Such attitudes can also be seen in modern works like Marqués's *La carreta* and
Jaime Carrero's Nuyorican play *Pipo Subway no sabe reír* (Pipo Subway
doesn't know how to laugh, 1972).

I DEFINE IMMIGRANT literature here as literature written by immigrants in their native language.[3] It is neither a literature about immigrants written by native American writers nor the literature written by
the children of immigrants, that is, writers who were born or social-
ized in the United States and write in English, regardless of their representation of family memories and experiences or even their firsthand
accounts of coming to the United States as young children. Although
this may seem to be stating the obvious, the point bears repeating,
especially since the past few decades have seen the appearance of numerous books of theory and literary criticism that treat Hispanic and

Latino writers raised in the United States, including Alvarez, Sandra Cisneros, Cristina García, and even Tomás Rivera and Rolando Hinojosa, as immigrant writers. For example, Alpana Knippling, in the preface to her edited reference collection *New Immigrant Literatures in the United States: A Sourcebook to Our Multicultural Literary Heritage* (ii), attempts to treat all "hitherto marginalized literatures, specifically the Asian-, Caribbean-, and Mexican-American ones," under the rubric of "new immigrant," erroneously considering the works of authors of Asian-, Caribbean- or Mexican-American ethnicity as immigrant literature while discounting their hyphenated American status; even when the authors studied are the products of generations of U.S. citizenship or residence and even of an indigenous or territorial residence prior to the establishment of U.S. dominion over their families' lands, their works are regarded as immigrant literature. Knippling's multiauthored volume includes studies on García and Hijuelos, Alvarez, Pedro Pietri and Piri Thomas, Ana Castillo, Cisneros, and Luis Valdez: all of these writers are U.S. citizens, having been born or raised in the United States and predominantly using English as their preferred literary language. And although Francisco Ramírez, Rivera, and numerous others discussed in this book wrote important works in Spanish, there is no reason to approach the works and subject matter of these native-born writers under the rubric of immigrant literature. Knippling and her contributing essayists are not alone. Even so august a body as the Modern Language Association has recorded and broadcast on its radio show "What's the Word" round-table discussions erroneously regarding ethnic literature as immigrant literature, including Hispanic ethnic autobiographies and bildungsromans in the tradition of Mary Antin, Louis Adamic, Jacob Riis, Henry Roth, James Farrell, Philip Roth, Richard Wright, and numerous others.[4] In their book *In a New Land: An Anthology of Immigrant Literature*, Sari Grossman and Joan Schur go to the other extreme and include all literature in the United States, except the Native American, as immigrant literature. Such native-born Hispanic writers as Alberto Ríos and Richard Rodriguez are treated not only on the same continuum as true immigrants but also alongside foundational, canonical American writers. Granted, Grossman and Schur do make a distinction in their section "Transplantings" that Ríos and Victor Hernández Cruz are first-generation Americans, or "transplants," as they put it, but this distinction was not made in reference to the other native-born Latinos in their anthology.

Katherine Payant and Toby Rose, in their edited collection *The Im-*

migrant Experience in North American Literature, likewise do not include any writing by authors I consider true Hispanic immigrants. Both Cisneros and Judith Ortiz Cofer[5] figure in the collection. While acknowledging that Cisneros is "a second-generation ethnic"[6] (107) woman and treating her work as typical border literature, Payant nevertheless directs her attention to Cisneros's depiction of a Mexican immigrant female protagonist in the short story "Woman Hollering Creek" and questions whether her depiction comes from a first-world American stance (96–97)—what other stance would one expect from someone born in the heartland of the United States, educated in and writing in American English, espousing latter-day American feminism? Carmen Faymonville, in her essay on Cofer in Payant's and Rose's collection, concentrates on the biculturalism of Cofer and her character Marisol in *The Line of the Sun* (123–125). In truth, Payant and Rose do not claim this is immigrant literature but "North American[7] literature" in which immigrants appear, although one essay in the collection, Wendy Zieler's "In(ter)dependent Selves: Mary Antin, Elizabeth Stern, and Jewish Immigrant Women's Autobiography," does treat immigrant works written in languages other than English. In sum, Payant and Rose see little difference between literature written in English and that written in a language other than English. More important, in their introduction the two editors actually articulate their justification for studying second- and third-generation writers with roots in the Third World: "This reflects the fact that first-generation, non-English speakers of any nationality seldom produce much literature" (xxii). It is precisely this ignorance of an entire corpus of literature that led me to write this book.[8]

William Boelhower, in his development of formulae for the immigrant novel, fails to consider works written in languages other than English, not seeming to understand that quite often the linguistic-cultural stance of works written in other languages supports a national identity in opposition to the national myths of the United States and deconstructs the American Dream. In fact, Boelhower goes to great pains to identify the pursuit of the American Dream as the motive for most immigrant novels. The choice of writing in a language other than English is in most cases the most important literary and ideological choice an immigrant author can make. In addition to defining national identity, that choice defines audience and means of distribution and even the mode of consumption by an immigrant reader or one in the homeland. In addition, Boelhower does not discriminate between works written

by immigrants and those written about immigrants, leading him, therefore, to identify such works as Upton Sinclair's *The Jungle* and Willa
Cather's *O Pioneers* as immigrant novels (8–10). His motive (a respectable one), like that of Payant and Rose, is to promote the insertion of
immigrant literature into the canon. But what in fact these scholars
are accomplishing is demonstrating how the writers they study are
quite adept at continuing the conventions of U.S. ethnic autobiography, many of whose texts, especially those written in the early twentieth century, have achieved canonical status. Homi K. Bhabha considers
the role of the native language of immigrants in deconstructing the
national myths of the receptor nations:

> I must give way to the *vox populi*:—to a relatively unspoken tradition
> of the people of the pagus—colonials, postcolonials, migrants, minori-
> ties—wandering peoples who will not be contained within the *Heim*
> of the national culture and its unisonant discourse, but are them-
> selves the marks of a shifting boundary that alienates the frontiers of
> the modern nation. They are Marx's reserve army of migrant labour
> who by speaking the foreignness of language split the patriotic voice of
> unisonance and become Nietzche's mobile army of metaphors, meto-
> nyms, and anthropomorphisms. They articulate the death-in-life of the
> "imagined community" of the nation; the worn-out metaphors of the
> resplendent national life now circulate in another narrative of entry
> permits and passports and work permits that at once preserve and pro-
> liferate, bind and breach the human rights of the nation. ("DissemiNa-
> tion" 315).

In the scholarly works cited above there is very little recognition of
the role native language plays in the literature of immigration,[9] just as
there is very little recognition of the differing experiences and conflicting identities of the immigrants themselves and their U.S.-raised children, not to mention depictions of the migrants by outsiders.[10]

David Cowart, who in *Trailing Clouds: Immigrant Fiction in Contemporary America* tries to distinguish the literature created by immigrants themselves from that of first-generation ethnic writers (2–3)
and touches upon the "language question" (7), nevertheless focuses on
works in English by first-generation writers like Alvarez, García, and
Díaz.[11] His study of such authors leads him naturally to the following
conclusion: "The immigrant must deal with prejudice and homesick-
ness but eventually becomes empowered by a new American identity"

(7). As will be seen in the following pages, this achievement of a new "American identity," the so-called new Adam, is antithetical to the majority of the works written by immigrants in Spanish and, rather than challenging the *Heim*, or homeland, in Bhabha's conception, supports and reaffirms it. Moreover, in support of this position Cowart cites Don DeLillo's rejection or "transcendence" of his native language and background: "It occurs to me that this is what a writer does to transcend the limitations of his background. He does it through language, obviously. He writes himself into the larger world. He opens himself to the larger culture. He becomes, in short, an American—the writer equivalent of his immigrant parents and grandparents" (10).

How can so many scholars be so confused? After all, it is acknowledged that the black novel is written *by* African Americans and the Chicano novel, likewise, is written by Mexican Americans; why does the immigrant category seem to be so muddled, pliable, unspecific? And in the case of Hispanic or Latino literature, why is practically the entire corpus of works written in Spanish by immigrants ignored and, instead, works about immigrants written by native Hispanic authors emphasized? Is it that the majority of critics who treat Hispanic immigrant literature do not speak or read Spanish? Is it that the works of such authors as Alvarez, Cisneros, García, Hijuelos, Nicholasa Mohr, Thomas, and others seem so foreign to these critics, despite their following the well-worn path of American ethnic autobiography and the American Dream myth? To treat the works of these authors as immigrant literature is to distance them from the canon, to condemn them to Otherness, on the one hand, while proclaiming, on the other, that they represent a recent, new story. In thus positing the notion of new immigrants these critics negate the roots and history of the Hispanic communities in the United States that have produced an oral and a written literature for more than two centuries. To marginalize or, in some cases, ignore the literature written in Spanish on American shores, furthermore, is to condemn that language and its speakers to perpetual foreignness and estrangement from the American nation. In the nonrecognition of literature written and published by working-class Hispanics from the nineteenth century to the present a literary marginalization may be at work, perhaps because most of this literature was published by newspapers rather than by publishing houses and because one of its significant uses was to be read aloud to workers. In fact, the working-class stance, the use of the vernacular and references to workers' culture and working lives, and the representation of their worldview are some of the greatest strengths of Hispanic immigrant literature.

ORGANIZATION OF THIS BOOK

My book considers the most important aspects of the literature of Hispanic immigration, from its ideological stances to its themes and overall meaning, and takes into account both the written and oral record as well as published and unpublished documents. In chapter 1 I present a schematic approach to understanding the literature of immigration by contrasting its purpose, articulation, and trajectory with those of the literature of Hispanics or Latinos who write as natives of the United States and have rights of citizenship and of national ownership and identity. In addition to native and immigrant literature, Hispanic writings also emerge from political exile from Spain and Spanish American countries. Far from overemphasizing the rigidity of these three constant currents—immigrant, native, and exile—the schema will indicate that they are permeable, flexible categories that allow for writers to assume different, even contradictory stances as they create works for specific publics or because of diverse economic and political circumstances. Nevertheless, over time the literature of Hispanic immigrants has distinguished itself from the other literary manifestations of Latinos in very important and salient ways.

To further situate the literary production by immigrant writers, I offer in chapter 2 an overview of print culture developed by Spanish-speaking immigrants from the nineteenth century to the present, highlighting the principal publishers, types of publications, and audiences addressed by the immigrant press. The cast of characters, that is, publishers and writers, has been ethnically and ideologically diverse, even while the motives for publication over almost two centuries have remained similar. Theoretically, therefore, one could compare the newspapers issued in Los Angeles and New York today with those published in San Francisco and New York during the mid-nineteenth century. Colombian, Salvadoran, Mexican, and other Hispanic immigrant writers and composers today produce works with characteristics similar to those of artists in the early twentieth-century periods of large migration and labor exploitation, phenomena that are being repeated today. Nevertheless, precisely how immigrant literature has evolved through the twentieth century and into the twenty-first will become clear, even as today's writers repeat forms and meaning without ever having read the earlier literature—although the same cannot be said about their never having heard the lore of earlier immigration, which lives on in song and tale.

Chapter 3 is an in-depth discussion of the explicitly articulated reason for creating immigrant texts: to convince readers or listeners to return to the homeland before they lose their identity in the United States, where the pressure to adopt materialistic and inhuman values is overwhelming and discrimination and poor treatment of immigrants are widespread. As such, the ideological underpinning for this literature is a deconstruction of the myths of the melting pot and the American Dream. The literature is counterhegemonic and nationalistic to the core. Nevertheless, over time and despite its resistance to hybridization, immigrant literature does change in its attitude toward majority culture in the United States: such writers as the Puerto Rican Guillermo Cotto-Thorner, the Mexican Teodoro Torres, and the Peruvian Eduardo González Viaña diverge from the conventional call for a return to the homeland as well as from the imperative to reject the Metropolis wholesale.

In chapter 4 I examine the nation-building mission of immigrant literature. By considering the theories of Homi Bhabha, Anthony Smith, and others, I decipher the codes embedded in the literature as part of the writers' desire to write the nation, whether as the geographic homeland or as a deterritorialized national space in the receptor land. I trace how the literature has evolved from a simple identification of culture and identity with the geography of the nation-state to positing such alternatives as hybridity and utopias as separate from either the homeland or the immigrant colony within the bounds of the receptor country, thus destabilizing both the sending and receiving nations. The chapter ends with a consideration of a novel, *El corrido de Dante*, which while essentially a novel of immigration nevertheless inverts nationalistic ideologies, making of the United States the destined homeland for Latinos.

The literature created by immigrant women and their perspectives on gender and nation is taken up in chapter 5. I analyze the development of a conservative feminism among female immigrant writers, who often wrote works that went beyond national concerns in an attempt to create an international sisterhood. The differences as to their motives for relocating to the United States and their social class identification will also be studied in their understanding of gender and nation. Their works, which represent a very small minority of crónicas,

essays, plays, and novels produced and published in the early twentieth century, contrast starkly not only in number but also in quality of
representation of women in works created by immigrant men, especially as they imagined women as central to engendering and sustaining the nation. I consider male perspectives on gender in chapter 6,
particularly as male cronistas and novelists, from a position of power
within the immigrant enclaves, sought to maintain traditional gender
roles. A crucial aspect of preserving Hispanic identity, this continuity
was seen as being threatened by the formidable pressure to assimilate
to American culture. Within the cultural struggle, as defined by these
male writers, women's bodies, social participation, and freedom to
define themselves were special sites of conflict.

The afterword briefly summarizes the conclusions arrived at in the
book and explores texts that seem to problematize the theses about
Hispanic immigration literature I put forward. A specific case will be
treated: that of the writer Gustavo Pérez Firmat, an American citizen
who came to the United States as a preteen and who rejects identifying himself and his writing either as immigrant or native, preferring to
consider himself an exile and his texts as products of the exilic experience. His case brings into high relief the differences among the various
literary positions of Hispanic writers in the United States—as natives,
immigrants, and exiles—and additionally reveals the basis for this extensive introduction: the tendency to confuse American ethnic autobiography for the literature created in Spanish by Hispanic transmigrants.

CHAPTER I

THE CONTEXT OF HISPANIC IMMIGRANT LITERATURE

Hay algo que no se hunde en los naufragios, que no vacila ni cae en los terremotos, que no se carboniza en los incendios, y ese algo inmutable y eterno, es el alma de la Patria, siempre lista a levantar a los caídos, a perdonar a los pecadores, a consolar a los hijos que por encontrarse ausentes, no se pueden refugiar en su regazo maternal. — NEMESIO GARCÍA NARANJO, *MEMORIAS*

TRANSNATIONALISM IS A concept developed by social scientists in the 1990s in order to understand the life and culture of people moving from one place to another, especially during the latter part of the twentieth century. The concept is often linked to another somewhat amorphous concept, that of globalization or the creation of a global economy that has the effect of uprooting populations. According to Linda Basch, Nina Glick Schiller, and Cristina Szanton Blanc, the people they call transmigrants participate in the nation-building projects of their land of origin and that of their receptor land, where they are often considered immigrants or ethnics (45–46). The concepts of transnationalism and transmigrants depart from earlier postulations that saw immigrants as people who gave up their land of origin in order to settle permanently in the host country — a popular concept extrapolated from the settlement patterns of earlier European immigrants to the United States, who were subjected to the pressures of the melting pot and the American Dream. Transnationalism challenges the earlier concept of assimilation to the host culture, as related to these two nation-building American myths, in favor of a model that goes beyond the limits of political and geographic borders, languages, and national allegiances.

These concepts are vital in the study of Latino literature, not only because the United States has been a destination of transmigrants from Spanish America and Spain since the early nineteenth century, but also because the geographic and political borders of the United States expanded at various times to incorporate Spanish-speaking peoples who likely felt a closer relationship with the peoples of Spanish America than with the American mainstream and its national imaginary. In fact, thousands of archival documents, some eighteen hundred books, and twelve hundred periodicals gathered by the Recovering the U.S. Hispanic Literary Heritage Project amply demonstrate how, by the end of the colonial period, the Hispanic peoples living north of the Rio Grande prior to and after U.S. expansion southward and westward were never cut off from communications and intercourse with the rest of the Spanish-speaking world.[1] This world and its pan-Hispanic imaginary provided the history, literature, and symbolism to Latinos in the United States in their construction of national identities, even if those identities were to be seen as existing within the American nationalization paradigm. The project's documents, especially those written or published in Spanish, demonstrate how the flow of literary discourse went northward and southward as well as across the Caribbean and the Atlantic.

These realities call into question certain premises asserted by academics in the past thirty or forty years. Among these are the Chicano movement's notion that populations in the Southwest were bereft of a written tradition and literature and therefore the academy needed to focus on the collecting and study of oral lore; and that Puerto Rican and Cuban letters in the United States are a recent phenomenon, intimately tied to the post–Second World War diasporas brought about by economic and political disruptions;[2] and that Hispanic communities in certain geographic areas of the United States are ethnically homogeneous and accordingly the literature and culture of each group can be studied in isolation. Other premises reign today and must be examined, such as those relating to English or Spanish language preference, what constitutes literary creativity, and how political discourse and literary creativity relate to each other. Most of all, the segregation of immigrant literature from Chicano, Nuyorican, and Cuban-American literatures must end, for these literatures are all intimately connected to transmigrant culture and its literary expression; they must be seen on the continuum of transnationalism.

NATIVE HISPANIC CULTURE

I want to propose a schema to illustrate the transnational dynamic of Latino literature from the 1800s to the present. The schema relies on my observation of three general trajectories of Latino expression in the United States since the 1800s. The first principle to merit discussion is the existence of a Hispanic native culture and identity which developed among the descendants of the Spanish, Hispanicized Native American, Hispanicized African, mestizo, and mulatto settlers under Spain and, later, Mexico. These people inhabited the areas stretching from Florida to Louisiana to Texas, the Southwest, and the West that would later be incorporated into the United States. The literary expression created by these groups through the generations presents a common stock of perspectives, whether one talks about the Isleños in Louisiana, the Floridians at the time of the U.S. purchase of Florida, or the Californios and Tejanos newly subjected to Anglo-American political and cultural domination after 1848, the end of the war with Mexico. These perspectives include (1) an identity or sense of place with geographic location; (2) a sense of history rooted in the Hispanic past; (3) a growing awareness of racial and cultural difference and resistance to assimilation within the new Anglo-Protestant majority overwhelming the native populations; (4) a sense of becoming a dislocated and oppressed minority within the new political, judicial, and economic arrangements resulting from defeat in war or being literally purchased by the United States; (5) despite all of the above, a sense of entitlement to civil and cultural rights, rights conferred by treaties and by American citizenship. Most of these ideas were forged during the late colonial period, before U.S. ascendancy, but certainly under the perception of threat from the expanding Anglo-American empire during the first decades of the nineteenth century. This colonial base became the bedrock for Hispanics in the United States considering themselves natives and assuming characteristic stances. In addition, texts generated by the descendants of these groups and by Hispanics raised in the United States or naturalized as citizens also display these characteristics.

THE CULTURE OF ECONOMIC AND POLITICAL REFUGEES

On the base of colonial/native culture and attitudes, the culture of economic refugees, one type of transmigrant, and that of political refugees, another type of transmigrant, planted themselves and grew, repeating certain patterns of thought and interaction, one with the other, from the beginning of the nineteenth century to the present. These economic and political refugees forged temporary and permanent relationships with native Hispanics and the American mainstream and also with their countries of origin. For the most part they settled among existing populations of Spanish speakers, often native Hispanics with a long history in the United States. Because of the geographic proximity of the United States to their lands of origin and because of economic and political circumstances, most seriously the U.S. interventions in their homelands, the flow of Hispanic transmigrants to the United States has been almost uninterrupted since the early nineteenth century. And with each wave of arrivals, newer, more up-to-date versions of culture from the lands of origin interacted with the Hispanic native culture in the United States, a phenomenon that continues to this day, perhaps now even more powerfully than ever owing to new technologies of travel and communications. This is not to say the native Hispanic populations were merely receptors of more advanced or more evolved culture from Argentina, Cuba, Mexico, and Spain. At each step it can be shown how advanced technology in the United States worked to the benefit of native Hispanic populations—as well as that of the transmigrants—in delivering their perceptions and even imagined nationhood to Spanish America.[3] Books have been written, for instance, on how Cuban nationhood was forged in the nineteenth century, not on the island but in the native and transmigrant communities of Key West, Tampa, and New York.[4] And while the dream of a united Spanish America may have originated with Simón Bolívar, countless native and transmigrant writers and activists from the late nineteenth century on have furthered this dream from the shores of the United States. And calls for solidarity of Hispanic peoples from the U.S. Southwest to Tierra del Fuego in confronting the Colossus of the North were issued long before José Martí's "Nuestra América" (1891) by such essayists as Francisco Ramírez in Los Angeles.[5]

In reviewing the schema and the accompanying chart, one must note there are two types of transmigrants important to this book: the economic refugee and the political refugee. Strictly speaking, in my treatment an immigrant is an economic refugee: someone who leaves the home country because its economy can no longer sustain him or her or the family and moves to a land in search of an opportunity to work and earn a living. Immigrant texts reveal, in part or in whole, the conditions for leaving the homeland, the immigrants' exploits on leaving and arriving in the United States, and their experiences while looking for and finding work; the texts reveal also the reflections of the immigrant narrators or protagonists, especially their desire to return to the homeland. The texts of political refugees, whom I designate as exiles, are usually produced by authors who have been persecuted for political reasons, were exiled or had to leave the homeland for fear of imprisonment, a death sentence, or losing their privileged social position or comfortable economic status. The schema does not account for texts of psychological or cultural exile but only those that express criticism or reveal ideological stances that would be dangerous to articulate in the homeland. These exilic texts often reveal an obsession with the internal politics of the homeland, often condemning the current regime there and expressing a rationale for effecting political or social change; ultimately, the political refugee dreams of returning home when political change has made it safe to do so.[6] Children born in the United States to immigrants and exiles are citizens of the United States and add to the native population; thus the texts of natives continue to grow and evolve with each generation. As a result, the views of immigrant and exile run counter to the American Dream myth, specifically the view that immigrants come to the United States to stay in order to benefit from the economic opportunities and upward mobility the country affords those who adopt its values, work hard, and persevere; the traditional or mythic view is that immigrants come or should come to leave behind their undemocratic governments and inferior culture. However, the majority of Hispanic texts, from the nineteenth century to the present, center not on an American Dream, but on a dream of return to the homeland. Whether the dreamed-of return is ever realized in the life of the authors or the community should not be of concern to the literary critic; what is of concern is the imaginary constructed in and by these texts and the impact they may have had in forging Hispanic culture in the United States while also defining a relationship with a specific homeland or the Hispanic world in general.

While it may be tempting to assign native, immigrant, or exile status to particular writers and communities, the schema more accurately relates to the texts writers generate and the narrative stances they assume with regard to the United States and the land of origin. An exiled writer is quite capable of writing from the point of view of an immigrant in one instance and from that of a political refugee in the next. Likewise, in some texts an immigrant may confront life in the grand U.S. Metropolis, while in the next he may represent his culture

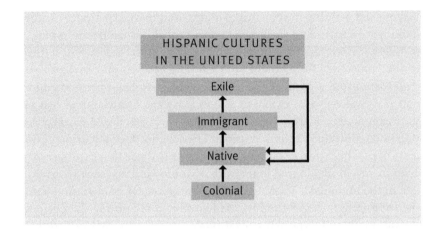

as exiled, as in *El México de Afuera* (Mexico abroad), that is, a Mexican colony existing outside of Mexico; and in another he may assume a native posture because, after all, as in the case of Adolfo Carrillo, he has lived in the United States for more than thirty years and become a voting citizen.[7] Ramírez, born and educated in California and trilingual (he spoke French, too), wrote as a native Californian while in Los Angeles but went into exile in northern Mexico, where he experienced the dislocation and uprootedness of the political refugee; he returned to California, where he worked for the San Francisco immigrant newspapers *La Voz de México* (The voice of Mexico) and *El Nuevo Mundo* (The new world).[8]

Below is an outline of the schema and an analysis of each of the categories (see table 1.1).

1

Native texts reveal an identity with the geographic location in the United States. There is no question of return to a homeland; this is the homeland. This attitude is as true of the Californio narratives and Tejano autobiographies of the nineteenth century as it is of Nuyorican and Chicano literature today. In fact, such texts as Rolando Hinojosa's Klail City Death Trip Series evoke the culture of the first Spanish-speaking colonists of the Rio Grande Valley in the eighteenth century and trace its development to the present. Immigrant texts created by immigrants, not by their progeny, serve as a bridge from the old country to the new. All immigrant texts have an implicit binary of contrast-

Table 1.1. Textual Characteristics of U.S. Hispanic Literature

Native	Immigrant	Exile
1. Sense of place in U.S.	A bridge from old to new country	Only relates to the homeland
2. Remain in the U.S. as citizens	Dream of return to the homeland	Return to the homeland when the political situation has changed
3. Protest injustice and effect cultural change in U.S.	Desire to preserve the culture of the homeland while living in the U.S.	Does not exhibit or support cultural change
4. Struggle for civil and human rights and against racism	Struggle for human rights and labor rights. Protest racism and exploitation	Protest politics in the homeland, colonialism, dictatorships, etc.
5. Working-class posture/ popular culture/minority consciousness	Working-class culture of the majority versus bourgeois posture of the minority of immigrants	Elite culture
6. Cultural synthesis, hybridization, and new identities and home spaces: Aztlán, Loisaida, etc. A new esthetic	The illusion of cultural purity, the colony as temporary: Little Mexicos, Little Havanas, and Little San Juans	Cultural purity: exile as Babylonian captivity, the homeland as Paradise Lost. Disillusionment
7. Culture conflict and cultural nationalism	Nostalgic and conservative nationalism	Political/revolutionary nation building
8. New, hybrid literary characters: Pachucos and Vendidos	Character types: the greenhorn, the flapper, the *agringado*, the *pocho*, the *pitiyanqui*	Heroes, epic and tragic figures, dictators, revolutionaries, and counterrevolutionaries
9. Themes: identity crisis, language and culture, race-class-gender, community	Themes: the Metropolis, the family, labor exploitation	Themes: political injustice, authoritarianism, etc.
10. Bildungsroman, autobiography	Picaresque narratives, road stories	Novels of the revolution, epic dramas and polemical treatises, editorials, and essays

ing the land and culture left behind with those encountered in the new land, including physical and cultural referents as well as language, religion, landscape, and a host of other markers. Exile texts are usually directed to the homeland, in expectation of effecting change or waiting for change to occur in the homeland.

2

Native texts reveal an awareness and acceptance of major American beliefs; they position themselves as American, although perhaps from a minority or marginal perspective. Immigrant literature promotes a return to the homeland and, in so doing, is antihegemonic and rejecting of the American Dream and of the melting pot. Immigrant literature, from the first immigrant novel, Alirio Díaz Guerra's *Lucas Guevara* (1914), to Daniel Venegas's *Las aventuras de Don Chipote* (1928) to René Marqués's play *La carreta* (1952), proposes return as the only solution to dying physically or culturally, that is, losing one's identity and personality in the Metropolis. In addition, immigrant texts often assume the position of speaking to readers in the homeland, warning them not to come to the United States, that the mythic streets of gold are really paths to modern wage slavery, indebtedness, and loss of identity. Exilic texts often see themselves as engaged in the battle to change the governmental order in the homeland and are often not concerned with politics and culture in the United States. As soon as their political cause has prevailed or there is amnesty, the authors plan to return home and end their exilic status.

3

Positioned as a literature of citizens with civil rights, native texts protest the discrimination, marginalization, and dispossession of Latinos in the United States. In addition, these texts exemplify a desire to reform the national culture and make it more equitable and accepting of linguistic, cultural, and religious differences. Immigrant texts promote an ideology of a Latino colony within the United States, one which must preserve the language, literature, and culture of the homeland so that upon return the transmigrants can resume the life they left behind. Immigrant texts often highlight and demonize symbols and representations of American culture, such as the Metropolis itself, capitalism, and social mores that represent threats to their family, reli-

gious, and societal arrangements, especially as related to the liberalized lives of women and the incursions of Protestant conversions of
Hispanic Catholics. During the early twentieth century, for instance,
the attacks on American flappers were equally vitriolic in works by
the Mexican Julio B. Arce, the Cuban Alberto O'Farrill, and the Puerto
Rican Jesús Colón. (As Colón assumed a more native position and
began writing in English, his attitudes toward American and Latina
women also became more liberal.) Exilic texts are not very concerned
with American social arrangements other than to see them as foreign
and very strange, a standpoint consonant with their metaphor of sojourn in Babylon. Their only version of culture is the one left behind
in the homeland; their imagined nation can be static, having become
frozen in time beginning with the moment of exile, or dynamic, envi-
sioning a completely new and liberalized social order or utopia. Culture
change, inevitable in the homeland, is rejected as deleterious and inauthentic in their imagined community. This attitude was taken to an
extreme for decades by Mexican exiled texts created during the Revolution; they envisioned the México de Afuera as the true Mexico and
the culture in the homeland as some deformed and degraded version of
the national culture.[9]

4

As citizens, Latinos are entitled to civil rights protected by the Consti-
tution, and they do not suffer the threat of deportation if they protest
inequities or injustices. Their texts reveal these entitlements as well
as others accruing to citizens. This empowers authors to use texts in
the battle to reform society and force it to live up to the principles of
equality and protection under the law which are codified in the national charter. Immigrants or economic refugees, whether documented
or not, do not feel they have the rights of citizens, and their texts, instead of protesting the lack of civil rights and exposing themselves to
deportation or further persecution, protest *in Spanish* the exploitation and oppression in industry and discrimination in the society. This
stance of marginality and implicit protest are evident from *Don Chipote* to Mario Bencastro's *Odisea del Norte* (1999). In addition, many
economic refugees worked historically in railroad construction and
maintenance in the Southwest, steel mills in the Midwest, tobacco factories in Florida, and manufacturing in the Northeast. In the late nineteenth and early twentieth centuries they became advocates of unions

as well as students and promoters of anarchism, socialism, and communism. Some were arrested, deported, and imprisoned for long terms. Many of their anarchist and radical texts eschewed nationalism in favor of uniting the working classes and revolutionizing society around the world. The workers' texts themselves were used for these purposes, from those published by the Mexican Villarreal sisters to the Sephardic Daniel De León to the Puerto Rican Luisa Capetillo to Luis Valdez during the Chicano movement.

Exilic texts are often polemic, attacking the government in the homeland and protesting against the colonial administration, dictatorship, and totalitarianism in the homeland; the numbers of these texts read like a political history of Spain and Spanish America, with attacks on the king of Spain in *El laúd del desterrado* (The lute of the exiled, 1856), to attacks on Francisco Franco in Leopoldo González's *Abajo Franco* (Down with Franco, 1937) and Lirón's *Bombas de mano* (Hand grenades, 1938), to protests against the regimes of Augusto Pinochet, the Argentine generals, and, in Ariel Dorfman's *La muerte y la doncella* (*Death and the Maiden*, 1992) and Tomás Eloy Martínez's *Santa Evita* (1995), Evita Perón. A subset of the texts is produced by writers who have been persecuted in the homeland for what the regime considers deviant sexual activities or attitudes, thus leading their authors to take political refuge abroad, where supposedly they will encounter a more tolerant reception. The Cuban expatriate author Heberto Padilla is a case in point.

5

Owing to what historians consider the proletarization[10] of the native Hispanic population of the Southwest with the advent of the Anglos in the mid-nineteenth century and to the overwhelmingly working-class culture of the majority of the economic refugees from the Mexican Revolution and the Puerto Rican and Central American diasporas in the twentieth century, the majority of native and immigrant texts and oral literature has represented a working-class perspective. These works exhibit an attendant reliance on oral and folk modes of transmission as well as on what Walter Ong calls secondary and residual oralities in written texts (37–57). Not only the Mexican *corridos* and the Puerto Rican *décimas* of immigration, but also the Tampa cigar rollers labor agitprop plays, such as "Vivan las Caenas" (1917), and Depression-era vaudeville sketches like Netty and Jesús Rodríguez's "Me voy pa'

México" and "Una mula de tantas," as well as the novels of immigration mentioned above, explicitly display working-class language, sensibility, and organizing ideology. Chicano and Nuyorican writers from the 1960s through the 1980s would echo these sentiments.

From the texts of José María Heredia and Félix Varela to the writings of Reinaldo Arenas, Dorfman, and Eloy Martínez, the literature of exile has been the product of cultural elites whose education and societal privileges in the homeland resulted in their texts standing as representatives of Spanish-language purity (*casticismo*), canonical European referents, and, at times, as in the case of the Porfirio Díaz regime in exile, a disdain for the working class and the racial inferiors (economic refugees) of their homeland now sharing their exile. It was often these elites who provided cultural products, such as popular theater, newspapers, and even books; it was they, too, who often promoted to the working classes—*las clases populares*, in their words—the idea of a national culture in exile alongside their propaganda against the regimes in power in the homeland.

6

From the 1800s to the present, native Hispanic texts have been written predominantly in Spanish; however, there have always been works written in English—today more than ever.[11] Since the late nineteenth century, native Hispanic texts have been synthesizing Latino and Anglo-American culture, creating a hybridism both in language and in outlook on life, relating both to mainstream American culture and the entire world of Hispanic letters and culture within and beyond the borders of the United States.[12] The most obvious manifestation of this is the bilingual poetry and song emerging in the late nineteenth century (Leal 92) and reaching its apogee in the poetic and theatrical works of such contemporary writers as Alurista, Tato Laviera, Carlos Morton, Gustavo Pérez Firmat, Valdez, and Evangelina Vigil. A characteristic of the intentional use of hybrid language is its contestation, often political in nature, which, as Mikhail Bakhtin explains (344), opposes monolingual, authoritative speech; one of the clearest examples in the literature is to be found in the unmasking and role reversals that take place in Valdez's and El Teatro Campesino's *Las Dos Caras del Patroncito* (The two faces of the boss). One of the few fiction projects to experiment with this code switching and heteroglossia, a highly political work in its contestation of official history, is Hinojosa's Klail City Death Trip

Series.[13] Some scholars have considered hybridization of language particularly characteristic of so-called border literature; in any case, this synthesis has led to a new esthetic in which a bilingual and bicultural reader is implicit and the definition of literature has been altered. In some writers' texts, for example, Alurista's *Spik in glyph?* (1981), the experimentation results in a metalanguage that is fully intelligible only to a reader who understands the interface of two languages and the resultant hybrid language.[14] Along with the synthesis and hybridism come new cultural spaces or homelands, such as the mythic Aztlán of Chicano literature, the Loisaida of Nuyorican literature, and even the mythologizing of Miami in Cuban American literature, as in Iván Acosta's *El super* (1977). An important transitional work in the creation of this type of mythic homeland is Guillermo Cotto-Thorner's *Trópico en Manhattan* (1951) (see chapter 4), which posits a "tropicalization" of El Barrio, a place where Puerto Ricans can maintain their culture and flourish, as exemplified by his iconic metaphor of a flower growing in the cracks of the cement. The "tropics of Manhattan" trope becomes fully realized, however, in the poems of such Nuyoricans as Victor Hernández Cruz and Laviera, especially in Hernández Cruz's book *Tropicalization* (1976) and in Laviera's birth-of-the-Nuyorican poem, "Doña Cisa y Su Anafre," in his *La Carreta Made a U-Turn* (1979).

Various immigrant texts, such as those of Teodoro Torres, Cotto-Thorner, and Eduardo González Viaña, tend toward or predict a hybrid culture but are not themselves hybrid works in style, form, or language. Most immigrant texts, however, tend to conceive and promote a pure culture as identified with the homeland left behind. They envision an enclave or a *colonia* as a temporary home where their culture can flourish until return to the true homeland is possible. Cultural synthesis and hybridism are incipient in these texts, as for example in the English loanwords and neologisms they deploy, but they offer themselves as pure and exempt from bastardization or degradation of what is to them the culture the immigrants brought with them and must preserve—even while the culture in the homeland is evolving and perhaps incorporating Anglo-American or metropolitan ways of its own. In the ideology of El México de Afuera no one is lower than the person who denies his culture of origin or forgets his native tongue (*el renegado*). The colonias, often the original ports of entry to the United States, are known in the English-speaking world and to many of the residents themselves as Spanish Harlem, Little Havana, Little San Juan, and Little Mexico; they are the spaces that later native literature will mythologize as Aztlán and Loisaida, for instance.

There is no question of cultural mixing and hybridity in exile literature; the texts represent the best of language and learning that privilege, education, and high culture can offer. Some of the best examples are the poems in *El laúd del desterrado* (1856). In many of them, as in much exile literature created to the present, the homeland is envisioned as a Zion longed for by the poet in Babylonian captivity, with the Metropolis configured as Babel. From the frigid shores of New York and the cement landscape of the Metropolis, Cuba and Puerto Rico are often configured as Paradise Lost. As political change in the homeland becomes more and more a lost cause, the plaintive literature of exile exhibits a grand disillusionment and lost hope and the narrators are forced to wander, rootless, in solitude through foreign lands and cultures. The greatest poet of this wanderlust and desperation was José María Heredia.

7

From the corridos forward to contemporary texts, culture conflict becomes a central motive and organizing force in Mexican-American and Chicano literature, as described in Américo Paredes's scholarly studies and illustrated in his literary works, such as *George Washington Gómez*, written in 1936.[15] Puerto Rican and Cuban American texts like Juan Flores's *Divided Borders: Essays on Puerto Rican Identity* (1993) attempt to resolve this conflict by celebrating the new hybridism; but in the end, according to Pérez Firmat's *Life on the Hyphen: The Cuban American Way* (1994), the loss of Latino culture will ensue, for he sees only his generation of Cuban Americans as able to balance the two cultures in opposition and conflict. However, the first phase of contemporary Chicano literature promoted cultural nationalism and separation from Anglo-American culture, regarded as oppressive and corrupt; today's Mexican-American literature, like much of Nuyorican and Cuban American literature, embraces hybridism, synchronicity, and synthesis.

Culture conflict was and still is integral to immigrant literature's binary structure and opposition of the homeland's culture to that of the United States. It is highly nationalistic, although the nation is imagined more through nostalgia and illusion than through a realistic assessment of the difficult life left behind and of the negative aspects of the national culture. One of the few immigrant texts to follow a protagonist back to the homeland and to elaborate on his rejection of what it has become is Torres's *La patria perdida* (1936); unable to fit in, he returns from Mexico to Missouri farm country and attempts to establish his own utopian version of the México de Afuera.

Exile literature is often part of a nation-building project, despite its location outside of the geographic *patria*. It can be very militant, supporting revolution, coups, and invasions. The first Hispanic exiled texts, in fact, provided a liberal ideology for the wars of independence from Spain as well as for the rise of democracy in *la Madre Patria*. To date, exiled texts support their imagined nation in opposition to the one currently institutionalized in the homeland.

8

Both positive and negative hybrid characters exist in Latino literature. Some hybrid characters proudly reap the benefits of bilingual and bicultural life, such as Laviera's Tito Madera Smith, raised in the barrio by a Puerto Rican mother and a southern black father. Hinojosa, too, has created in Becky Escobar, in *Los amigos de Becky* (1990), not a type but an individual who is a strong, capable navigator of both Anglo and Mexican cultures; her mixed Anglo-Mexican parentage makes her a match for Hinojosa's bilingual and bicultural alter egos, Rafa and Jehú. The two most important character types to represent hybridism in native literature are the Pachuco, uncomfortable in Mexican as well as American culture, and the Vendido, or Sell-Out, who trades his Mexican-American ethnic and cultural allegiance for personal gain in the system of racial and economic oppression. Valdez produced the most enduring representations of the Vendido and the Pachuco in, respectively, *Los Vendidos* (1967) and *Zoot Suit* (1979), but the types are ubiquitous in Chicano drama and narrative. Hinojosa has portrayed the Vendido in Becky Escobar's husband, Ira, in *Mi querido Rafa* (1981; *Dear Rafe*, 1985).

Ultimately, the Vendido is the native version of the negative immigrant stereotypes of earlier generations, such as the *agringado*, the *pelona* (flapper), and the renegado in the crónicas and the novels of immigration—not to be confused with the *pocho*, who was never considered a Mexican to begin with. Another frequent stereotype in immigrant literature, like the others born in oral lore, is the *verde*, or greenhorn, who misinterprets American language and culture and becomes the subject of extreme exploitation. The literature of exile, however, does not embrace culture change and hybridism. Instead of characters that represent these social evolutions, it has historically produced both epic heroes and tragic heroes, as in Francisco Sellén's play *Hatuey: poema dramático en cinco actos* (Dramatic poem in five acts, 1891), as well as bloodthirsty dictators, as in Gustavo Solano's play *Sangre: Crímenes de Estrada Cabrera* (Blood: The crimes of Estrada Cabrera, 1920), based on the Guatemalan strongman Manuel Estrada Cabrera.

9

As a literature struggling for recognition and respect of place in American society and culture, native literature develops themes around such issues as identity crisis, bilingualism and biculturalism, race, class, and gender discrimination, and the importance of community. These issues have been central to such foundational works of contemporary Latino literature as Acosta's *El Super* (1977), Rudolfo Anaya's *Bless Me Ultima* (1972), Nicholasa Mohr's *Nilda* (1973), Tomás Rivera's *. . . y no se lo tragó la tierra* (1971, *And the Earth Did Not Devour Him*, 1985), Piri Thomas's *Down These Mean Streets* (1967), and even such religious conversion narratives as Nicky Cruz's *Run, Baby, Run* (1968). In the second and third waves of contemporary Latino literature, published by mainstream presses, these issues remain strong, as in Alicia Gaspar de Alba's *Sor Juana's Second Dream* (1999), Julia Alvarez's *How the García Girls Lost Their Accent* (1991), Sandra Cisneros's *Caramelo* (2002), Junot Díaz's *The Brief Wondrous Life of Oscar Wao* (2007), Cristina García's *Dreaming in Cuban* (1992), and Virgil Suárez's *Latin Jazz* (1989), among many others. The latest waves have coincided with the increased number of Latinos writing in English and graduating from university creative writing programs and thus being fully versed in the American literary canon and decidedly engaged in broadening it.

From the early twentieth century on, immigrant literature has focused on writing the nation through a rejection of the Metropolis as the vortex of values antithetical to the culture of the homeland: materialism versus idealism and spirituality, individualism versus family and community, labor exploitation and discrimination versus equal opportunity and egalitarianism, liberalism that verges on libertinism[16] versus traditional gender roles, and so on. These binary oppositions remain strong from Díaz Guerra's *Lucas Guevara* (1914) to the current manifestations, for example, Roberto Quesada's *The Big Banana* (1999) and *Nunca entres por Miami* (2002, Never enter through Miami). Despite the persistence of this binary, a growing immigration literature is not positing a return to the homeland, as in González Viaña's *El corrido de Dante* (2006).

Exile literature today remains as committed to political causes as when José Alvarez de Toledo, Félix Megía, and Varela attacked the French intervention in Spain and the Spanish monarchy and cultivated the Spanish Black Legend in support of their wars of independence in the first decades of the nineteenth century. Today, despite the restoration of democratic rule in Argentina, for example, a writer like Eloy Martínez, who has found a home in the American academy, continues to elaborate his attack on Argentine authoritarianism in *Santa Evita* (1995), *The Lives of the General* (2004), and *The Tango Singer* (2005). Similarly, the Mariel generation of exile writers, as represented by Arenas and others, continues to attack Castro and Cuban communism.

10

Autobiography and memoir writing began among Latinos in the mid-nineteenth century, as exemplified by Juan Nepumoceno Seguín and other writers who documented their disillusion with the newly installed Anglo-American legal and governmental system in Texas and the Southwest. These genres became more popular as the influence of American Protestantism increased, and a number of converts documented, in ways faithful to American canonical patterns, how they reformed their ways and accepted Christ. The most influential of these conversion narratives—José Policarpo Rodríguez's *"The Old Guide," Surveyor, Scout, Hunter, Indian Fighter, Ranchman, Preacher: His Life in His Own Words* (1897)—went through multiple editions from 1897 to 1968, its last edition. Although the genre has remained strong among Latinos, in fact producing in contemporary times the all-time bestseller in Latino literature, Cruz's *Run, Baby, Run*, some of the most recognized Latino novels have followed the bildungsroman and *künstlerroman* patterns of American ethnic autobiography, especially as practiced by the children of Irish, Italian, Polish, and Jewish immigrants in the early twentieth century. Prominent works in contemporary Latino literature have been considered coming-of-age novels, their protagonists struggling as Latinos to come of age in American society. Among these works are Anaya's *Bless Me, Ultima* (1972), Cisneros's *The*

House on Mango Street (1984), Mohr's *Nilda* (1973), Thomas's *Down These Mean Streets* (1967), José Antonio Villarreal's *Pocho* (1959), and, in the years since these foundational works were published, a legion of works by first-time Latino novelists issuing from mainstream commercial presses. This type of writing, which usually reinforces the canons of American literature, seems to announce the presence and Americanization of the particular ethnic at a specific time in history, petitioning for admission to the American imaginary by adopting the national values of individualism and persistence in the face of discrimination and by shucking off the old-country language and values that hinder assimilation into American society, as in Richard Rodriguez's *Hunger of Memory* (1981).

Many immigration narratives refer to the Hispanic novel par excellence, *Don Quijote*, as their protagonists pursue fortune or fame in the United States. Closely linked to the broad pattern canonized by Cervantes is the picaresque novel, also an influence on immigration novels. Despite emerging from popular anecdote and lived experience, Venegas's *Las aventuras de Don Chipote* glosses on these two sources. In its examination of the life and culture of the United States, the novel of immigration, like the *Quijote* and many picaresque novels, is a novel of the road in which the characters suffer physical and emotional pain, exploitation, and discrimination during their journey, experiences that demythologize the the alleged land of equality and opportunity. Such has been the case from Conrado Espinosa's *El sol de Tejas* (1926) to Bencastro's *Odisea del Norte* and González Viaña's *El corrido de Dante*. Unlike the contemporary novel of native Hispanics, which explores the psychological conflicts and evolution of the protagonist as an individual, the novel of immigration remains more focused on the protagonist as a representative of his people in a plot that is often epic in scope.

The greatest flowering of exile narrative has been in the novels of the Mexican Revolution that were published in the United States from 1915, when Mariano Azuela's *Los de abajo* (*The Underdogs*) was issued in El Paso, to 1935, when Alberto Rembao, in *Lupita, A Story of the Revolution in Mexico*, adapted the genre in English to promote his religious ideology. From 1910 to the mid-1930s, Mexican political discourse accounted for much periodical and literary publishing in the Southwest; in the East, nonfiction prose, fiction narrative, and poetry from the 1930s to the post–Second World War period often supported the Republican cause in Spain, as in the works of Prudencio de Pereda. And the historical realities of contemporary Central America, Cuba,

Chile, and Argentina have made familiar the impact of politics on the literature being produced by political refugees from those countries. Nevertheless, at this juncture no genre has been so foundational to the national literature of a homeland or to the development of Latino literature in the United States as the long-lived novel of the Mexican Revolution.

THE GENERAL SCHEMA of Latino literature in the United States illustrated above is meant not to bind or limit interpretation of the various texts and their authors, but to serve as a general guideline to understanding how native, immigrant, and exile texts relate to each other as well as to problematize the relationship of these texts and authors to their homelands and, indeed, to the whole Hispanic world. In essence, I have sought to illustrate that Latino literature, from its origins in the early nineteenth century to the present, has been a transnational phenomenon, one that crosses borders physically or symbolically or in both ways, constructs more than one national identity at a time or deconstructs and rejects them all, always gazing either at the land it left behind or at the land of reception and reinvention. And even when reinventing itself in English along the lines of the American canon, it nevertheless continues to gaze upon "our house in the last world," as Oscar Hijuelos phrased it in the title to his first novel. For natives, the "last world" is the general Hispanic background in Spain and this hemisphere and the history of their land that became part of the United States. The economic and political refugees, on the other hand, continue to erase the borders separating them politically and geographically from very specific residences prior to their American sojourn.

CHAPTER 2

AN OVERVIEW OF HISPANIC
IMMIGRANT PRINT CULTURE

El periódico en las modernas sociedades respresenta un gran
esfuerzo hecho por el progreso humano. . . . Instruye, moraliza,
civiliza y prepara a los hombres para que sean útiles en las
grandes faenas del trabajo en la incansable lucha por la vida.
—*EL LABRADOR*, LAS CRUCES, N.M., JULY 16, 1909

THE IMMIGRANT PRESS

From the mid-nineteenth century on, Hispanic transmigrants in the United States have written and published books and periodicals and sustained other forms of print culture to serve their enclaves in their native language.[1] That culture not only allowed transmigrants to maintain a connection with the homeland but also helped them adjust to a new society and culture in the United States. Hispanic immigrant print culture shares many of the distinctions Robert Park identified in 1922: (1) the predominant use of the language of the homeland, in (2) serving a population united by that language, irrespective of national origin, and (3) the need to interpret events from immigrants' own peculiar racial or nationalist point of view, and to promote nationalism (9–13).[2] According to Park, the immigrant press serves a population in transition from the land of origin to the United States by providing news and interpretation to orient them and facilitate their adjustment to the new society while maintaining the link with the old society. Underlying Park's distinctions are the concepts of the American Dream and the melting pot: that the immigrants came to find a better life, implicitly a better culture, and that soon they or their descendants would become Americans and thereby obviate the need for this type of press. For Park, immigrant culture was a transitory phenomenon, one that would disappear as the group became assimilated into the melting pot of U.S. society.

The following chapters of this book will show in detail how the concepts of assimilating and disappearing as a culture distinct from what was thought to be the American mainstream were anathema to the writers and publishers who served the transmigrant community. An attitude of *not* assimilating or melting has characterized Hispanic transmigrant culture and its use of the printing press. The advice of *El Horizonte* (1879–80), a newspaper published in Corpus Christi, to its Mexican readership was typical of that given in many immigrant newspapers, novels, poetry, and other publications: do not become citizens of the United States because there is so much prejudice and persecution here that "permaneceremos extranjeros en los Estados Unidos y como tal nos considerarán siempre" (March 24, 1880) (we shall always be foreigners in the United States and they will always consider us as such).

To Park's observations I would add that the defense of the community was also important to the immigrant press. Hispanic newspapers in particular were sensitive to racism and abuse of immigrant rights; this attitude also characterized the creative literature and folklore produced by the transmigrants. Almost all Hispanic immigrant newspapers announced their service in protection of the community in their mastheads and in editorials, and some of them followed up on this commitment by leading campaigns to desegregate schools, movie houses, and other facilities and to construct alternative institutions for the Hispanic community's use. Contrary to Park's prognosis for the ethnic identities of immigrants, the history of Hispanic groups in the United States has shown an ethnicity that refuses to melt, and given that immigration from Spanish-speaking countries has been almost a steady flow ever since the founding of the United States, there seems no end to the phenomenon at this juncture in history or in the foreseeable future.

IMPORTANT IMMIGRANT PUBLISHERS

While Hispanic immigrant newspapers had existed since the late 1820s,[3] it was not until much later, when larger Hispanic immigrant communities began to form, that more characteristic immigrant newspapers were founded to serve a burgeoning community of transmigrants from

Mexico and the entire Hispanic world.[4] These people had been drawn mainly to the San Francisco Bay Area during the gold rush, when collateral industrial and commercial development in the city proliferated. From the 1850s through the 1870s, San Francisco supported the largest number, longest running, and most financially successful Spanish-language newspapers in the United States, among them two dailies named *El Eco del Pacífico* (1856–?) and *El Tecolote* (The owl, 1875–1879). The San Francisco Spanish-language press covered news of the homeland and generally assisted the immigrants in adjusting to their new environment. The newspapers reported on discrimination and persecution of Hispanic miners and generally considered the defense of the *colonia* to be a top priority, denouncing abuse of both immigrants and natives.[5]

Although the Hispanic population in San Francisco was the state's largest in the nineteenth century, Los Angeles received the largest number of Mexican immigrants in the mass exodus of economic refugees during the Revolution of 1910. In the twentieth century Los Angeles, along with San Antonio and New York, supported some of the most important Spanish-language daily newspapers, periodicals, and publishing houses. Newspapers were the primary publishers of creative literature and had the most direct impact on the transmigrants owing to their immediacy and pervasiveness in the communities. Publishing houses were few and far between, and their products were costly, in comparison to the price of a newspaper, which were underwritten by advertisers. Between 1910 and the Great Depression, approximately one million Mexican immigrants settled in the United States, Los Angeles and San Antonio being the most popular destinations.[6] These two cities saw the rise of an entrepreneurial class of refugees with enough cultural and financial capital to establish businesses of all types to serve the rapidly growing Mexican enclaves. They constructed everything from tortilla factories to Hispanic theaters and movie houses, and through their cultural leadership in mutual aid societies, churches, theaters, publishing houses, and periodicals they disseminated a nationalistic ideology that ensured the solidarity and insularity of their communities, which is to say, their markets.[7] They settled in cities where Hispanic populations lived and where the industrial base was expanding rapidly enough to offer employment for economic and political refugees as well as investment opportunities for themselves. Los Angeles and San Antonio offered large labor pools for the entrepreneurs and were far enough from Mexico to protect the political refugees from their enemies there while offering them opportunities to continue their political and cultural work.

Hispanic immigrant print culture throughout the Southwest, the Northeast, and the Chicago area was sustained principally by the Spanish-language newspaper and, on a much smaller level, by publishing houses that were often associated with the newspapers. While many of the periodicals and publishing houses functioned as business enterprises, numerous community-based periodicals were published by various interest groups, such as clubs, mutual aid societies, and writers' associations as well as labor unions, political organizations, and individuals. The business-oriented enterprises tended to be operated by educated elites, while often the small weekly publications, not geared to make a profit, were written, designed, and operated by working-class organizations and individuals. Then, as now, the majority of the Latino community was made up of working-class people.[8] While virtually all of the highly commercial publications to issue from the big-city Spanish-language presses targeted the immigrant community, immigrant workers themselves were quite successful during the first half of the twentieth century in representing themselves in their own weekly and occasional publications.[9]

Among the most important big-city daily newspapers were *El Heraldo de México*, founded in Los Angeles in 1915 and called a "people's newspaper" (Chacón, 48–50); the two newspapers owned by Ignacio Lozano, *La Prensa* (1913) in San Antonio and *La Opinión* (1926) in Los Angeles; and *La Prensa* (1913) in New York.[10] All four ostensibly catered to immigrant workers while serving the entrepreneurial class by promoting its business enterprises and purveying an ideology of a Hispanic culture in exile. All of them, at one time or another, led campaigns through editorials and even community action to protect immigrant rights, to protest discrimination, and to raise funds to assist in community crises. While *El Heraldo de México* and the Lozano newspapers promoted specifically Mexican nationalism, *La Prensa* promoted pan-Hispanism to its more diverse immigrant community. Nevertheless, the underlying, at times not so subtle message of all of these periodicals was to preserve Hispanic identity and resist assimilation to Anglo-American culture.

The entrepreneurs who ran the cultural enterprises, including newspapers and publishing houses, generally had arrived, as noted, with enough resources to start their businesses. They often employed politi-

FIGURE 2.1. A customer purchasing *La Prensa* at a newsstand.

cal refugees as journalists, editorialists, and columnists because they were educated, literate, and, owing to the internal political problems in their homeland, both abundant and in need of sustaining themselves and their families, especially if they had arrived without financial resources. These intellectuals understood their mission as one of preserving Mexican and Hispanic identity and culture in exile. Unlike the usual roles they had played in the homeland, where they generally interacted with a professional and intellectual class, in the United States they were faced with relating to large masses of uneducated, working-class transmigrants. Hundreds of newspapers were founded to serve these masses, first of Mexicans in the Southwest and, later, of Puerto Ricans in the Northeast. While many newspapers had specialized audiences, such as political refugees or industrial workers, for instance, in the large population centers large commercial newspapers were founded to serve broad segments of the transmigrant communities, with articles that appealed to workers as well as to middle- and upper-class readers and, through the fashion and food pages, even to middle-class women. But all of the commercial dailies were obliged to cater to the working classes, by far the largest market for their information. For instance, *El Heraldo de México*, founded and run by Juan de Heras and Caesar Marburg, reserved most news space to cover events in the homeland, followed by news that directly affected the transmigrants in southern California. Among its other functions, the newspaper saw its mission as protecting the interests of the transmigrant community through reporting and editorials dealing with discrimination and exploitation of Mexican workers, especially the abuse of workers committed by foremen (Chacón 50, 62). In 1919 *El Heraldo de México* assumed the role of activist by assisting in the formation of a labor union, the Liga Protectora Mexicana de California (Mexican protection league of California).

The defense of workers and their families, which, as noted, was openly announced on mastheads, extended from the West to the East Coast and was common not only in Mexican communities but also among the Cubans and Spaniards of Tampa and the Cubans and Puerto Ricans in the New York area.[11] In the Southwest, publishers, editorialists, columnists, novelists, poets, and playwrights were almost unanimous in developing and promoting the idea of a *México de Afuera*, in which it was the duty of the individual to maintain the Spanish language, keep the Catholic faith, and insulate children from what community leaders perceived as the low moral standards of Anglo-Americans. Basic to this belief system was the imminent return to Mexico when the hostilities of the Revolution were over. Mexican national culture was to be preserved during what the intellectuals conceived of as an exile in the midst of iniquitous Anglo Protestants, whose culture was aggressively degrading even while discriminating against Hispanics. On the other hand, the expatriates believed that Mexico had been so transformed by the *bolchevique* hordes who had won the revolution that the only true Mexican culture survived in exile, precisely in these colonias.[12] The ideology was most widely expressed and disseminated by cultural elites, many of whom were the political and religious refugees from the Mexican Revolution. They often represented the most conservative segment of Mexican society in the homeland; in the United States, their cultural and business entrepreneurship exerted leadership in all phases of life in the colonia and solidified a conservative substratum that characterized Mexican-American culture for decades to come. While the political refugees truly believed this ideology, they exerted themselves to promote it through publications to the economic refugees, that is, the true immigrants whose descendants make up the largest portion of the Mexican-American community today. Nemesio

García Naranjo, one of the primary promoters of the México de Afuera ideology and former minister of education under the dictator Porfirio Díaz, believed this nationalist ideology had deep historical and political roots in the Southwest:

> Y la Patria vive. Los Estados Unidos debieran tener presente que hace más de dos tercios de siglo se firmaron los tratados de Guadalupe, y sin embargo, aún no se han americanizado los mexicanos que viven en Texas y Nuevo México, Arizona y California. Nuestra raza es persistente y en medio de sus odios y divisiones, conserva inalterables su homogeneidad y carácter. Y un país así, que no se confunde fácilmente con los demás pueblos, que no se fusiona sino excepcionalmente con las otras razas, que conserva sus tradiciones y perpetúa sus leyendas, que, en una palabra, mantiene siempre creciente la fuerza maravillosa de su genio, no se domina con la ocupación de tres o cuatro plazas militares, ni aun con la absorción total de su territorio.
>
> México, por consiguiente, no perderá su nacionalidad, aun cuando llegare a ser vencido. Nuestra vitalidad, como la de Polonia e Irlanda, como la de Armenia y Bélgica, está por encima del desastre mismo.[13] (García Naranjo 8:195–196)

Among the most powerful of the political, business, and intellectual figures in the Mexican immigrant community was Ignacio E. Lozano, founder and operator of the Casa Editorial Lozano and of the two most influential and widely distributed daily newspapers, *La Prensa* (1913–1963) and *La Opinión*, founded in 1926 and still publishing today, principally for the transmigrant community.[14] With the business training and experience he received in Mexico, Lozano was able to contribute professionalism and business acumen to Hispanic journalism in the United States. These traits were reflected in his hiring of well-trained journalists, starting at the top with his appointment of Teodoro Torres, known as the father of Mexican journalism, to edit *La Prensa* (see chapter 4). Lozano also employed García Naranjo, with whom he also had family ties, and Naranjo himself was publisher of a monthly magazine, *La Revista Mexicana*. The ideas of men like Torres and Lozano reached thousands, not only in San Antonio but throughout the Southwest and Midwest; and when President Alvaro Obregón liberalized Mexico's policy toward exiles, *La Prensa* was allowed to circulate throughout northern Mexico (García Naranjo 8:341). Lozano was an astute businessman who, unlike the owners of many exile newspapers, targeted

FIGURE 2.3. Nemesio García Naranjo.

Sr Ignacio E. Lozano

FIGURE 2.2. Ignacio Lozano.

the immigrant and Mexican-American communities as well as other Spanish-speaking nationality groups, including something for everyone in his paper. He even tried to extend the nationalist ideology of México de Afuera to Mexican Americans, writing and publishing his own contribution to this extensive literature: *Narraciones históricas mexicanas: leyendas y tradiciones; libro destinado a cultivar el sentimiento patrio en el corazón de los hijos de México* (1915; Historical Mexican narratives: legends and traditions; a book designed to promote patriotic sentiment in the hearts of the sons of Mexico). Even in his practical book for businesses, *Perfecto secretario mexicano: los preceptos y modelos para escribir toda clase de cartas* (1915; The perfect Mexican secretary: the principles and models for writing all types of letters), Lozano included a small anthology of occasional poems, many of them patriotic.

La Prensa was distributed through a vast network that included newsstand sales, home delivery, and mail. Lozano and many of his prominent writers and editorialists became leaders of the Mexican, Mexican-American, and Hispanic communities. They shaped and cultivated their market for cultural products and print media as efficiently as others sold material goods and Mexican foods. The community truly benefited in that the entrepreneurs did offer needed goods, information, and services that were often denied by the larger society through official and open segregation. And the writers, artists, and intellectuals provided high as well as popular culture and entertainment in the native language of the Mexican community, something also not offered by Anglo-American society: Spanish-language books and periodicals, silent films with Spanish-dialog frames, and Spanish-language drama and vaudeville, among other entertainment and popular art forms.

Various newspaper companies operated publishing houses, the Lozano enterprise and *El Heraldo de México* among them. They also imported books and published reprint editions under their own imprints. The largest publisher, Casa Editorial Lozano, advertised its books in the family's two newspapers and sold them via direct mail and in the Lozano bookstore in San Antonio. *El Heraldo de México* also operated a bookstore, in Los Angeles. In San Antonio and Los Angeles as well as in smaller population centers many other newspapers published books also.

San Antonio, which became the acknowledged publishing center for Hispanics in the Southwest, housed more Spanish-language publishing houses than any other U.S. city. During the 1920s and 1930s, San Antonio was home to the Casa Editorial Lozano, Viola Novelty Company, Whitt Publishing, Librería de Quiroga, Artes Gráficas, and various others, all of which both published and imported books and printed catalogs for mail order.[15] Lozano and Viola Novelty, which were connected to newspapers, also published book listings in their parent newspapers, *La Prensa*, *La Opinión*, and the satirical *El Fandango*—quite often the authors of their books were members of their newspaper staffs. Those that were proprietors of bookstores, such as Lozano, Quiroga, and Librería Española, had a ready sales outlet. The San Antonio publishers' catalogs included titles on everything from the practical to autobiographies by exiled political and religious figures, to sentimental novels and books of poetry. Whitt Publishing issued religious plays appropriate for parish Christmas festivities, along with numerous books of Mexican folklore and legendry. The Librería de Quiroga seems to have concentrated on supplying leisure reading for housewives, especially those of the middle class, with such sentimental fare as María del

Pilar Sinués's novel *El amor de los amores* (The love of loves), Rafael del Castillo's novel *Amor de madre* (A mother's love), Joaquín Piña's novel *Rosa de amor* (Rose of love), Harriet Beecher Stowe's *La cabaña de Tom* (*Uncle Tom's Cabin*), and Antonio Plaza's poetry collection *Album del corazón* (Album of the heart). Catholic and Protestant publishing houses issued hundreds of religious books from their presses in San Antonio and El Paso, and much of this fare established a culture of the Church in exile from Mexico.

These offerings contrasted with the literature oriented toward the working class that often was issued by these same presses. The extent to which cultural elites were able to create and promote a literary and cultural identity for working-class transmigrants, who made up the majority of the community, is astonishing. This is not to say the working class lacked the capacity to create its own sociopolitical identity and culture without the intervention of elites. They did so not only through their songs, oral literature, and theater, but also by publishing and reading their own newspapers, such as Daniel Venegas's *El Malcriado* (The brat) (see chapters 4, 6) and P. Viola's *El Fandango* in San Antonio. Both papers were noted for their use of the working-class dialects of the transmigrants they called *chicanos* (which back then meant precisely Mexican immigrant worker), and both satirized the cultural elites.

THE LABOR PRESS

Both immigrant and native Hispanic workers have engaged in the founding and building of unions throughout their history as industrial and agricultural workers in the United States. The fact that since the nineteenth century Hispanic workers have been imported on a large scale by industry makes their labor press mostly a phenomenon of immigrant life. Historically, the Hispanic labor unions and their periodicals were created by and for Latinos working in very specific industries, industries often associated with their native cultures or old-country backgrounds: cigar rollers, miners, and agricultural workers, cowboys, copper miners, and fruit harvesters. In more contemporary times, Hispanics have been leaders in organizing other trades and industries, such as the steel mills, the needle trades, hospitals, and manufacturing.[16]

One of the first, largest, and most significant industries to rely almost exclusively on Hispanic labor was the cigar manufacturing industry, which had factories in Key West, Tampa, New York, and San Antonio, among other locations. In 1886, the first transfer of a whole industry from Latin America to the United States began when Spanish and Cuban entrepreneurs acquired Florida swampland near Tampa and built a cigar manufacturing town, Ybor City. By 1890 the population of Tampa and Ybor City was fifty-five hundred, and that number tripled by 1900. The tobacco entrepreneurs hoped to attract a docile workforce, unlike the labor union activists in Cuba, avoid U.S. import tariffs, and get closer to their markets in the United States. In addition, the Cuban wars for independence were raging and continually disrupting business. The industry in Ybor City grew to ten factories by 1895 and became the principal cigar-producing area in the United States at a time when cigar smoking was at its peak. By 1900 there were about 150 cigar factories in West Tampa and Ybor City, producing more than 111 million cigars annually (Henderson and Mormino, 34).

The cigar company owners soon discovered they were wrong about escaping the labor unrest that was endemic to the industry in Cuba, as the greater freedom of expression afforded on U.S. soil allowed the cigar workers to organize more openly and to publish their periodicals more extensively. They formed the strongest unions of any Hispanic workers in the United States, calling strikes in 1899, 1901, 1910, 1920, and 1931 (Henderson and Mormino, 40–45).[17]

Workers in the cigar crafts in Cuba and Puerto Rico had traditionally been more politicized because of the high level of informal education obtained through the institution of the *lector*, a person selected and paid by the workers to read to them throughout their laborious and boring work day rolling cigars.[18] The lectores would read extensively from world literature as well as from national authors and newspapers and magazines.

The roots of the Cuban American labor press are to be found in Cuba in this tradition of tobacco workers.[19] Cuban tobacco workers in Tampa established their first labor newspaper, *La Federación*, in 1899 as the official organ of their union. Before that, their interest in organizing and in anarchism had been addressed by their local newspapers, *El Esclavo* (The slave) in 1894 and in *La Voz del Esclavo* (The voice of the slave) in 1900 (Chabrán, 157). Other important union newspapers from the Tampa area were *Boletín Obrero* (Worker bulletin, 1903–?), *El Federal* (1902–1903), *La Defensa* (1916–?), *El Internacional* (1904–?), and *Vocero de la Unión de Tabaqueros* (Voice of the tobacco workers'

FIGURE 2.4. Luisa Capetillo.

unions, 1941–?). The unions and their newspapers as well as individual working-class writers published a steady stream of books and pamphlets to disseminate their ideas.

One of the most important of these writers was Luisa Capetillo, a lector who had worked in Puerto Rico, Tampa, and New York and was an activist labor organizer. Celebrated today as an early Puerto Rican feminist (she was known to have been the first woman to wear men's clothes in public), Capetillo published five books and wrote plays and numerous newspaper articles to convey to workers the details of her anarcho-syndicalism and free love ideologies (see chapter 5).[20] Her plays, published in her book *Influencia de las ideas modernas . . .* , were performed in union halls and, for the most part, took the form of truncated melodramas in which the female protagonists developed their theses through monologs and occasional action. The themes included the benefits of a return to Nature, equality among the sexes, the evils of wage slavery, and the conflict between true love and money. In adapting and subverting the conventions of melodrama, Capetillo was attacking the system of social classes and gender roles.

At the end of the nineteenth century New York was the scene of a large influx of Spanish working-class immigrants; they joined their fellow Spanish-speakers in Harlem and Brooklyn and on 14th Street, and many ultimately participated in the work of raising working-class consciousness through such newspapers as *El Despertar* (1891–1912, The awakening), *Cultura Proletaria* (1910–1959), and *Brazo y Cerebro* (1912, Arm and brain), all of which were primarily anarchist periodicals (Chabrán, 157). *Cultura Proletaria* became the longest-lasting anarchist periodical published in Spanish in the United States. Edited by the noted Spanish anarchist and author Pedro Esteves and published by Spanish workers, the paper passed into the hands of Cubans and Puerto Ricans over the years, as the composition of the workforce changed. Puerto Ricans early on established their own labor and radical press in such organs as *La Mísera* (1901, The miserable one), *Unión Obrera* (1902, Worker union), and, much later, *Vida Obrera* (1930–1932, Worker life).

IMMIGRANT WRITERS

The most interesting story of working-class print culture emerging from the barrios of New York, Tampa, and the Southwest goes beyond the labor movement and subscription to any specific ideology, such as the anarchism or socialism so widely studied and promoted by workers in the early twentieth century. Working-class immigrant writers and intellectuals developed their own newspapers and published books that represented their perspective on life in the United States as individuals immersed in an epic displacement of peoples, relocated to the U.S. Metropolis.[21] Often through the medium of weekly community newspapers and monthly magazines, but also in published books, these authors documented the experiences of Hispanic immigrants, often autobiographically and often employing the vernacular dialects of their working-class readers. Much of the writing was infused with an orality that came from lived experience, anecdotes, and jokes snatched from that experience as well as from popular entertainments, including vaudeville performances.

One genre, closely associated with journalism, was the *crónica*, or chronicle, a short weekly column that often humorously and satirically commented on current topics and social customs in the local community. Rife with local color and inspired by the oral lore of the immigrants, the crónica in the United States came to serve purposes that went beyond those of its forerunners in England, Spain, and Spanish America.[22] From Los Angeles to New York, Hispanic moralists assumed pseudonyms in the tradition of earlier crónicas, such as *Chicote* (The whip), Samurai, and Az.T.K. (Aztec), and in these guises became community moralists commenting in the first person as witnesses to the customs and behavior of the immigrant colony. It was the *cronistas'* mission to promote Hispanic cultural identity and battle the influence of what they saw as Anglo-American immorality and Protestantism; their principal weapons were satire and humor, often directed at the immigrants' supposed degradation of the Spanish language by mixing English words and concepts in their speech, their gawking at Yankee ingenuity and technology, and their penchant for deriding everything associated with the old country as backward. While cultural elites often wrote crónicas to promote such conservative ideologies as el México de Afuera, in the hands of such working-class writers as the Puerto Rican Jesús Colón and the Cuban Alberto O'Farrill of New York there was more ground-level representation of the working man and his struggles and aspirations. Under the pseudonym Tiquis Miquis—one of three names he employed in his crónicas—Colón railed against the overcrowded, filthy conditions of the tenements, the hordes of Latino con men ready to fleece greenhorn immigrants, and the uncultured, chaotic behavior of the transplants from the rural tropics.[23] With a humor tempered on the vaudeville stage, O'Farrill created the persona of an unemployed mulatto *pícaro*, who week after week narrated his struggles to find work during the Depression, at times through such marginal employment as passing out handbills, shoveling snow, or wearing a sandwich board on the streets of Gotham;[24] his downfall as a picaresque rogue was his laziness, his lack of understanding of English, and his ogling of flappers. The most syndicated and highly popular of the cro-

FIGURE 2.5. Julio G. Arce, alias Jorge Ulica.

nistas was the journalist Julio G. Arce, who wrote under the pseudonym Jorge Ulica. A Mexican political refugee who relocated to San Francisco in 1915, swearing never to return to the homeland, he soon purchased a newspaper. Amid news and advertising, Arce launched his weekly column, *Crónicas Diabólicas*, as a literary entertainment and soon attained a popularity and impact no other Mexican writer had in the Southwest in the early twentieth century (see chapter 6).

Outside of newspapers, writers like Venegas, Conrado Espinosa, and Miguel Arce created novels of immigration in which they charted lives and misadventures in the United States and deconstructed the Metropolis. In almost all of them the world of work was the subject, as in Gustavo Alemán Bolaños's *La factoría* (1925), a detailed chronicle of dehumanizing, boring, dangerous work in a New York factory. Like many an immigrant who was unable to find work in the Metropolis commensurate with his experience and training, the Salvadoran journalist Alemán Bolaños created a subtle protest of the working conditions facing immigrants.[25] So, too, the Cuban Wenceslao Gálvez, also a cronista for the Tampa Hispanic newspapers, extended his first-person narrative, published as *Tampa: Impresiones de un emigrado* (1897), to revealing the humiliation and marginalization of immigrant life as his protagonist struggles to make a living as a door-to-door salesman in the

African American ghetto, where his limited English and lack of knowledge of American culture and the Jim Crow South lead him to realize the futility of his marketing enterprise.

While so much of the lived experience of these writers created an immediacy and almost documentary chronicle of immigrant and working-class life, oral lore and journalism in the immigrant communities also provided much ink for the pens of intellectuals, who created a more self-consciously literary rendition of life in the United States as seen by people displaced from the homeland by politics and economic circumstance. From the early crónicas of José Martí and Pachín Marín, which voice some of the same concerns about the cold, dehumanizing, materialistic American Metropolis, to the voluminous novels of immigration by such authors as the Colombian Alirio Díaz Guerra in his *Lucas Guevara*, the Puerto Rican J. I. de Diego Padró in his *En Babia* (Head in the clouds, 1940), and the *La Prensa* editor Torres in his also appropriately titled *La patria perdida* (The homeland lost, 1935), the same binaries appear as in the working-class novel: the constant comparison of life in the United States with that of the homeland; the inability to adapt to the new land and the inability to return home in constant tension; admiration for the advances of American society conflicting with the perceived dehumanization, racism, and exploitation of the poor; more progressive gender roles in the United States threatening the integrity of the family and Latino male-female relationships; and so forth. However, all of these narratives bring to bear the more elevated perspective of educated authors who ground their narratives in a wide array of historical and literary allusions and underpinnings, from biblical passages to the writings of philosophers. Their rhetoric is not meant to be read aloud around a campfire or in a saloon but pondered and meditated upon by an individual educated reader. Perhaps that reader is also displaced under similar circumstances but desirous of continuing the life of elite culture and breeding he or she once enjoyed in the homeland, an elite self-concept that may allow them to survive the poverty or humiliating blue-collar work that has befallen them in the United States as a political or religious refugee. Whereas both Díaz Guerra and Padró at least metaphorically reproduce the resolution of most novels of immigration, that is, return to the homeland or death,[26] Torres's narrator returns to Mexico City only to discover that he feels just as displaced in the homeland as in the United States; in a highly ingenious turn for these formulaic novels, Torres has his protagonist return to his extensive farm outside Kansas City to create a utopia for his family and his workers. He has thus resolved the binary of opposites: here versus there, the past versus the present, American versus Mexican culture. By opting for neither and both, his utopia will combine the best of both societies while remaining isolated from both; this scenario comes to be symbolized by his son, adopted from Anglos but raised by Mexican parents.[27] Ironically, the authors who most strenuously advocated a return to the homeland, such as Arce, Díaz Guerra, and Venegas, lived out their lives in the United States as permanent residents, while Torres, whose protagonist returns to create his utopia in the U.S. heartland, returned to Mexico and became a famous editor and professor of journalism.

Today, there is an equally vibrant literature of Hispanic immigration that takes both oral and written form. The epic story of pulling up roots and resettling in the United States while experiencing the continuing tug of the homeland and the need to preserve language and culture is still sung and finds voice in the ever-renewing *corrido*, *décima* and *salsa* lyrics not only sung in dance halls but packaged on CDs and music videos. Both working-class and elite immigrant authors continue to confront the Metropolis in their novels and first-person chronicles in Spanish, as in the works of Ramón "Tianguis" Pérez, Mario Bencastro, Alicia Alarcón, and others. And the language is key here, as is the lived experience of immigration. And Spanish-language newspapers serving the large transmigrant communities in Chicago, Houston, Los Angeles, Miami, New York, and elsewhere are undergoing somewhat of a boom while English-language dailies are cutting staff and the number of pages and idling their presses in the face of rapidly falling circulation. Through the newspapers and, to some extent, the small Spanish-language publishing houses, the literature of transmigration is once again flourishing.

CHAPTER 3

THE DREAM OF RETURN TO THE HOMELAND

Tal vez sería mi destino
venir a tierras extrañas
pero algún día a las montañas
de Adjuntas yo volveré
y mis despojos dejaré
guardados en sus entrañas.
— "LAMENTO DE UN JÍBARO," ANÓNIMO

PAUL WHITE HAS asserted that "amongst all the literature of migration the highest proportion deals in some way with ideas of return,
whether actualized or remaining imaginary" (14). Most Hispanic immigrant literature likewise promotes a return to the homeland and, in
so doing, is antihegemonic and rejecting of the American Dream and
of the melting pot. The ethos of Hispanic immigrant literature is based
on the premise of return after what authors and community expect
to be a temporary sojourn in the land where work is supposedly ubiquitous and dollars are plentiful and the economic and political insta-
bility of the homeland is unknown. Authors or their narrators (or both)
dissuade readers from investing in the American myth of creating a
new life, a new self in the United States, where one is supposedly free
to develop one's potential, climb the social ladder, and become inde-
pendently wealthy. With equal conviction they discredit the idea of a
melting pot in which all races and creeds are treated equally and have
equal opportunity to attain the benefits the United States has to offer.
The last lines of Daniel Venegas's novel *Las aventuras de Don Chipote,
o Cuando los pericos mamen* (1928) state this disdain in no uncertain
terms: "Los mexicanos se harán ricos en Estados Unidos, cuando los
pericos mamen" (Mexicans will become rich in the United States when

parrots suckle their young, 159). The attitude of not assimilating goes back to early days of Hispanic immigration. An editorial of March 24, 1880, in *El Horizonte* expressed it as follows:

> Los mexicanos, bien lo sean o hayan renegado de este título, son siempre tratados con injusticia y prevención, por los jueces, los ciudadanos, los pudientes, y en general todos los hijos de esta nación.
>
> Por consiguiente, si no se ha de lograr ningún mejoramiento, y de ello estamos todos convencidos, ¿a qué renegar el título de hijos de la República de Méjico . . . [ya que] permaneceremos extrangeros en los Estados Unidos y como tal nos considerarán siempre?[1]

It is noteworthy that at this early date the writer employs the term *renegado* (renegade) to invoke the fear of identity loss in the United States. The term will be used time and again in the twentieth century in Mexican immigrant literature, both oral and written, to bring home a moral lesson about the dangers of assimilation. One's ethnic or national identity can disappear under the crushing pressures exerted by the American mainstream and its national myths. Of the three terms employed by public commentators and writers, *pocho*[2] (non-Mexican, applied negatively to Mexican Americans), *agringado*[3] (gringoized or Americanized), and *renegado*, the last is by far the strongest, reminiscent even of the New Testament reference to those who denied Christ. Agringado, on the other hand, was widely used in the nineteenth century, for example in an editorial in the El Paso newspaper *El Monitor* on August 13, 1897, chastising agringados for not donating money for the celebration of Mexican independence day: "A esos agringados que niegan ser mexicanos, por el solo hecho de haber nacido en los Estados Unidos, les preguntamos, ¿qué sangre corre por sus venas? ¿Acaso pertenecéis a la raza sajona y sois trigueños por el hecho de haber nacido en la Frontera? ¡Qué barbaridad!" (We want to ask those agringados who deny they are Mexican based on the sole reason that they were born in the United States: What blood flows in your veins? Can you possibly belong to the Saxon race, and are you dark-skinned only because you were born on the Border? How ridiculous!) As can be seen from the quote, identity and national allegiance at this time were becoming associated with racialization.

It is ironic that transmigrants, who were inclined to identify themselves regionally or tribally and had no real awareness of national identity before immigrating to the United States, suddenly found themselves imagined by the receptor nation as Mexican, Cuban, Puerto Rican, or Spanish, terms often applied indiscriminately to a host of Spanish and Spanish-American nationalities;[4] they also found working-class sojourners from other regions of their countries, which led to recognition of their common background.[5] The authorities and employers in the United States grouped them together under these national titles, employed labor recruiters and foremen fluent in their dialects, and often housed them together in the perceived nationality groups. These practices developed out of perceptions of racial inferiority and reinforced racialization, especially in industries that created a pay scale that distinguished among the supposedly varied racial and ethnic workers they employed.[6] On the other hand, the transmigrants, in building up their communities in the United States, often felt (and many still do) more Mexican, more Cuban, more Puerto Rican, than their compatriots back in the homeland. There were various reasons for such attitudes, including the cultural destruction visited on their countries by revolutions and the export of American industrialization and modernization that transformed the national culture. For example, the narrator in *Trópico en Manhattan* proclaims that the character Antonio, "se sentía más Boricua en Harlem que en la apacible serenidad de Barranquitas" (8) (felt more Puerto Rican in Harlem than in the peaceful serenity of Barranquitas). The same notion can be seen in the speeches of Nemesio García Naranjo that deal with the theme of the deterritorialized Mexico that extends north of the Rio Grande.[7] This discourse was crucial in the creation and sustenance of the ideology of *México de Afuera*, which promoted the extreme idea that the true Mexico existed in the barrios of San Antonio and Los Angeles and everywhere the transmigrants established themselves in the United States, given that the so-called Bolshevik revolution had destroyed the *patria*. Discussing the elites who disseminated this nationalist ideology through newspapers, literature, and theater consumed by the transmigrants, Juan Bruce-Novoa has written,

> Many of the editors and writers who had fled were not welcomed back in Mexico. And when exiles cannot return, they justify their existence in a dual manner: they manipulate the image and significance of their residence outside their country by discrediting what the homeland has become; and, two, they set about proving that they are the authentic bearers of the true tradition of the homeland and even of the ideals of the attempted revolution. Thus, they must declare the revolution a

failure, at least temporarily, because only they have remained faithful to the true patriotic ideals. Eventually the exercise in self-justification leads to the claim that the homeland has actually moved with the exiles, that they have actually managed to bring it with them in some reduced form, and if the opportunity should arise, they can take it back to plant it in the original garden of Eden.[8]

Longing for the return home is depicted in the majority of immigrant works, and in some an actual return is represented. In the texts, the return may be physical—preferably during one's lifetime but even, as in the case of the jíbaro whose verses appear in the epigraph above, in death if need be—or metaphorical. The representations of the return are as varied as the idiosyncrasies, class standings, genres, and ethnicities of the authors. The first *corridos* of immigration[9] in the late nineteenth century, documented by Américo Paredes, for instance, concentrated on the vicissitudes of the arduous trip *al norte* but always presupposed a return home,[10] even "after twenty or more years of residence in the United States" (*Folklore and Culture* 11).[11] All of these elements—the reasons for leaving home, the description of the journey, the observation of and conflict with U.S. culture, worker oppression and discrimination, the desire to return home—first appeared in song and oral lore but have come to inform much of the written literature of immigration, regardless of the Hispanic ethnicity of the writers. These characteristics, it turns out, provide an implicit plot structure in most of the immigrant novels and plays that appeared during the twentieth century: the economic reasons for leaving home and the expectations of improved wages and working conditions in the United States; the confrontation with the brute realities of quasi–slave labor and working conditions; disillusionment and rejection of the American Dream; and return to the homeland or a loss (often seen as a figurative death) of identity or actual physical death.

THE INIQUITOUS METROPOLIS AND THE DREAM OF RETURN HOME

While the first known immigrant novel in Spanish, *Lucas Guevara* (1914), by Alirio Díaz Guerra, conveys that the protagonist should leave the iniquitous environment of New York and return to his edenic small town of Santa Clara somewhere in Spanish America, Lucas's unwitting progression into a New York that is likened to Sodom and Gomorrah as well as Hell makes return impossible and leads to his annihilation. Midway through the novel, Lucas decides to leave the Inferno and return home (137), but his corrupt sponsors in New York make it impossible for him to receive the funds his father has sent to allow him to purchase passage for his return home. Thus stranded and victimized by hosts of grifters, pimps, and other underworld types in an infernal Hampa (a reference made in Golden Age Spanish picaresque literature to the ghettoes in which rogues rule), he descends further and further into libertinage and sin, losing his chaste Hispanic Catholic identity as a convert to the immorality and amorality of the Metropolis.[12] Ultimately, as noted earlier, he commits suicide by leaping into the East River from the Brooklyn Bridge, a symbol of American technology and advancement, while the Statue of Liberty, the putative symbol of American freedoms and economic opportunity for immigrants, looks blankly on. The novel thus cynically deconstructs the American Dream and all it purports to offer in Emma Lazarus's poem inscribed on the statue's base: "Give me your tired, your poor,/Your huddled masses yearning to breathe free." For the narrator, Lady Liberty does not "lift [her] lamp beside the golden door"; instead she is the perverted Lady of Libertinage, the idol and representation of all the women, as opposed to men, who rule U.S. society and prey on men, especially Hispanic immigrant men, for their sexual gratification.[13] Having been lured to the Metropolis by the myth of American know-how, progress, and prosperity, Lucas has become the victim of American materialism, cupidity, and licentiousness and consequently has lost his identity as a Hispanic; figuratively he died as a Hispanic as he descended into the depths of Gomorrah and into pennilessness and homelessness, his suicide in the last chapter serving merely as the physical representation of his loss of moral compass and cultural identity. This loss is emphasized as Lucas contemplates his suicide on the bridge and scans the metropolitan panorama, once again compared with the homeland he left behind:

> Allá lejos, el hogar abandonado; la madre cariñosa llorando el amor ausente, perdido ya para el calor de sus besos; la blanca cabeza paterna, doblada no tanto por el peso de los años cuanto por la pena intensa á que el hijo sin entrañas quiso condenarlo; los crepúsculos patrios, antes llenos de luz y color, esfumados ahora en tiniebla impenetrable; los afectos íntimos de la niñez, ya casi olvidados por completo; todo el conjunto, en fin, de los primeros años de su vida sepultado por largo tiempo en como una penumbra de indiferencia y hastío; pugnando

FIGURE 3.1. Alirio Díaz Guerra.

ahora por alzarse en lo íntimo de su sér con todos los lineamientos
de la infantil intensidad. Aquí á su alrededor, la ciudad formidable y
arisca; una aglomeración de condiciones adversas, de realidades pavo-
rosas, de seres humanos ajenos á todo sentimiento noble; un caudal
de odios brotando de su alma, sorda ya á la voz generosa del perdón;
la amargura de la esteril lucha; el desaliento de la voluntad vencida,
la noche de una desesperación espantable y el espectro de un porvenir
aterrador sin miraje alguno de esperanza.[14] (310)

In numerous other immigrant works characters meet their demise
while in pursuit of the American Dream. Time and again they are done
in by symbols of American technological advance and materialism: ele-
vators, drill presses, train locomotives, subways, bridges, skyscrapers,
explosives, and other such inventions that win the *verdes'*, or greenhorn immigrants', admiration and respect, not only for the technology
itself but also for the masters of innovation and progress that Americans appear to be in the eyes of the newly arrived innocents from rural,
preindustrial settings. Even the most intellectual of observers, such as
José Martí in 1881, marvel at the American technological and industrial
advances and the culture springing from them:

Es lo cierto que nunca muchedumbre más feliz, más jocunda, más bien
equipada, más compacta, más jovial y frenética ha vivido en tan útil
labor en pueblo alguno de la tierra, ni ha originado y gozado más for-

tuna, ni ha cubierto los ríos y los mares de mayor número de empave-
sados y alegres vapores, ni se ha extendido con más bullicioso orden e
ingenua alegría por blandas costas, gigantescos muelles y paseos brillantes y fantásticos.[15]

In the 1890s the Puerto Rican chronicler and poet Francisco Gonzalo
"Pachín" Marín recreated the vision of the Metropolis as first seen
through the eyes of a newly arrived, penniless Hispanic immigrant:

> Sus edificios, sus obras portentosas de arquitectura; sus ferrocarri-
> les elevados que cruzan fantásticamente por los aires; sus calles, an-
> chas arterias por las cuales discurre un gentío inagotable de todos los
> pueblos del mundo; sus parques, de corte severo y aristocrático; sus
> máquinas de vapor; sus poderosas empresas periodísticas; sus muje-
> res alevosamente bellas; sus maravillas todas producen a primera vista
> cierto malestar al forastero, porque se le antoja a uno que estas grandes
> ciudades, ensordecedoras por su progreso, son así como la boca de un
> horrible monstruo ocupado constantemente en tragar y vomitar a la
> vez a seres humanos.[16]

Seen from the point of view of the more humble worker, as experienced and written about by the self-taught Venegas, even the dusty
border town of El Paso in the 1920s astonished the poor greenhorn Don
Chipote, who on his arrival entertained wishes of sweeping up "todo el
oro que hay por allá" (all the gold they have over there).[17] The narrator
of *Don Chipote* describes his countrymen's astonishment in what may
be considered the working-class rhetorical equivalent of the prose of
Martí and Pachín Marín:

> Creían estar soñando al ver semejantes casotas y tan elegantes, ya que,
> la mayor que habían visto era la del dueño de la hacienda y ésta les
> parecía un jacal en comparación de los edificios que de tan altos les
> parecía que se les venían encima; luego, eso de ver las calles tan listas
> y que toda la gente vestía tan a lo *curro*, y sobretodo tanto carretón que
> corrían sin mulas, eran cosas que no podían caberles y los hacía abrir
> las quijadas hasta soltar la baba.[18] (36)

Díaz Guerra's metaphor of New York as Babylon, a frigid, gray ex-
panse of industrial buildings touching the firmament and particularly
inhospitable to Hispanics, is repeated throughout the twentieth cen-

tury in the literature of immigration.[19] As such, New York becomes the symbol of the totality of American culture for its cold indifference, extreme materialism, and inhumanity, its luring of transmigrants from around the world into its factories, devouring and spitting out masses of them. The freezing weather in winter is especially trying to the Spanish Americans who have left behind tropical climates. In his renowned poem appropriately entitled "Nostalgia" (1916), the Puerto Rican poet Virgilio Dávila elaborated on the following folk quatrain:

¡Mamá! ¡Borinquen me llama!
¡Este país no es el mío!
Borinquen es pura flama,
¡y aquí me muero de frío![20]

Carrying on the *décima* folksong tradition, the schooled Dávila created a stanza glossing on each of the verses of the original quatrain and, in so doing, captured the essence of Hispanic repulsion by the Metropolis and his nostalgia for and dream of return to the homeland:

Tras un futuro mejor
el lar nativo dejé,
y mi tienda levanté
en medio de Nueva York.
Lo que miro en derredor
es un triste panorama,
y mi espíritu reclama
por honda nostalgia herido
el retorno al patrio nido.
¡Mamá! ¡Borinquen me llama!

¿En donde aquí encontraré
como en mi suelo criollo
el plato de arroz con pollo,
la taza de buen café?
¿En dónde, en dónde veré,
radiantes en su atavío,
las mozas, ricas en brío,
cuyas miradas deslumbran?
¡Aquí los ojos no alumbran!
¡Este país no es el mío!

Si escucho aquí una canción
de las que aprendí en mis lares,
o una danza de Tavárez,
Campos, o Dueño Colón,
mi sensible corazón
de amor patrio más se inflama,
y heraldo que fiel proclama
este sentimiento santo,
viene a mis ojos el llanto . . .
¡Borinquen es pura flama!

En mi tierra, ¡qué primor!,
en el invierno más crudo
ni un árbol se ve desnudo,
ni una vega sin verdor.
Priva en el jardín la flor,
camina parlero el río,
el ave en el bosque umbrío
canta su canto arbitrario,
y aquí . . . ¡La nieve es sudario!
¡Aquí me muero de frío![21]

Dávila not only captures the essence of the rural immigrants' re-action to the Metropolis, but also develops his poetic structure using the binary opposition of *here* compared with *there* that provides the backbone of most of the literature of immigration. In this binary, every-thing from the climate to foods, customs, gender roles, and family re-lationships is explored as a reason to return to what is familiar, to a place where one is comfortable, wanted, and loved. Nostalgia supplies the energy motivating this binary that ultimately results in a return to the homeland.[22]

Probably the most detailed and incisive depiction of the freezing, snowy New York winters is to be found in José de Diego Padró's *En Babia (El manuscrito de un braquicéfalo* 1940, Head in the clouds [The manuscript of a many-branched brain]), a sprawling second novel in a trilogy that features a poor struggling writer working as a clerk in a New York office.[23] More than a novel of immigration, *En Babia* presents biting satires of the novelistic genre itself, expanding its boundaries to include treatises on philosophy, biology, the black arts, and so forth. The penniless bohemian protagonist, who between work hours and at times on the job is writing the novel the reader is reading, is forced to reside in working-class boardinghouses. He does not identify his principal residence as part of Spanish Harlem but does state that it is located uptown on Lenox Avenue. Daily he escapes the confines of his room to roam the city streets as a *flâneur*, often eduring ice storms and snowstorms, at times accepting the kindness of well-off acquaintances who offer him shelter from the weather and food in the establishments of Chinatown, Little Italy, and the Bowery. For him, as for many of the other writers discussed here, New York is "denso, babélico, con su apretada crestería de *skyscrapers* agujereados de luces, y rosnando su clásico industrialismo entre las gasa de la niebla invernal" (54, dense, Babel-like, with its tightly spaced skyscrapers riddled with little lights, snorting its classic industrialism amid the gauze-like wintery clouds). And, reminiscent of Díaz Guerra's descriptions, places like the Bowery are

> de los suburbios más peligrosos de Nueva York. Hay que ir allí con infinitos cuidados y precauciones. En el Bowery abundan las pandillas de profesionales del crimen: estafadores, carteristas, matones, licenciados de presidio, bootleggers, traficantes de narcóticos, explotadores de juegos prohibidos, extorcionistas, agentes del *white slavery*. . . . En fin, todo el detritus social, toda la carne delincuente de la metropolis ha hecho de aquella zona el cuartel general de sus maquinaciones y fechorías. (38)[24]

In all of Hispanic immigrant literature, Padró's descriptions of the cold and snow the immigrants from the tropics face are the most indelible:

> La primera cosa que hice al salir fue alzar el cuello de mi sobretodo. Después sepulté las manos en los bolsillos, dejándolas allí acurrucadas como reptiles en su agujero . . . ¡y andando!
> Hacía mucho frío. Una copiosa nevada caía sobre Nueva York, empañando el aire y envolviendo la extensión de la ciudad en una tristeza grave, aterida. El cielo, ceñudo, carbonoso en el cenit, aparecía inyectado de un rojo denso al ras de la masa de edificios, se obscurecía más allá y presentaba grises y verdes palúdicos, desviados hacia el bajo horizonte. El viento soplaba fuerte, hinchándose y levantando por intermitencias del suelo, de las cornisas de las casas, de todas partes, furiosos torbellinos de un polvo fino y seco de nieve.

. . . Las ráfagas de viento azotaban de continuo mi rostro. Llevaba la nariz y la barbilla un tanto insensibilizados por todas partes; y las orejas, si es que se puede metaforizar así, me chillaban, gemían, lanzaban ladridos de ardor.[25] (31–32)

As he makes his way through the frigid wind and the snow-covered streets, passing landmarks that still exist today, he slips and falls on the ice, provoking laughter from an anonymous passerby; the narrator sees the fall as a terrible omen of his destiny in the Metropolis and takes the opportunity to unload his wrath on the city: "¡Miren qué calles, qué aceras, qué hostia! . . . ¡Mal rayo parta Nueva York! . . . Pensaba: 'Ese resbalón que acabo de dar, algo quiere decir, algo. ¡A saber lo que me aguarda por ahí! Siempre determina algo un resbalón." (34) (Look, what streets, what sidewalks, damn! A thunderbolt should rend New York! . . . I was thinking: That fall I just took, it must mean something, something. Let's see what the future brings! It always means something.)[26]

What is intriguing about the protagonist is his skeptical eye, his censure of the corruption and debauchery that accompany assimilation into metropolitan life ("Nueva York es una cloaca" [New York is a sewer], 77), as represented by his wealthy Cuban friend, Sebastián Guinard, a hedonist and libertine.Like Lucas Guevara, Guinard has become completely assimilated into metropolitan culture but serves as a foil for the protagonist's pessimism and artistic ideals. It is in the voice of Guinard that Padró places the most cynical and outrageous attacks on Yankee materialism and pragmatism:[27]

—Ahí tienes—decíame irónicamente—a tus correligionarios: los defensores y guardianes de la razón práctica, del buen sentido. Ahí tienes a los profesores de energía y rastacueros de la pan-beocia. ¡Ja, ja! De tal manera arraiga el móvil utilitario en la contextura íntima de esta gente, que aun en sus tipos más idealizantes (soldado, artista y poeta) se percibe invariablemente el fetor característico del curial o del tocinero. Dice Schopenhauer que el carácter propio de los norteamericanos es la vulgaridad en todas sus formas: moral, intelectual, estética y social. Una afirmación incontrovertible. Porque, en verdad, nada más huérfano de elegancia ideológica que el cerebro de un norteamericano. Es una gaveta, un archivo de pensamiento bursátil, rutinario, mediocre. No da un paso el yanqui que no esté sujeto al cálculo, a la línea recta, al cinco por ocho cuarenta. Todo lo tasa a razón de pesos y centavos: desde la abstracción tiempo hasta las más elevadas realizaciones del genio humano. Para el yanqui un hombre vale y pesa por lo que rinde en metálico. (110)[28]

Probably the most sophisticated and experimental of the novels of immigration, the trilogy's last installment chronicles a return to Puerto Rico (Pardó himself returned). *En Babia* is a masterwork of Spanish-American literature, but unfortunately, because of its massiveness, it is largely unread and forgotten.[29] By any measure the most recognized and even canonized work, although never before studied as a sterling example of immigration literature, is René Marqués's play *La carreta* (1953), one of the foundational works of Puerto Rican literature and highly esteemed by the Puerto Rican diaspora. The carreta, or oxcart, is developed as a symbol of migration, transitioning at each phase of the play into a technologically more advanced means of migration, such as the automobile and the airplane. *La carreta*, as literature, is also the most noteworthy example of the use of death as poetic justice for abandoning the homeland and investing one's talents and destiny in the Metropolis. The highly poetic play, famous in Puerto Rican letters for its groundbreaking employment of working-class and rural vernacular (by now a standard of immigrant literature), follows the travails of a family forced to leave their highland farm to eke out a living in Puerto Rico's major city, where they are forced to live in a slum. The onset of major ethical and moral as well as economic problems compels the family ultimately to migrate to New York. All the while, it is the illegitimate eldest son, Luis, who prevails on the family to leave rural life to take advantage of the opportunities for advancement and betterment offered in the Metropolis. Luis, who has been secretly raised by an adoptive mother, is fascinated with American technology and know-how, especially the mysteries of its machines. Migrating to New York is part of his search for identity and a mother; it leads him, one might say, to crawl into the womb of a machine, where he is devoured. In the absence of a male head of family, it is up to Luis's half sister Juanita and his adoptive mother, Doña Gabriela, to decide to return home to the simple, chaste customs of the mountains, to lovingly care for the land that nurtured them and gave them their identity, to remain as strong as the symbolic *ausubo* tree in weathering the economic storms and vicissitudes of a rapidly modernizing Puerto Rico. However poetically articulated, Marqués's call for a return to the homeland, as personified by Juanita and Doña Gabriela, is among the most forcefully expressed statements of nationalism. Although the two women are the heroes of the tale, characters who take the reins of their destiny or oxcart in their own hands and return home to build the nation, *La carreta* is not a feminist work: rather, like much immigrant literature, it personifies the nation as a woman and is meant to embarrass men for their cowardice in not confronting and opposing American colonialism and the export of the island's manpower for the building of the American empire. In an extended essay, *El puertorriqueño dócil: literatura y realidad psicológica* (1967; *The Docile Puerto Rican: Essays*, 1976), Marqués expands on this view, stating that men's characteristic reaction has been *ñangotamiento*, a tendency to withdraw almost into a fetal position rather than face adversity; the first act of the play also portrays the patriarch as *ñangotao*. As in other works, such as *Las aventuras de Don Chipote*, it is the women who represent the nation and reestablish the natural order by bringing their duped husbands home; Doña Chipota quite literally searches for her husband and drags him back to the border and the tenant farm.

A more contemporary and down-to-earth rejection of the Metropolis and a rewriting of *La carreta* to fit the Cuban diaspora following Fidel Castro's takeover of the government is Iván Acosta's play *El súper* (The superintendent, 1977). In the play, a working-class family lives in a basement apartment in the city, forced by poverty and adverse circumstances to see the world from the bottom up, as Roberto, the barely English-speaking paterfamilias, struggles to keep the family afloat by working as the superintendent of the building they live in. The bittersweet drama includes outrageous monologs and dialogs querying and cursing American culture; bemoaning the long, frigid winters; expanding on the garbagemen's strike to envision the Metropolis as a pile of garbage, and so on. Ridden with nostalgia and disappointed in their unwed daughter's adoption of gringo ways and her ensuing unwanted pregnancy, Roberto and his wife, Aurelia, long to return to Cuba, which is politically impossible under Castro. Apolitical from the start but drawn into the hysteria surrounding the exodus from the island under the new Communist regime they did not understand, they realize, like many other transmigrants, they have traded Eden for the monster city. Their only recourse is to return, but they can return only to the simulacrum of Cuba that is the Cuban community of Miami, the only return possible, the geographically and culturally closest place to Cuba that exists for them.

NUEVO CIRCULO DRAMATICO presenta

La Carreta

DE RENE MARQUES

direccion de
Roberto Rodriguez Suarez

Del
9 al 12 de diciembre
1954

HUNTS POINT PALACE

FIGURE 3.2. Poster in New York announcing a performance of *La carreta*.

One of the most recent installments in this ever-evolving but consistently negative portrayal of the Metropolis is *Paraíso Travel* (2001; *Paradise Travel*, 2007), a novel by the Colombian author Jorge Franco, which, starting with the title itself, contests the myth of the United States as a Promised Land. In *Paraíso Travel*, the obsessive love of the protagonist Marlon drives him to accompany the venal, adventurous Reina to the United States, where he promptly loses her and all of his possessions, including his clothes. He becomes almost catatonic on the sidewalks of the city as indifferent, uncaring citizens ignore him in his destituteness and despair during a severe winter. Befriended by the owners of a neighborhood Colombian restaurant, he begins his climb back to sanity and works to acquire some meager means, first by cleaning toilets. The novel explains: "El último que llegue lava los baños . . . una de las leyes de inmigración" (*Paraíso*) ("The last one here [meaning the latest immigrant group] cleans the bathrooms . . . one of the immigrations laws") (*Paradise* 87). Able now to survive, albeit barely, in the United States, Marlon hits the road in search of Reina, and the novel becomes another road tale depicting a bus rider's view of American culture. He eventually finds her in Miami, only to have his particular version of the American Dream, a life of prosperity with the one he loves, explode in his face: Reina has become a prostitute and has a child engendered by one of her customers. His parting words contest their whole reason for coming to the United States in the first place: "Hasta entiendo el dolor y la incertidumbre de ser colombiano; y que cuando quisiste cambiar de patria, Reina, no entendiste que la patria es cualquier lugar donde esté el afecto. Ahora sé donde van mis pasos" (*Paraíso* 242) ("I understand that when you wanted to change countries, Reina, you didn't understand that a person's country is wherever there is love and affection. Now I know where my steps are taking me") (*Paradise* 228). The reader assumes that those steps lead back to Colombia.[30] In *Paraíso Travel* a role reversal has the female motivating and taking the lead in migrating to the United States and the male maintaining and protecting the national values. This rare plot twist is represented in only one earlier work, a series of rhymed *crónicas*, "Tanasio y Ramona," published in 1928 in a Texas newspaper by Ignacio G. Vázquez. In this humorous satire, a husband abandoned in Mexico searches throughout the Southwest for his iniquitous agringada wife in order to bring her back home; as in *Paraíso Travel*, it is the woman who bears the blame for having betrayed the Nation (see chapter 5).

The message to return to the homeland can also be emphasized against the backdrop of those who remain in the States and suffer the consequences. From the very first pages of Conrado Espinosa's *El sol de Texas* (1926) it is obvious that the major motivation for the family's working the fields is to earn enough money to pay for the journey home, "a México, a su rancho de donde nunca debían de haber salido y trabajar lo suyo, su tierra . . . podrá hacerlo ahora sin recurrir a los préstamos (4)" ("to Mexico, to the ranch he should have never left. He'll go back to work his own land. And he'll be able to do it now without having to borrow any money from anybody") (142). But unlike the authors cited above, Espinosa handles the question of return by positing three alternatives, each of which successfully contests the myth of the American Dream. Espinosa's narrator follows two families hailing from rural Michoacán: the generically named Quico and Cuca and their son and daughter, and Don Serapio with his two sons. Despite hard going both in finding work and in making a living, the two families persist, traveling the roads of Texas through railroad camps, ranches, and cities, as far as the oil-exporting port of Port Arthur. Serapio's son, José, who had been fascinated with the power of the locomotives when they worked in railroad construction, is run over by a locomotive one night; from then on, it is his father's and brother's lot to make their way back home with José's broken body.

Serapio's family is developed by the narrator as a positive example of integrity, morality, and loyalty to the motherland; their quick disillusionment with the United States as well as their maintenance of their cultural and religious values is seen as praiseworthy. On the other hand, Quico's quixotic pursuit of the American Dream is unwavering despite the many challenges he faces, including racism, fraud, and oppression on and off the job, and despite Cuca's entreaties to return home. He is resigned to pursue a marginalized life in Texas close to his son and daughter, who have now become essentially Mexican Americans by adopting what the narrator has presented as the worst of American culture: materialist pursuits, which lead his daughter to sell herself as a prostitute and his son to become a drunkard and a slave to maintaining his second-hand car. Quico says, "Yo no puedo regresar ya a mi tierra. No soy rico, vivimos, nada más vivimos, gracias a que hay trabajo duro que podemos desempeñar . . . soy tan probe como cuando vine, y ahora tengo lo que antes no tenía, un hijo borracho, perdido" (*El sol de Texas* 109) ("I can't go back now. I'm not a wealthy man. We're able to survive, but no more than survive, thanks to the fact that there's hard work that we can do. I am as poor now as when I got here, and now I have something I didn't have before, a son who is a drunk, a lost soul") (*Under the Texas Sun* 255). "Perdido" is the one word that sums up their American Dream. For Espinosa, those who stay in the United States are fated to lose their identity, becoming that hideous distortion of Mexican and American hybridism, the pocho. Others die in pursuit of their dream, while those who return regain their cultural integrity.

The righteous Serapio and his son Matías, despite the death of José, experience a bittersweet return to the homeland:

> Qué placer estar ahí, frente a la patria, junto a la patria, cuya tierra podía pisarse con sólo atravesar aquel puente. México. Otra vez en su seno, otra vez a sufrir y a gozar, pero a sufrir con los dolores de todos, a gozar con las alegrías de todos. Ahora se sabía lo que significaba patria, ahora se perdonaba a los caciques del pueblo y a los caciques de la nación. Cierto que eran crueles, pero ya pasarían, eran hombres, ya bajarían a dormir el sueño eterno, mientras que ella, la patria, aquella tierra bendita, aquella raza hermana, era inmortal. Sería libre, sería feliz, y con ella lo serían también todos los hijos buenos, los que pusieron su esfuerzo noble, los que tuvieron fe en el porvenir, trabajo en el presente, respeto y veneración para el pasado.[31] (108)

It is far better to suffer oppression and poverty among one's own people in the homeland than on foreign soil; furthermore, it is the patriotic duty of the sons of Mexico not to abandon their native land to live on foreign soil, but to invest in their country's future and to respect its history and culture. The irony, the tragedy, represented by José's dead body, is that the family had to leave home to learn to love their nation, to become patriots. The message to the Mexican reader is not to leave home for the glitter of the North; if you are already in El Norte, return as soon as possible, lest you meet the fate of José or of Quico's family, which has totally disintegrated and suffered the death of its Mexican identity.

Immigrants in real life suffer untold tragedies and death on their trek northward and through the deserts of the Southwest. The literature is rife with examples drawn from everyday incidents. Recent narratives, such as Alicia Alarcón's *La migra me hizo los mandados* (2002; *The Border Patrol Ate My Dust* 2004), Mario Bencastro's *Odisea del Norte* (1999; *Odyssey to the North* 1998), and Ramón Tianguis Pérez's *Diario de un mojado* (2003; *Diary of an Undocumented Immigrant* 1991),[32] draw on personal experiences and news items relating to the deaths of would-be immigrants to the United States or those already on the job in the Metropolis. In fact, the opening chapter of *Odisea del Norte*, which has been called "the foundational epic of Salvadoran

migration and settlement in the North" (Craft 156), relates the acciden-
tal death of a window washer who has fallen from his perch high up
on a building in Washington, D.C.: "Pobres diablos. . . . Mueren lejos
de su tierra, desconocidos. ("Poor devils. They die far from home, like
strangers") (3). As in his works on the civil wars in El Salvador, Bencastro includes a collage of newspaper articles, court transcripts, and
testimonies of transmigrants. In Becastro's young adult novel *Viaje a la
tierra del abuelo* (2004; *Journey to the Land of My Grandfather* 2004),
Sergio, a Salvadoran high school student from Los Angeles, takes it
upon himself to fulfill his grandfather's dying wish to be buried in his
homeland ("la tierra es mi ombligo") ("the land is my umbilical chord")
(32) and accompanies the coffin on a journey to El Salvador and an exploration of his ethnic roots and family history. However enriching the
experience, Sergio goes back to the City of Angels, for this is his true
homeland. The reason the funereal task falls to Sergio is that his parents are too wrapped up in the world of work and materialism in the
Metropolis to take time off to perform this duty, which seems beyond
their understanding.

MAKING A HOME IN THE METROPOLIS

Trópico en Manhattan, *La patria perdida*, and *El corrido de Dante* are
three novels that may be seen as a transition to a native U.S. Hispanic
or Latino literature that develops in the 1960s and has become slowly
integrated into mainstream publishing in English. The first two offer
alternatives to the definitive return home, and the last stakes a claim
on U.S. territory (or a portion thereof) that is typical of the discourse in
Chicano and Nuyorican literature.

Guillermo Cotto-Thorner's *Trópico en Manhattan* (1951; The tropics
in Manhattan) may be considered to exemplify a new stance regarding
return to the homeland; even more, it may be considered a transitional
work springing from a hybridization of culture and leading to a new,
native literature in the following generation. Cotto-Thorner, educated
and ordained as a Protestant minister in the United States, fully embraced the ethos of his adopted home; for him it opened the doors to
a successful career within the church and allowed him to direct his
ministry to Spanish-American immigrants. As expressed by the narrator in his novel, he also sees Puerto Ricans as already hybridized:
"Y la maldición que ha caído sobre nosotros es la falta de una conciencia acabada de puertorriqueñismo. Por ser políticamente americanos,

y de sangre y tradición hispana, no somos ni gringos ni jíbaros, sino una mezcla indefinida de características a veces opuestas" (68) (And the curse that has befallen us is the lack of awareness of what it means to be Puerto Rican. Because we are Americans politically and have Hispanic blood, we're neither gringos nor Ricans but an undefined mix of at times opposing traits). The duty of good Puerto Ricans is thus to identify the good in American culture while preserving the best of the home culture of the island. That is why various characters and the narrator condemn not only those who deny their Puerto Rican origins, but also the lumpen who bring uncivilized and uneducated behavior patterns with them from their island homeland. The narrator presents at great length the low life and criminal habits of these immigrants, from prostitution to *bolita* (a gambling game), but he also presents a series of "good" Puerto Ricans, in contrast, who truly wish to better themselves and avail themselves of the opportunities the United States has to offer the long-suffering masses. He provides an example of such a person in Miriam Santos, a young woman raised almost from infancy in El Barrio. She has preserved the best of Puerto Rican customs and morality despite having grown up in the alien environment. Miriam's marriage to an upstanding teacher, Juan Marcos, who has immigrated to further his education, much like the author himself, portends the possibility of the preservation of Puerto Rican culture in New York in perpetuity; it is their example that will gain the respect of the mainstream: "levantar nuestro prestigio cultural ante el pueblo norteamericano" (152) (to raise our cultural prestige in the eyes of the Americans).

To be sure, Cotto-Thorner does recognize the ills and pitfalls of the Metropolis, with its anti-Hispanic discrimination, materialistic values, and proclivity to immorality and criminality, but he does not call for a return to the homeland. Rather, while centering home values and culture on a woman as the symbol of the Nation, he projects that portions of New York, like El Barrio, and of the United States as a whole can become a homeland for Puerto Ricans, a home where their values and customs can take root to flower like a "tropics in Manhattan" and thereby obviate a return to the island. From this vantage point, Puerto Rican values and culture can flourish in a democratic society that emphasizes the work ethic and education, so willingly and consistently embraced by the narrator as the salvation for immigrants. As presented in the "Nota Inicial" (Opening note) of the novel, "Sobre la roca dura de Manhattan, y en torno a la masa de piedra de sus rascacielos, se esconde este jardín cuyos abrojos no pueden impedir que revienten día a día sus capullos de esperanza" (On that hard Manhattan rock, and surrounded by the massive stone of its skyscrapers, a garden is hidden where even the thistle cannot impede the daily buds of hope from appearing); thus the island culture can take root in the interstices of American life, the figurative cracks in the cement. Although Cotto-Thorner embraces the hybridity of Puerto Rican culture on the island and the mainland, never positing some long-standing purity or inherent antagonism of one for the other, either of American or Rican culture, his stance is not that of the Nuyoricans, Chicanos, and others who will appear in the 1960s and begin to promote bilingual and bicultural identities.[33] For Cotto-Thorner, some identifiable purity and essence of Puerto Rican language and culture can survive and flourish within the Metropolis.

Teodoro Torres's *La patria perdida* (1935; The fatherland lost), on the other hand, explores the option of returning to the homeland but with a surprising outcome to the journey home.[34] The novel follows the life of an expatriate named Luis Alfaro, a scion of Mexican wealth and privilege who many years earlier went into exile in the United States with his sickly wife. Torres, who, as noted, had served as an editorial writer for *La Prensa* in San Antonio and was well steeped in its ideology of México de Afuera, imbues Alfaro and his wife with nostalgia for the homeland and the dream of returning as soon as possible. He describes their efforts at preserving Mexican culture and the Spanish language in their expatriate home and farm outside Kansas City, Missouri, on which a community of Mexican immigrants work and reside. It is Luis's wife, Ana María, who feels the most uprooted and, as in many other immigrant narratives, comes to represent the Nation; she is the one who will die on Yankee soil and have to be taken by Luis to be interred in the patria: "Quiero que me prometas que si muero, no me dejarás en esta tierra que no ha sido mala con nosotros, pero que no es la mía. Llévame a donde seguramente irás tú cuando yo te deje. A Morelia, a Pátzcuaro, a México, a donde yo sienta, después de muerta, que estás cerca de mí" (19) (I want you to promise me that if I die, you won't leave me in this land that has not been bad for us but is not mine. Take me where for sure you'll go when I leave you. To Morelia, to Pátzcuaro, to Mexico, where after I die I'll feel you close to me). The couple adopts a blue-eyed, blond American child, whom they raise on their farm; he will come to personify cultural hybridism. At first Luis Alfaro is not as taken with the child as his adoptive mother Ana María, who had encouraged the adoption as a solution to her infertility—can it be that Mexican culture is infertile outside of the homeland? Alfaro's attitude toward cultural and linguistic purity is staunchly conservative and vehemently opposed to hybridism throughout most of the narrative. He repeatedly criticizes the pochos, agringados, and *ayancados* (Yankeefied), and in part 2, which deals with his return to Mexico, he reacts unfavorably to modern Mexico's adoption of Yankee ways.

The Alfaros' dream of return involves taking their son back to Mexico with them. They openly reject the American Dream, as they reveal in their conversations with Italian, German, and Polish immigrant acquaintances, who have wholly subscribed to it and never intend to return home: "Como en un conjuro, con la plática del italiano, se levantaba la ola de la emigración europea que viene a buscar el vellocino de oro, y realiza el milagro de labrar al mismo tiempo que la fortuna de cada emigrante, la riqueza fabulosa de esa Norteamérica, alquimista gigantesca, que torna en oro el sudor de la frente y la fatiga de los pechos" (35) (As if in a trance, through the Italian's conversation the wave of European immigrants was invoked, who come in search of the golden fleece, and each immigrant is able to accomplish the miracle of making a fortune, the fabulous wealth of the United States, the giant alchemist that turns the sweat of your brow and the fatigue of your breast into gold). The Alfaros are chagrined to observe how these European immigrants soon become truly American via the children they raise and school at the best institutions. They develop an attitude that proclaims them superior to the rest of the world's inhabitants: "Con los convencionalismos yanquis, que engendran el orgullo de la raza nueva, el producto puro del famoso 'melting pot'" (37) (With the Yankee conventions that engender the pride of a new culture, the product of the famous 'melting pot'"). Torres seems well steeped in the ideology of the American Dream and its implicit opportunity to remake oneself, to become a New Adam in American society; it is precisely such Americanization that receives his censure in the character of Magdalena (61–64), Alfaro's old lover from Mexico who has moved to the United States and appropriated the customs of a liberated woman, one who contrasts with the saintly personification of Mexican womanhood in Ana María: "la mujer buena, la dulce, la casta, la del amor tranquilo" (17) (the good, sweet, chaste woman of peaceful love). Torres's deft touch at narration is quite a bit more subtle than this obvious New Testament Magdalena-María dichotomy.

Although the Alfaros have the wealth to live in comfort and continue their lifestyle of *latifundistas* (large landowners), they still recoil at the grand American Metropolis, in this case Kansas City:

Kansas le parecía como todos los grandes poblados del país del norte, una ciudad de hierro, fría, estruendosa y dura como ese metal, hecha en férreos moldes, a golpes ciclópeos. Una fragua inmensa que nunca dejaba de trabajar para seguir elevando hasta el cielo las Torres de Babel de aquellos edificios gigantescos, para fabricar sus millones de carruajes que desfilaban por las calles congestionadas, en una línea sin solución de continuidad; para refaccionar el desgaste fabuloso de las mil máquinas que en todas partes jadeaban ayudando al individuo en los más nimios menesteres, hasta en el barrido de las calles y en las labores culinarias, como para dar oportunidad al hombre y a la mujer a que dedicaran más tiempo al negocio, al trabajo, al afán loco de la vida y del dinero.[35] (47)

The two spouses constantly voice their nostalgia for the homeland and the old ways, if only they could somehow relive their lives and work for a more equitable society in Mexico and avoid revolutions. The Alfaros have purposely removed themselves from the political exile community in San Antonio (15), which the narrator criticizes severely, as well as from the "agitada vida yanqui" (frenetic Yankee life) by buying a large farm and re-creating their hacienda on Missouri soil: "Bellavista había sido el primer débil lazo de unión entre la desterrada pareja que no dejaba nunca de suspirar por su rincón nativo, y la tierra extraña" (16) (Bellavista had been the first connection of the exiled couple, who never stopped missing their corner of the world, with this strange land). The Alfaros commit themselves to being more caring and equitable to the many Mexican peons who work on Bellavista, whom they call *colonos* (colonists). The narrator unself-consciously describes the workers' utopia the Alfaros have set up as only an elitist author would dare; there seems to be no irony or satire in his depiction of the patronizing relationship between masters and servants. Throughout the novel the narrator is condescending when depicting working-class culture and lack of education—although he does describe at some length the trials and tribulations of the economic refugees who migrated, including the use of their working-class dialect and grass-roots, self-deprecating humor: "Nos dijeron que aquí se barría el dinero con escobas. Las escobas sí las hallé, pero el dinero no. Yo barro las calles en Arley" (114) (They told us you could sweep up money here with a broom. I found the brooms, okay, but no money. I'm a street sweeper in Arley). Torres himself was a member of dictatorial regimes overthrown during the Mexican Revolution and was forced into exile in San Antonio.

The whole idea of refuge in this idyllic Bellavista, separated from the hurly burly of U.S. life as well as from the chaos and disorder of Mexico, tests credibility:

No era, no podia ser una nueva patria, porque las patrias, como las madres, son insustituibles; pero allí, en la soledad de la hacienda el país adquiría el encanto de una isla virgin, sin el ruido de las fábricas ni el anhelo civilizador de sus ciudades indiferentes y orgullosas; pro- porcionaba, además un rincón donde vivir en paz, y hacía un silencio amable en torno de aquellos dos extraños que apoyados en su propio cariño esperaban siempre el regreso, sin las ansias mortales de los pri- meros días, pero con la terca ilusión del que nunca renuncia al bien soñado.[36] (16)

Bellavista is the perfect model for the ideology of *México de Afuera*, an island populated only by Mexicans, where only Spanish is spoken, and the religion and customs of Mexicans are preserved and honored until the community can return to the beloved homeland. The celebra- tion of Mexican independence day even affords Luis an opportunity to give a speech on the subject of patriotism to his colonos. After the nar- rator has commented on how intensely the working-class colonos feel their patriotism despite having been treated so poorly in the homeland, Luis nevertheless finds himself reinforcing their and his Mexican iden- tity and desire to return home:

No olviden que tenemos la obligación de querer a México sobre todas las cosas, de honrarlo, de vivir de tal modo que conquistando el respeto para nosotros, lo conquistemos para él. Saquemos de esta aventura del exilio el provecho de ser más mexicanos que ninguno por haber vivido fuera de México. Aprovechemos las lecciones de dolor que nos ha dado el destierro, con la conciencia de que no hay patria como la nuestra, y con la esperanza de que al reintegrarnos a la casa paterna hallaremos en ella más calor y más cariño. . . . México se nos va a presentar con un rostro nuevo cuando volvamos.[37]

On this last prophetic note, Luis expounds eloquently on how the transmigrants have changed, as has Mexico, and that a period of adjust- ment will follow on their return for the betterment of both the patria and its wandering children. The last pages of part 1 end with an elo- quent, lengthy representation of the dream of return to the homeland.

Part 2 explores, like no other novel or play to this point in Latino history, the theme of the changed homeland and the protagonist's disillusionment upon return.[38]

After some ten years of residence in the United States, Ana María reacts strongly: she is tired of the foreignness of the surroundings and the culture and blinded to the beauty and enchantment of some ways of life in the States, which throughout the first part of the novel are compared consistently with Mexico's positive attributes. The return journey, in which Luis accompanies Ana María's casket, presents the inverse of the previous comparisons: Mexico is now unfavorably compared to the United States:

> Experimentaba Alfaro el primer síntoma de un mal que había de darle muchas amarguras en su viaje: la fatal revisión que daña de igual modo a las patrias que dejan marchar a sus hijos, y a los hijos que vuelven, al cabo de una ausencia prolongada y de haber adquirido, sin darse cuenta, modos de vida y de pensar extraños. El mal de la comparasión, inevitable, que busca paralelos y pretende ajustar a los mismos cartabones vidas tan distintas como las de estos dos pueblos, México y Estados Unidos.[39] (252–53)

Luis's journey home has the effect of dissipating his previous nostalgia and calling to mind the ills and backwardness of Mexican culture: "Tierra de castas y prejuicios. . . . Clases. División y subdivisión de clases" (218) (Land of castes and prejudices. . . . Social classes. Division and subdivision of classes); the relationship of racial features to class and privilege (219); a land of disorder and useless laws (221); a land of human misery side by side with the most ostentatious riches (221, 251); even the grandeur of the capital city brought down by zones of poverty, garbage, and misery (327): "La ciudad opulenta tenía aledaños de mendiga" (327) (the opulent city surrounded by zones of beggars). But Mexico had indeed changed in Luis's eyes: there had been an invasion of Yankee ways: "la invasión del cemento y de la cursilería progresista" (258) (the invasion of cement and progressivist jabber); the growth of American tourism, popularizing the manly customs of gringo women (263); past traditions forgotten and now, as in the United States, people living only for the moment in irrevocable forward movement (269). In sum, the Mexico he had known was now turned upside down, with women wearing pants, smoking in public, getting educated, and populating the government and business bureaucracies (291, 297), and the privileged social classes supported by past dictators, to which he had belonged, now penniless and marginalized (294) while laborers were ascending into a new middle class (298). Even the food was insipid, the product of canning and industrialization: "Alimentos industriales, en fin, que tenían el gusto de la máquina" (302) (industrial foodstuffs which, after all, tasted of machinery). And that "mayar de gatos" (caterwauling) and "rebuznar de jumentos" (ass-braying) music, jazz, was displacing traditional Mexican music (305). Not just American customs but even the English language was penetrating popular culture in Mexico (338), recalling the narrator's earlier railing against the mixing of the two languages and against hybridism. Luis's reaction to all of these shocks caused him to wonder if he was seeing everything through gringo eyes (299). And that was not all: Luis did not recognize anyone and never felt as alone as he did in Mexico, a stranger in his own land: "extranjero en su propia tierra" (349), someone who "se acercó con los brazos abiertos a un antiguo afecto, que respondió fríamente al cariñoso halago" (323) (approached a former loved one with open arms, only to receive a cold response).

There comes a point, however, when Luis realizes he has changed more than his beloved Mexico. Days had already passed since Luis had been feeling the call of Bellavista (324); the catalyst that sends him rushing home, however, is news that his son has taken ill. Luis returns to his son and to Bellavista committed to undoing past errors, those that in his homeland had produced class oppression and injustice and eventually a revolution, and to forging a utopia, not in his patria and not really in the United States but in a hybrid space, where the best of Mexican culture may thrive in the land and economy of the Yankees: in Bellavista. When a train loaded with emigrant workers passes him on his journey north, he wants to cry out to them to turn back, "para librarlos del mal que a él le destrozaba el alma" (380) (to free them from the malady that was tearing at his soul). Yet his is not the usual warning made explicit in most immigrant literature, that is, beware of false dreams of wealth and opportunity in the United States. Rather, what Luis would warn them of is the transformation of the self. He has changed so much he can no longer reside in the patria; he has become "un hombre que había perdido su patria" (381) (a man who had lost his homeland).

Although this is a loss of identity comparable to the ones in the works discussed above, in reality it is an existential affirmation of forging one's life, one's identity out of a hybridization imposed on the individual by circumstances, be they economic or political or even psychological. It is not a positive transformation for Luis or for the author. Luis becomes the mirror image of his son, who is an American adopted by a Mexican family; Luis has lost his mother country and has become an orphan adopted into American geographic space. It is a destiny Luis bemoans; he has joined the ranks of all those souls he has accompanied within the diaspora, so often referred to condescendingly throughout the novel.[40] Luis's transformation at the end is not an affirmation of cultural hybridity but a warning against it, although it implies a future that has potential for him and for his son. Implicit in this recognition of the hybridity that follows upon diaspora is the questioning of the concept of nation. No other text cited above challenges so deeply, so psychologically, this concept both from the foreign shore as well as from the national territory.

In his magical realist road novel *El corrido de Dante* (2006; *Dante's Ballad* 2007), Roberto González Viaña's articulation of the return home is more nuanced than many of the other versions. It goes further than both Cotto-Thorner and Torres in recognizing that the United States has changed immensely by becoming a land of Latinos. Like Luis in *La patria perdida*, the title character in *El corrido de Dante* must also transport the remains of his beloved wife back to the homeland, in this case to the small town in Michoacán where the couple had lived. Dante's wife, Beatriz, represents the territorial nation and its past and must be interred in her native soil. Like many transmigrants, however, Dante must remain in what is presented as an Inferno, but, as I explain below, becomes much more positive than earlier depictions of the United States, even if his Donkey Virgil is the metaphorical guide through the nether rings, or in this case the highways, of Hell. Dante is unable to return home because his fifteen-year-old daughter, Emmita, born in the United States and thus a U.S. citizen, does not identify with Mexico and sees herself strictly as an American. Dante cannot abandon her. In fact, the motive for the road trip that structures the novel is Dante's pursuit of Emmita, who has run away from home on the very night of her *quinceañera*, or fifteenth birthday party. Unlike many of the immigrant narratives that preceded *El corrido de Dante* in the twentieth century, however, this novel recognizes an amazing transformation in the States: wherever Dante travels, Spanish Americans of various ethnicities, whom the narrator calls Latinos, have succeeded in planting and nurturing their culture on American soil, so much so that they need not return to their respective lands to be in charge, to forge their own destinies, to live lives that are enriched by all of their cultural means, from food and music to religion and superstition. And in his dreams Dante is commanded even by God to stay in the United States and procreate:

> Aquí es donde debes trabajar y vivir. Mutiplicar, lo que de veras es multiplicar, no es lo que te estoy ordenando porque sólo tendrás una hija, pero tampoco te quejarás, yo sólo tuve uno. Si haces memoria, yo soy quien sacó a tu mujer y a ti de las tierras de Michoacán para traerlos, a ti caminando a través de los desiertos y a Beatriz raptando por un tunel oscuro.
>
> Acuérdate lo que te voy a decir: ésta es tu tierra y la tierra de los hijos de tu hija y de los hijos de los hijos de tu hija. No me preguntes si podrás volver a Michoacán porque eso no te lo quiero decir. . . . No, no en vida, no volverás a oler la fragancia de los chiles picosos ni a contemplar las tunas más rojas del universo. . . . Comerás el pan con el sudor de tu frente y con el dolor de tu alma y con la nostalgia de tu tierra, y a veces será pan duro bien diferente de los tamales de Michoacán. Serás feliz con la compañera que te he dado pero odiarás haber sido tan feliz cuando la pierdas y cuando lleves de regreso su cuerpo a Michoacán.[41] (166–167)

Even in the metaphorically infernal United States, Dante is able to find his divinely ordained and edenic destiny in the appropriately named Mount Angel in the state of Oregon. He has traveled far enough north to figuratively reach the sky, leaving behind the inferno of migrant farm labor and other forms of exploitation he experienced. While Beatriz must return to rest in her native soil, Dante is stymied, afraid he will not be able to return ever to the United States and to Emmita if he ventures over to the other side, even to El Paso, where his musical *conjunto* performs. Emmita represents the new land, the land of milk and honey, and Dante as a father is committed to her. The novel ends with Emmita and her father reunited: now a university student, she teaches him to read and write English, and father and daughter look to that future prophetic vision of children and grandchildren and great-grandchildren in the United States. González Viaña's epic tale of migration, of love lost and gained and lost again, of nostalgia for the homeland and discovery of a new world as rich in opportunities as it is in idiosyncratic characters never before treated in literature, protests the suffering and persecution of transmigrants while celebrating their love of life, their beliefs, and their imagination in legendry, literature, and, most of all, song. Ultimately, the novel is a lyrical call for a revision of national identities and boundaries, geographic, political, and cultural.

CHAPTER 4

NATION AND NARRATION

La patria, aquella tierra bendita,
aquella raza hermana, era inmortal.
Sería libre, sería feliz,
y con ella lo serían también
todos los hijos buenos,
los que pusieron su esfuerzo noble,
los que tuvieron fe en el porvenir,
trabajo en el presente,
respeto y veneración para el pasado.
—CONRADO ESPINOSA, *EL SOL DE TEXAS*

THE MAJORITY OF the works discussed in the preceding chapter imagined the nation as a geographic area in which the audiences addressed
in their narrations must reside to maintain their cultural and political
integrity. Remaining in the host country or subscribing to the American national myths or both were regarded as a sign of disloyalty and
treachery to the homeland that had nurtured the transmigrants and
given them an identity, a worldview, often a complex of shared historical, racial, and even religious orientations. In no uncertain terms,
these authors presented negative, often stereotyped examples of these
denizens of a cultural space that was neither of the homeland nor of
the host country; while aspiring to be Americans, they became *pitiyanquis*, gringoized ingrates, and, in the case of Mexican nationhood,
persons completely unrecognizable as Mexican: *pochos*. The exhorta-
tions of Daniel Venegas, Conrado Espinosa, and René Marqués, for example, were for the humble *campesinos* and *jíbaros* to return to their
home soil and invest in or, even more preferable, literally grow the nation. The plaintive tones of the *corridos* and *décimas* called upon the

transmigrants to return to the fields, hillsides, and mountains of their beloved lands, if not in life, at least in death—implicitly to restore the natural order, if not enrich the soil: Mexicans in Mexico, Puerto Ricans on the island, and so forth. No greater lesson could be learned from the follies and disillusionment of those who heed the siren call of American ingenuity, technological progress, and wealth than to be destroyed by the same machines and technology that had beckoned them, as in *Lucas Guevara*, *El sol de Texas*, and *La carreta*. And it often was the lot of women to be cast in these works as the purveyors and protectors of the national culture and the rescuers of men who were losing themselves in the Metropolis; on the other hand, these works also insisted on presenting the negative examples of frivolous, materialistic Eves who led the transmigrant Adams astray (see chapter 6).

THE NATION AND HOMELAND

I want to consider how the diasporic literature that develops from Hispanic transmigration begins to challenge concepts of nationhood as identical to territorial and cultural affiliation, especially in the works of intellectual writers from the mid-twentieth century to the present, including Guillermo Cotto-Thorner, Teodoro Torres, Eduardo González Viaña, and Iván Acosta, among others. My discussion in no way implies a chronological evolution, given the fact that authors like Jorge Franco, Roberto Quezada, and Mario Bencastro, among many other transmigrant writers today, continue to promote homeland geography or territory as the major determinant of national identity.

To be sure, such writers as Venegas and Espinosa implicitly and explicitly imagine a history and culture rooted in the homeland from ages past, a foundational myth, as Branislaw Malinowski would call it, that "supplies a retrospective pattern of moral values, sociological order, and magical belief, the function of which is to strengthen tradition and endow it with a greater value and prestige by tracing it back to a higher, better, more supernatural reality of initial events."[1]

Despite Venegas's identification with the common man, the working-class Chicano immigrant, his initial literary project patterned itself after the national narrative par excellence of Spain, *Las aventuras del ingenioso caballero Don Quijote de la Mancha*, perhaps at first as burlesque in creating the more humble character parallels of Don Quijote/Don Chipote (a name which means a bump on the noggin), Sancho Panza/Policarpo, Rocinante/Sufrelambre ("Starved Hack"/"Suffers

Hunger") and Maritornes/Pelona, but ultimately emphasizing the Hispanic roots of the culture he designates as Chicano. Despite grounding his greenhorn character in the arid soil of rural northern Mexico and appropriating its *campesino* dialect, foodways, religiosity, and other customs, Venegas rarely, if ever, invokes an indigenous past or present, attending more to the Hispanic patterns represented in Cervantes's novel, the Hispanic-*mestizo* patterns of the corrido, and especially the picaresque novel, whose structure provides a strong pattern for the journey through the U.S. Southwest taken by Venegas's main character. And *Las aventuras de Don Chipote, o Cuando los pericos mamen* is populated with numerous *pícaros*, or rogues, who take advantage of the greenhorn Chipote. This type of walkabout, which Benedict Anderson has identified as a primary nation-forming structure in novels, occurs in *Don Chipote*: "The movement of a solitary hero through a sociological landscape of fixity that fuses the world inside the novel with the world outside. The picaresque *tour d'horizon*—hospitals, prisons, remote villages, monasteries, Indians, Negroes" (35). During this tour Venegas, as a witness/narrator, interrupts the flow of the narrative to remind the reader that he, himself, witnessed these events and characters and to editorialize in protest of the injustice and inhumanity visited on real people as well as on the fictional characters. In Venegas's binary of U.S./Mexican homeland, his effort at demythologizing the United States surveys modern technology in the form of streetcars and the railroad Chipote and Policarpo help to build, hospitals, highway construction, foremen and the class system, Negroes and the vestiges of slavery, the urban underworld with its sex trade and its exploitation of greenhorns, and so on, all the while indicting the governments and corporations of Mexico and the United States alike for their inhuman exploitation of innocent, poverty-stricken transmigrants. By always sympathizing and identifying with the *chicanada* (chicanos as a group) and its humble values of family, noninstitutional religiosity, and work ethic, Venegas makes it clear that rural Mexico, with its wholesome Hispanic-mestizo folkways and mores, is the nation his characters and readers must embrace as theirs even as they must reject the American national myths as illusions that mask dehumanization, materialism, and racism in the United States. It is to this rural, poverty-stricken area of northern Mexico that the characters return in order to remain whole and preserve family and identity.

Espinosa, even more of a Hispanophile than Venegas and more moralistic in emphasizing patriotism as a sacrosanct duty, resuscitates a key episode in *Don Quijote* to present his vision of national origin. As Regis Debray has written, "A point of origin is fixed, the mythic birth of the *Polis*, the birth of Civilization or of the Christian era, the Muslim Hegira, and so on. This zero point or starting point is what allows ritual repetition, the ritualization of memory, celebration, commemoration—in short, all those forms of magical behavior signifying defeat of the irreversibility of time" (27).

Don Quijote's famous speech, known as "The Golden Age" and delivered in the chapter entitled "Bodas de Camacho" (Camacho's wedding)—perhaps the same passage that inspired Anderson to apply this name to the motive in nationalist literature—is invoked and adopted by Espinosa in chapter 12 of *El sol de Texas*, appropriately entitled "El Tricolor" after the red, green, and white Mexican flag. In describing the patriotic speeches given in honor of Mexico's founding fathers during San Antonio's commemoration of Mexican independence, the elitist narrator lightly satirizes the humble, patriotic speechifying of workers unaccustomed to speaking in public; but more serious is his censure of hybridity, of the inauthentic and uneducated remonstrance of love of country, because they can only be pure and authentic in the homeland itself. The only recourse the workers have in this imperfect copy of a national Mexican holiday is to use folkspeak, despite their grandiloquent intentions: "Señores y señoras: Porque semos [instead of the grammatically correct *somos*] mexicanos . . . necesitamos estar unidos todos los mexicanos, para demostrarles a estos hombres que también somos civilizados, que también sabemos honrar a nuestra patria. ¡Necesitamos que todos nuestros hijos mamen la santísima leche de la Patria!"[2] (77).

In response comes a wisecrack from someone in the audience: "¡Los alimenta mejor la de su madre!" (Your mother's milk would nourish them better!). With this burlesque of the Fiestas Patrias celebrations of September 16, the omniscient narrator, who identifies himself as a shadow in the crowd, launches into an extensive discourse on the meaning of patriotism and nation. He is inspired by the festive scene, which reminds him of the "Bodas de Camacho" chapter in *Don Quijote*, in which the Knight of the Sad Countenance delivers his inspired discourse on the Golden Age. The narrator imagines what Don Quijote's speech would have been like in this contemporary setting:

¡Oh tiempos y edades aquéllas en que los hombres no conocieron fronteras circunscritas por la codicia! ¡Oh días felices en que ni el color, ni la lengua, por ser una misma y armoniosa, encajaban diferencias entre los hijos de Adán!

¡Oh dorados días de aquella época en la cual los fuertes gastaban su energía en el socorro y el remedio de los débiles, sin más mira que el anhelo ardiente de verter el caudal de sus amplios, generosos y fraternales pechos!

¡Oh, hombres felices aquéllos que no conocieron la férula de gobiernos descastados y aviesos, que se forman para expoliar multitudes, para repartirse la tierra y su ganado humano y entregarse celosos y desconfiados a su esquilma!

* * * * *

¡Oh soles aquellos que desconocieron todo este pervertido progreso de máquinas y vicios! Cuánto mejor el tardo paso por la agreste senda, que este correr sobre pulimentadas carreteras, en carros que, trasuntos mejorados de la magia clavileñesca, llevan en una fiebre de ambiciones nunca satisfechas y en un retorcedor de siempre aumentadas congojas. . . .

¿Qué necesidad ni qué apremio hubieran tenido estos hombres sencillos para dejar las llamadas y las sierras de su patria y para echarse en busca de las fementidas ollas de Egipto?[3] (79)

Seemingly returning to ancient, pastoral times, when all men were equal despite the color of their skin and the language they spoke, the narrator anxiously indicts modernity, capitalism, and corrupt governments as well as the uprooting of the chosen people from their ancestral lands to labor as slaves in Egypt, in a clear analogy to the transmigrants' dislocation from rural Mexico to the Metropolis. The narrator continues pondering the exploitation of their labor, the injustice of their suffering at home and in the host country, rhetorically asking if this was God's design, but he suddenly switches to a messianic vision that often characterizes nationalist narratives and political speeches:

¿Quién me dice que no son éstos los medios para resucitar en un mañana lejano por cierto, toda la bondad moral de la Edad de Oro, aumentada y mejorada con las conquistas que en este camino de dolor lograron los hombres?

¿Quién me dice que este medio de circunscripciones para patrias y razas, no será el camino mejor para choques de compenetración, para fusión de intereses, para desarrollo de propias e íntimas virtudes y para futura conjunción amorosa y óptima?

¡Para qué inculpar a estos hombres rubios, como verdugos cal-
culistas y fríos de estos hombres morenos? Son reos los primeros en
haber robado al misterio esa su energía y esos sus arrestos y ese su
aserto para desarrollar toda una época de capitalismo, para dar un
matiz especial a la civilización para poner a flote y facilitar el estudio y
el examen de toda una serie de peligrosas virtudes y nefandos vicios.

Y los otros, los morenos, ¿son culpables de la vecindad de éstos?
¿Tienen alguna culpa de haber sido engendrados por razas hechas
para épocas de batalla heroica, de vivir épico, de empresas conquista-
doras y grandes? Si aún persisten y guardan su rico solar, a pesar de que
estos tiempos han mermado el prestigio de la espada y de la fantasía, si
siguen cultivando tan fervorosos el rito de la ilusión y del honor, ¡allá
el secreto que florecerá mañana! ¡Allá la página que aún no voltea el
dedo de Dios para mostrarla a nuestros ojos!

¡Que pase el tiempo . . .

Quizá entonces . . .[4] (81)

After considering the possibility of "fusion," that is, a resultant hybridity after the shock of the two races (although he makes reference to
the darker people, "raza" is not used in the biological sense but the cultural) confronting each other, the Anglo and the Mexican, the narrator
in the last full paragraph above peers into a future destiny in which his
own people will flourish. He bases his vision on the past grandeur of
the conquistadores—although it is not clear if he includes the Aztecs
in his time and place of origin of people born for the heroic and epic
gesture, or he means to refer to modern Mexicans as "morenos," that
is, mestizos.[5] Most important, that racial memory relies on the sword
and on imagination, following dreams and achieving honor: "la espada
y la fantasía" and "la ilusión y del honor"—all motives of *Don Quijote*
and Golden Age Spanish literature in general. And this has been pre-
ordained by God . . . "allá," repeated. (Over there . . . over there.) That is,
in Mexico, on national terrain. Thus in this one passage, so emphati-
cally set off from the rest of the text as a speech inspired in deep racial
memory, Espinosa has alluded to the three Old Testament concepts
Hans Kohn has identified in nationalist texts: "the idea of a chosen
people, the emphasis on the common stock of memory of the past and
of hopes for the future, and finally national messianism" (9). One day
Mexico will fulfill its destiny and exceed Yankee conquest and rule
of the material world through spirituality, the arts, literature, cultural
understanding. It is left unsaid precisely how the illusion and honor

will combine with the sword and fantasy, but some indication may be found in the passage quoted as an epigraph to this chapter.

Torres invokes the pre-Hispanic past more directly in his vision of Mexican origins in *La patria perdida*. On his return to Mexico, Torres's protagonist Luis makes a steady ascent to the highlands of Michoacán, his and his wife's place of birth, and on a moonlit evening climbs to a vantage point overlooking the valleys below and imagines the history of the peoples that populated the land from time immemorial. The omniscient narrator details at length Luis's analysis of the major themes of the history of Michoacán, which can be extrapolated to all of Mexico. If there is a central focus in his summary of indigenous and Spanish governments succeeding each other, it is the errant nature of the people, destined to migrate throughout time. His history also foregrounds a common theme among late nineteenth-century Mexican intellectuals: Mexico as a mestizo nation. Luis begins by recognizing a grand history, an epic of struggles and deeds that continues to resound today but that started with primitive peoples emerging from the forests and jungles to fight each other for dominance over the land (279). They built large temples and edifices but were always driven by the need to migrate: "El impulso errante que las movía sin descanso, que las trajo de ignorados y remotos orígenes, y las revolvía y las agitaba, en el curso de los siglos, como si estuvieran condenadas a no asentarse nunca en un lugar definitivo" (280–281) (The errant impulse that kept them moving without rest, which had brought them from unknown and remote origins, and mixed them together and agitated them, for centuries, as if they were condemned to never settle in a final place). The most noteworthy of the lot were the *puherepechas*, who despite their "espíritu nómada, hecho al viaje y al eterno caminar" (281) (nomadic spirit, made for travel and endless wandering) stayed and ruled Michoacán for a long time until they were replaced by other wanderers, such as the Aztecs and, ultimately, the Spanish conquistadores and settlers. The missionaries came and brought the light into the "alma oscura" (dark soul) of the indigenes, and the mestizo was born from the miscegenation of Spaniards and indigenous peoples, but Luis highlights the upper-class mating that took place among them rather than the more humble couplings. Periods of extermination of the primitive *michoacanos* followed, until a patriarch, Bishop Vasco de Quiroga, who "loved the Indians like a father" (284), came and ruled more equitably, establishing laws and policies that have survived to this day.

The long rhetorical presentation of Luis's imaginings circuitously arrives at his millenary vision of redemption of the indigenous past through the rise of the mestizo. Torres is here using *mestizaje*, like many Mexican intellectuals of the time, in its nationalistic implications for unifying a diverse Mexico.[6] In referring to the indigenous past and foregrounding mestizaje, Torres is echoing the postrevolutionary nation-building process that Robert Young has identified: "If the cult of *mestizaje* enabled the construction of a national identity marked by mixing, then *indigenismo* provided the framework for pulling the internal exteriority of the Indian into the national mix. The former exalted a national trait; the latter interpolated a heretofore alienated subject. Together, they worked in the service of hegemony: the forging of an integral body politic" (67). Torres, who was part of the regime of the dictator Porfirio Díaz, is continuing, some thirty years after Díaz was deposed, the construction of the Mexican nation on the back of the mestizo. As Young summarizes, "It is under Díaz, then, that *mestizaje* achieves it apotheosis, and becomes the norm of both a hegemonic nationalization of identity and a sovereign institutionalization of state" (88). Joshua Lund contends that the need to transform the vast hinterland of Mexico into a productive geography, in a capitalist sense, was a primary motive for the advancement of theories on race and mestizaje.[7] Torres's protagonist, a reformed *latifundista*, intends to construct a mestizo utopia on his American hacienda, Bellavista.

In Luis's vision the heavenly, eternal bodies in the skies above are personified in their waiting for the indigenes/mestizos to fulfill their destiny:

> Esperaban, con la paciencia y dulzura de las cosas eternas, el día que la doliente[8] raza india fuera por fin dueña de su tierra, sin sobresaltos ni quebrantos, sin conmociones ni revueltas, sin guerras que la arrancaran de su hogar, sin miserias que la obligaran a vagar por los caminos, llevando a cuestas el producto de sus pobrísimas industrias, sino asentada firmemente en este vasto espacio que promete acomodo y sustento no sólo para los hijos del país, sino para humanidades enteras.[9] (284)

This uncovering of ancient roots is what Anthony D. Smith calls the "purification," "a golden age that can act as an inspiration" to help solve contemporary problems (450). Luis's vision of the past and his prescience of a time when Mexican wandering would cease and give way to an epoch of justice for all humanity foreshadows not only the

next part of the passage but also the denouement of the novel. After independence, Luis remembers, there followed an entire century of wars,
revolutions, and migrations:

> En la peregrinación sin fin que comenzaba en la oscuridad de los tiem-
> pos y seguía aún, muy civilizadamente, pero con el mismo andar me-
> droso de la fuga, en trenes y automóviles, por caminos asfaltados; era
> la misma peregrinación la que veía ahora, encadenando las escenas
> grandiosas de su larga visión de aquella noche, con las escenas que aca-
> baba de presenciar en la frontera de los Estados Unidos, en los cami-
> nos poblados de emigrantes que volvían en derrota pero con esperanza,
> huído ya el nuevo Nuño de Guzmán que los echara fuera—el ham-
> bre, la discordia—en busca de la paz, de la abundancia que tanto se les
> había negado.[10] (286)

Here, the narrator, in relating Luis's thoughts, brings the thesis up
to the present and directly indicts the Revolution for once again having
uprooted the people and condemned them to ceaseless wandering,
driven by hunger, discord, and hope. As Smith writes, "The past then
becomes the standard against which to measure the alleged failings of
the present generation and contemporary community" (450). And the
rest of Luis's journey will transpire in judgment of postrevolutionary
Mexico. There is no doubt that the Revolution and Mexico fail in Luis's
eyes, and the author's.

Luis's imaginary survey of Mexican history from the heights of Michoacán is immediately followed by episodes in which he becomes
increasingly aware of the awful changes that have transpired in contemporary Mexico. As I noted in chapter 3, he becomes a stranger in
his own land, where in addition to lamenting the Americanization or,
more accurately, the hybridization of Mexico, which is anathema to
him, he repeats another theme of the *porfirista* exile: that the men
who have taken over his *patria* are from the unwashed and uneducated
masses (298–299)—later it will be his duty as the educated and benefi-
cent *hacendado*, the *patrón* of Bellavista, to slowly bring his uneducated farmhands to their future illustrious prominence. The Mexico
Luis rejects has been inherited by men in "zambra perpetua" (289) (perpetual commotion) "por esa fiebre de placer que le había quedado como
herencia de una larga etapa revolucionaria, subvertidora de los valores
sociales. . . . veía también en aquel muestrario humano la transforma-
ción social que se había operado en un pueblo. Todo un cataclismo que

cambió conceptos, ensanchando los límites de una clase, reduciendo los de otra, poniendo lo de arriba abajo y lo de abajo arriba"[11] (290–291) (because of that feverish pursuit of pleasure that remained as an inheritance from a long period of revolution that subverted all social values. . . . he also observed in that sampling of humans the social transformation that had taken place in the people. It was a complete cataclysm that changed concepts, broadening the limits of one social class, reducing those of another, lowering what was on top to the bottom, raising the bottom to the top). Thus Luis finds himself on the horns of an existential dilemma: he feels at home neither in the United States nor Mexico; his identity and values are at odds with the national myths and realities of both nation-states.[12]

Luis's final judgment relates directly to his vision from on high: a people condemned to eternal migration:

> Volvía a presentársele a Alfaro el espectáculo de un pueblo inquieto que carece del arraigo del lugar y vive en perpetua movilidad. La raza errante, podía llamársele a la suya que no podía o no quería establecerse en un sitio, hacerse un plan de vida, aferrarse al patrimonio familiar, explotar el suelo, la única salvación de este gran país desierto. . . . ¿Emigrar? ¿Moverse de un punto a otro con la incorformidad del que no se siente a gusto en ninguna parte? ¿Para qué, Dios santo? ¿Por qué no volver a los campos, a los villorios, ahora que el peligro había pasado? ¿Por qué había en el extranjero esos millones que persistían en la emigración a pesar de sus dolorosas condiciones de elementos indeseables en el país vecino, que los invitaba a salir de mil maneras, y que a pesar de todo se quedaban, unos por la absoluta imposibilidad de regresar y otros porque estaban ya ligados a la nacionalidad nueva y no podían desprenderse de ella?[13] (341–342)

THE NATION BEYOND THE HOMELAND

Luis will return to Bellavista to form his own nation, a refuge where his beleaguered indigenous/mestizo people can stop their wandering, settle down under the protection and care of an enlightened, educated leader who will preserve the best of Mexican tradition while embracing cultural change and hybridity for the forging of a new humanity, which will eventually inherit the land.[14] Torres recognizes and reemphasizes time and again in Luis's observations and his own uprootedness, first of all, that his nation exists in the state of diaspora, and because of that, second, his nation really exists beyond the geographic and political limits of the Mexican state. These two realizations, plus Luis's personal guilt for having participated in the oppression of the working class as not only a privileged *hacendado* but also as part of the political regime that provoked the Revolution that would scatter his people from their homeland, lead him to create a utopia beyond the bounds of Mexican and American politics and social organization.

Torres's utopia in Bellavista has arisen from the transitional moment in Mexican life following the great upheaval of the Revolution; it posits an alternative state and culture to the one being implemented in postrevolutionary Mexico and the one to be found in the much-mythologized El Norte. It has been created by the author, narrator, and protagonist looking to the past for a narrative of origin, for answers and orientation, and projects to the future in Bellavista. Rather than some radically changed nation, Bellavista is an "abstract utopia" that results from an impulse to repair the present, to follow Ernst Bloch's typology of utopias.[15] If Bellavista is to be taken as a model society for the Mexican nation, as "a way of telling and making modern history" (Wegner xvi), it promotes not a representative democracy but a republic led by a humane class of educated, enlightened leaders—the sort of *científicos* that Torres and his intellectual cohorts had belonged to under the deposed Díaz dictatorship. However, the government would be repaired to eliminate the abuse and exploitation and create the path leading to greater education and empowerment of the mestizo masses. In time they would truly be able to administer a democratic republic, purportedly within the geopolitical boundaries of a state under a *patrón* such as Luis (a reincarnation, a new and improved Porfirio Díaz, possibly). Torres's vision does not merely look to the past in the formulation of a national narrative; it recognizes social evolution and the inevitable process of hybridity, however noxious it may feel to Luis and national essentialists. The Luis-Luisito dyad, father and son, ultimately recognizes and accepts the merging of American and Mexican cultures for the betterment of both and of humanity in general. *La patria perdida* engages in what Phillip Wegner has called a "re-territorialization" that is "producing new strictures and bounds, 'norms and forms,' that are imposed upon and within the social and cultural environment" (25). Out of the present disorder and even chaos of the errant Mexican nation, Torres prescribes an original cultural program for the future.[16]

If Torres's utopia is planted in the agricultural fields of rural America, as have been many experimental communities in U.S. history, Guillermo Cotto-Thorner's *Trópico en Manhattan* proposes the planting of an ideal "jardín" right in the heart of the Metropolis, an ideal garden—can one extend the metaphor to a Garden of Eden in which the characters Juan Marcos and Miriam Santos are the foundational couple?—in El Barrio, that is, East or Spanish Harlem. In a prescient analysis of the relationship between the external colony, Puerto Rico, and the internal colony, Spanish Harlem, Cotto, at every step in his novel, separates cultural nationalism from political nationalism by consigning the debate over Puerto Rico's and the Boricua immigrants' political status to the sidelines. At the same time he makes a case for the ascension and flowering of Boricua culture in New York—and in the entire continent, by extension—through education and acceptance of the opportunities offered by the American citizenship that Puerto Ricans have enjoyed since 1917. Cotto, as noted earlier, came to New York as a theology student at Columbia University, was ordained a Baptist minister in 1942, and went on to minister to Spanish-speaking immigrants, mostly Puerto Ricans in New York and other cities.[17] Textual and biographical information attests to his having achieved his American Dream through access to higher education and the profession it enabled him to have.[18] The "Nota Inicial" and the metaphors in the last chapter announce and reinforce his utopian vision: "sobre la roca dura de Manhattan . . . se esconde este jardín" (on the hard rock of Manhattan . . . this garden is hidden) and "somos parte de un azulejo incrustado en la roca dura de Manhattan" (242) (we are part of a ceramic tile cemented onto the hard rock of Manhattan). The flowers of the hidden garden produce buds of hope, and the tile, with its many tropical colors and its glaze, adds to the diversity of the city, allowing the richness of Puerto Rican culture a permanent space in the Metropolis.[19]

As I mentioned in chapter 3, Cotto develops his thesis by pairing the educated, hardworking characters, who are confident of the value of their Puerto Rican culture and open to the opportunities of the American Dream, with those who bring their ignorance and underclass lifestyle with them into Gomorrah. That indolent way of life will flourish and bring about their demise just as surely as the attributes of the exemplary characters will lead them to succeed. Unlike much of the literature of immigration, U.S. and homeland cultures are not cast in opposition, and a return to the homeland is not emphasized; instead Cotto embraces a hybridity not unlike Torres's: a space where authentic Hispanic culture can survive, surrounded by the larger multicultural society. Cotto's cultural nationalism, however, depends greatly on identifying with American national myths while at the same time celebrating and preserving his idea of Puerto Rican culture—even if that culture, he realizes, is diverse and hybridized itself.

The character Antonio introduces Juan Marcos, the newcomer, to their colony, Spanish Harlem, where, as in the U.S. colony of Puerto Rico, their culture thrives, but thrives in the manner of a colony, that is, where the wealth generated benefits outsiders: "Este—respondió Antonio—es nuestro Barrio. Se dice que los latinos mandamos aquí. Y así nos creemos. Mientras los americanos se llevan la mayor parte del dinero que circula por aquí, nosotros pensamos que esta parte de la ciudad es ya nuestra" (21) ("This," answered Antonio, "is our Barrio. It's said that we Latinos rule here. And that's what we believe [or: That's our illusion]. While the Americans take out most of the money that circulates here, we think this part of the city is already ours"). The similarity between the two "colonies" is immediately emphasized in the next chapter, when Juan Marcos realizes, "El, que creía estar tan lejos de Puerto Rico, se encontraba ahora, a tantas millas de distancia, de nuevo en un pedazo de su amada tierra" (23) (He, who thought he was so far from Puerto Rico, after so many miles of distance found himself on a piece of his beloved land). The reasons for Juan Marcos's migration to New York probably mirror the author's own reasons and lay the basis for his embrace of the American Dream: "buscar más amplios horizontes" (28) (looking for broader horizons); "venirme para acá a fin de civilizarme" (24) (to come here to get civilized) and pursue "esta nueva vida" (32) (this new life).[20] And immediately Juan Marcos finds work and economic and social success, at first earning as much as a teacher on the island but later giving up that job for one with higher prestige but lower pay at the public library—the pursuit of money is not his sole motivator. Moreover, Juan Marcos's new task is to ensure the flourishing of Spanish Harlem by raising "el nivel cultural de la colonia" (79) (the cultural level of the colony); he establishes and leads a cultural club patterned on the island's famed Ateneo (Athenaeum), where concerts, dramatic performances, exhibits, and literary readings are held. Ultimately, Juan Marcos is concerned with raising the opinions Americans have of Puerto Ricans: "Le haremos ver al pueblo americano que tenemos talento, que tenemos bagaje cultural, y que ellos muy bien podrían aprender muchas cosas de nosotros" (213) (We'll show the American people that we have talent, that we have cultural baggage, and they very well may learn many things from us). His words reveal an inferiority complex much concerned with deflecting discrimination and prejudice by an oppressed minority group and, as such, may be typical of what Smith considers to be an *ethnie*, a group very much like a nation but lacking a public culture (*Nationalism* 13). This "public culture" is very much what Juan Marcos wants to establish for his community.

Throughout the novel Juan Marcos contests arguments about discrimination, poor living conditions, and labor exploitation as barriers that should send the immigrants home. His counterarguments rely on the Protestant ethic and his confidence in the opportunities for advancement offered by American society: "Aquí no hay tantos prejuicios como dice la gente. Es mera propaganda, aquí uno vale por lo que es" (52) (There aren't as many prejudices here as people say. It's just propaganda, here one is valued for what he is). If Puerto Ricans and Latinos have to work hard and in humble jobs at first, it is the character of the individual that matters; and hard work builds an honorable character: "Hacer un trabajo humilde no significa ser inferior. Uno vale por su carácter, por su dignidad, y por la vergüenza que uno tiene, y no por la ropa que viste o por las míseras pesetas que se gana" (101) (Having a humble job does not mean being inferior. A person's value resides in his character, his dignity and his honor, not from the clothes he wears or the miserable wages he earns). Moreover, there is an explicit warning against expecting easy success in the land of opportunity without working hard for it: "Nuestro más grande pecado consiste en aspirar a la Gloria sin la voluntad de cargar la cruz" (212) (Our greatest sin consists of aspiring to Glory without wanting to carry the cross). Prejudice and labor exploitation are part of the price to be paid to earn the privileges and opportunities in this society. One of those easy responses for lack of social progress, according to the narrator, is to blame everything on discrimination and to invest in ideological politics to reform the society for the immigrant. Large sections of the novel are directed toward contesting communist propaganda in the barrio, often showing how it is destructive of cultural life, even threatening to his own culture club, which is named after the Puerto Rican patriot Eugenio María de Hostos (besides fighting for independence, Hostos was known as "the great educator"). In fact, one salutary effect of the Hostos club is its diminishing "cierta tendencia nacionalista y chauvinista que había imperado entre los miembros" (148) (a certain nationalist and chauvinistic tendency that had dominated some of the members). *Trópico en Manhattan* was published at the beginning of the decade that would see Puerto Rican nationalists assault Congress and when numerous *independentistas* were imprisoned. Cotto's novel perhaps had the additional purpose of resolving the political antagonisms that were tearing Puerto Rican culture apart.

What Cotto advocates instead of political organizing in this novel, although he does advocate educating oneself on the issues and voting, is following the inner light of the soul and persevering through the adversity the city offers new arrivals like Lencho, as explained in a preacher's sermon (60): "El secreto de la vida feliz consiste en poseer el don espiritual que nos capacita para afrontar serenamente, con mucha fe y esperanza, lo adverso e inesperado . . . si hay valor y fe, en la más oscura noche siempre hay luz" (62–63) (The secret to a happy life consists in possessing the spiritual gift that prepares us to calmly and with great faith and hope confront adversity and the unforeseen . . . if there is courage and faith, in the darkest of nights there is always light). The very root beliefs of American society are presented in the context of the Protestant teachings within which they originated. Even Lencho, the vengeful antagonist driven by a "conciencia enferma" (113) (sick conscience), is temporarily persuaded to follow the golden path. But ultimately he, like many other negative examples in the novel, fails due to the lack of "perseverancia y responsabilidad" (127) (perseverance and a sense of responsibility), giving into their passions, not following reason and not trying to improve themselves (127). Cotto's most powerful declaration of cultural nationalism, and a spirituality to accompany it, is Juan Marcos's rebuttal to a communist intellectual's assault:

> A nosotros no sólo se nos explota económicamente, sino en lo espiritual e intelectual. Para los dueños y directores de las corporaciones, ¿qué somos? Pues instrumentos de producción. Y la idea de ellos es producir más y más, amasar grandes fortunas, a expensas del sudor de los otros infelices. ¿Y en lo social y cultural, qué somos para ellos? Basura. Nos consideran bárbaros, atrasados, incultos, y semi-salvajes. Así que, del mismo modo que tenemos que luchar por el mejoramiento económico, es nuestro deber luchar por levantar nuestro prestigio cultural ante el pueblo norteamericano. . . . Cuando los americanos nos lleguen a respetar por nuestra cultura, entonces estaremos en vía de resolver otros problemas también importantes.[21] (152)

If Cotto embraces the American Dream, he most definitely does not advocate the melting pot. He does, however, identify negative attitudes and behavior that impede immigrants' road to success in the United States; most notably, such attitudes are incarnated in self-destructive characters like Lencho. For Cotto, it is possible to be both Puerto Rican and American: culturally and linguistically Puerto Rican, politically and economically American.²² And there is no stronger exemplar of this dual identity than Juan Marcos and his bride-to-be, Miriam Santos, who represent a confidence in their cultural identity, which they will foster in the Metropolis, as well as a willingness to pursue the opportunities that continue to confirm the American Dream. Miriam, in particular, is the embodiment of this sacrosanct duty, for she is presented as almost saintly, having been raised in Manhattan but remaining more Puerto Rican than many who reside on the island. Despite having lived twenty years of her life in New York and not remembering her homeland at all (81), Miriam speaks perfect Spanish (not the Spanglish Cotto censures throughout) and preserves the customs of the homeland. But Miriam's cultural steadfastness is not so surprising, given the example set by her seventy-nine-year-old "abuela santa" (saintly grandmother), Doña Emilia, who is not her blood relative but a mentor who has lived her life in the service of others. Doña Emilia counsels the young couple to be parsimonious and not ostentatious in their upcoming wedding ceremonies—unlike the pretentious, grotesque display their immigrant brethren are known to put on to impress relatives back home. In Doña Emilia's house, the couple is able to partake of a completely Puerto Rican meal, which reductively represents the survival and flourishing of their culture in New York (160). Juan Marcos and Miriam are prepared to be the perfect couple to live in and populate the hidden garden, creating a future for their people in the heart of the Metropolis.

Except for the language difference, *Trópico en Manhattan* resembles the novels of immigration that colonial subjects and former colonial subjects have written to record the experience of moving from the islands of Jamaica and Trinidad to London, such as Sam Selvon's *The Lonely Londoners*. In these works the same themes of the Metropolis and its dehumanization and discrimination as well as nostalgia for the homeland, are highlighted within a general didactic framework of how to survive and prosper in the alien environment. *Trópico en Manhattan* is overwhelmingly didactic in its illustration of the ills and pitfalls as well as the opportunities for transmigrants in the Metropolis. What's more, its moralizing tone and undercurrent of Christian teaching almost take the narrative to the level of allegory in which these first parents will engender a nation—or *ethnie*, if one gives Smith his due—prepared to assume its rightful place alongside the other social constituents of a multicultural United States. In the eyes of both Cotto-

Thorner and Selvon, their people have earned this right through citizenship and through having rendered service, military and otherwise, to the state. This is quite a different position from the works of immigrant literature discussed in chapter 3, in which the authors and their characters have no rights of citizenship, only human rights. *Trópico en Manhattan* ultimately confirms and encourages the right of Puerto Ricans to dream the American Dream but without having to sacrifice their language and culture to do so—a sacrifice European immigrants thrown into the melting pot traditionally were expected to make.

A NEW HOMELAND

Eduardo González Viaña in his contemporary tale of immigration *El corrido de Dante* purposefully sets about mythmaking and utilizes the themes and techniques of nation building in providing a basis for a new, bicultural United States in which Latinos are part of not only the official history but the national identity, for this is truly the land of immigrants. Around the plot of Dante's divided family—his separation from his beloved wife, Beatriz, who was left behind in the homeland for years, and from his runaway daughter Emmita in the United States— that gives rise to his travels through the contemporary West and Southwest of the United States, González has developed a whole magical realist cosmography of religious and superstitious practices, epic landscapes, and heroic figures to legitimize the Latino demographic explosion and future cultural preeminence in the United States. The narratives discussed above stake out a limited utopia in which to correct historical mistakes and prepare for a future hybridity, thus resolving the binary of cultural and geopolitical conflict, or the dream of maintaining cultural purity in an edenic garden right in the middle of the monster Metropolis. González, by contrast, has elevated the struggles of Mexican transmigrants and other Latinos to mythopoetic stature, using Old Testament stories as well as Latino folk songs and legends to write his new history of Latinos and of the United States.

Borrowing most heavily from the epic-narrative tradition and performance of Mexican corridos, the Peruvian immigrant González does not, however, project specific nationalities as the basis for a Hispanization of the United States. In this regard he differs from Torres, who dealt solely with Mexicans, and with Cotto-Thorner, who was mainly addressing Puerto Ricans. González fashions his tale as an exemplar for all the Hispanic ethnic groups in the United States and populates the episodes with, among others, Cuban, Colombian, Mexican, Chicano, Peruvian, Puerto Rican, and Venezuelan characters, all engaged in the same transmigrant remaking of the United States. González's foundational myth, in fact, takes the reader back to Genesis, when God divided the world into northern and southern hemispheres with two particular types of inhabitants:

> Los del norte le salieron calladitos, ordenados, ahorrativos y buenos para la mecánica, rubios y castos, con la carne un poquito cruda como si el Hechor era mal cocinero, y a lo mejor no sazonaba muy bien. Pero al hacer los del sur, se excedió en la sal, y los hizo intensos, algo tostados, amigos del revoltijo y de las fiestas, intrépidos, frenéticos y enamorados. Aprovechaban de cualquier momento que los dejara solos para hacer crecer y multiplicarse.[23] (64)

And realizing that greater balance was required in the world, God made life very difficult for the southern folk through famine and wars and dictatorships and natural disasters, effectuated by the Devil. God came to the southern folk in dreams about the wealth to be made in the North in order to inspire their exodus—read here, a new myth on top of the old myth of the American Dream—and he created guides such as Facundo to bring these "tostaditos" and "intensos" north to procreate and multiply (65). The divinely created "coyote," or labor smuggler, Facundo, later ascended to sainthood, and Facundo's children had taken on the role of Moses for Dante's people and led them to the Promised Land (110), in which Dante's burro Virgilio, because donkeys are the animals closest to God (279), has served as his guide. In this magically populated landscape, phantom mariachi groups lure the transmigrants to their death in the southwestern deserts, like the sirens who lured the sailors in *The Odyssey*; people hide their identities with false Social Security cards but eventually take on the personalities and biographies of the original owners; hosts of Spanish-language radio call-in shows are capable of foretelling the future of the callers; saints intervene to protect the migrants en route; and Dante not only has the virtuosity to become the accordionist for the most popular corrido band but also becomes mythologized himself in corridos that are sung from Oregon to the Mexican border.

Numerous times in the novel it is stated that Latinos were born to migrate, like the butterflies returning north (105), like salmon swimming upstream: "Es como si comenzáramos a nadar en el vientre de nuestras madres y, al salir, siguiéramos nadando hacía el norte" (74) (It's as if we started swimming in our mothers' wombs and, on coming out, we continued swimming northward). Latinos come to enrich the lives and culture of the people of the more frigid regions: "Deben acceptar a todos los que quieren entrar. No sólo eso. Deben invitarlos para que vengan a mejorar las razas frías del norte" (142) (They should accept everyone who wants to enter. Not only that. They should invite them to come and improve the cold peoples of the North). And so by the time Dante and Beatriz come on the scene (as much in love with each other as their Italian namesakes), the United States is populated everywhere with Latinos, who have obeyed God's order to migrate north and multiply. When their daughter Emmita was conceived, "Tal vez todos los latinos en los Estados Unidos estaban haciendo el amor al mismo tiempo y generando más vida, temblorosos y brillantes por los naturales hervores de la pasión que son entre nosotros veinte veces más cálidos y fosforescentes que los de la gente de las regiones frías del mundo" (127).[24]

So much immigration and so much multiplying have gone on that even Dante is surprised at the penetration of *hispanos*: "Ya estaba en casi el corazón de los Estados Unidos. Le extrañó encontrar tanta gente en todas partes que hablara y luciera como él, y que incluso los policías no fueran gringos ni hablaran inglés" (228) (He was already nearly in the heart of the United States. He was surprised to find so many people everywhere that spoke and looked like him, and even policemen who were not gringos and did not speak English). And each group, Mexicans, Cubans, Colombians, Chileans, Venezuelans, and so forth, has a saint charged with watching over the transmigrants on their journeys: La Santa Muerta, María Lionza, María Sabina, Santa Bárbara, Sarita Colonia, San Jesús Malverde. Facundo/Moisés is not the labor smuggler on the nightly news reports but a saint leading his people through the desert, like Moses leading the Israelites of the Old Testament. And he is not breaking laws in leading the transmigrants northward but following divine revelation and leading his people on a holy pilgrimage, one during which they must behave in a religious manner: "Les prohibió detenerse en las ciudades, beber tequila y entrar en burdeles, y los obligaba a rezar, a meditar y a soportar prolongados ayunos" (61) (He prohibited them from staying in cities, drinking tequila, and going to brothels, and he obligated them to pray, to meditate, and fast for long periods of time). Facundo/Moisés and his family themselves become mythologized: Facundo's face appears in the clouds above the desert to warn the transmigrants not to venerate the idols of the gringos or they will be transformed into pillars of salt (64); here one myth subverts and replaces the other, as the force driving the transmigrants must not be the prospect of sweeping up gold from the streets; they are not seeking to enrich themselves, they are following a divinely inspired imperative to migrate. Even the common coyotes ascend to the level of legendry: "Tienen ojos para ver detrás de los cerros, del agua y de la noche. Pueden cambiar de forma y transformarse en árboles, pájaros y serpientes. Por eso, nada pueden contra ellos los de la Migra" (279) (They have eyes that can see behind hills, under water and in the night. They can change form and transform themselves into trees, birds and snakes. That's why the Migra [the Immigration and Naturalization Service] can't do anything about them).

In this novel of light political protest and strong celebration of Latino culture and literature, both oral and written, there is an explicit call for the elimination of political and geographic borders: Dante envisions the stars twinkling in the firmament as the souls of transmigrants "volando hacia las fronteras de un universo sin fronteras" (57) (flying toward the border of a universe without borders). And the transmigrants' songs to their patron saints tell of a world without immigration agents and without borders: "La frontera sin agentes/el mundo sin fronteras" (274). Many make their way back and forth, repeatedly eluding the Border Patrol, white supremacists, and people who prey on the unwary travelers; many are here to stay, like Dante and his daughter, to see generations of their descendants becoming the mainstay of life in this country. As God had revealed to Dante in his dreams, "Esta es tu tierra y la tierra de los hijos de tu hija y de los hijos de los hijos de tu hija" (166) (This is your land and the land of your daughter's children and the children of your daughter's children).

In *El corrido de Dante*, González Viaña acts as translator and disseminator of texts across cultures, taking two series of myths, those of the sending nations and those of the receiving nations, rewriting them, and generating a new imaginary, one just as fictitious and beautiful and outlandish as the two originals—and also just as historical or ahistorical as foundations for a people's identity. In the process he seems to exercise what Homi K. Bhabha described as "a temporality of representation that moves between cultural formations and social processes without a 'centered' logic" (*DissemiNation* 293). Bhabha continues, "The power of supplementarity is not the negation of the preconstituted social contradictions of the past and the present; its force lies . . . in the renegotiation of those times, terms, and traditions through

which we turn our uncertain, passing contemporaneity into the signs
of history" (*DissemiNation* 306). In his narrative González Viaña, to
borrow from Bhabha once again,

> contests genealogies of "origin" that lead to cultural supremacy and
> historical priority. Minority discourse acknowledges the status of na-
> tional culture—and the people—as a contentious, performative space
> of the perplexity of the living in the midst of the pedagogical represen-
> tations of fullness of life. Now there is no reason to believe that such
> marks of difference—the incommensurable time of the subject cul-
> ture—cannot inscribe "history" of the people or become the gathering
> points of political solidarity. (*DissemiNation* 308)

Whereas Torres may have provided an argument for the historical priority of Mexican culture and Cotto-Thorner an argument for a
public culture for Puerto Ricans to flourish within the United States
alongside majority culture, neither author attempts to truly disas-
semble the armature of myths that sustain the receptor nation; rather,
one proposes an alternative, a Porfirian utopia, and the other a program for participating in and benefiting from the supposed rewards
given to the authorized believer-participants in the nation, U.S. citizens. González not only subverts and replaces the U.S. national myths
but treats the present as past: the United States is no longer an Anglo-
European geopolitical-cultural state. That was the past; the Latino
States of America is the present and future, in praxis, not just in fiction
and myth. The long-predestined integration of the Americas has taken
place; Simón Bolívar's dream has become a reality, at least as far north
as the Canadian border. González's discourse is directed at readers who
are familiar with the conflicting histories, myths, and politics of the
two peoples confronting each other; these readers' initial disbelief is
assuaged through irony and a subversive humor that allows the author
to propose what otherwise would be a preposterous mythopoesis; but
it is made palatable, indeed, enjoyable, through the techniques of magical realism. The fantasy and the magic have led the reader to greater
truths and to an insight into the reality of not only, to use Bhabha's
words again, the "pagus—colonials, postcolonials, migrants, minorities," but also "the *Heim* of the national culture and its unisonant discourse" (315).

CHAPTER 5

IMMIGRATION AND GENDER:
FEMALE PERSPECTIVES

*Los tiempos cambian. La mujer . . . está en vías de una completa
emancipación, y si en otra época la represión del pensamiento
femenino fuese excusable por el ambiente absurdo en que se
vivía entonces, en la hora presente no hay derecho a vedarle
su desarollo intelectual. La mujer debe surgir al lugar que le
corresponde.*
—HORTENSIA ELIZONDO, "LA MUJER MODERNA,"
EL CONTINENTAL (EL PASO), JUNE 11, 1935

THE QUESTION OF GENDER has often been related to the concept
of nation, as so many theorists and critics have demonstrated. This
chapter and the next, therefore, may be considered as a continuation
of chapter 4, whose subject was the nation as imagined by transmigrant authors. In the following pages, I will first outline how and what
Hispanic women wrote from within the context of immigration to the
United States, and then, in chapter 6, present a detailed account of
how male authors imagined Hispanic women, mostly from the traditional perspective as symbols, protectors and generators of the nation.
This chapter will not be an exhaustive treatment of the subject, given
its vastness as well as the current inaccessibility of texts which are
only now being discovered. Rather, this brief exposition will only mention how some women authors, even while ascribing to and furthering
male-initiated and -dominated projects of nation-building, were able to
find interstices and develop strategies from which to write themselves
into the public sphere, the nation, the world. Others were able to es-
chew nationalism in order to construct a world not divided by class,
nation, and gender, or they sought to create an international sisterhood
of Hispanic women.

From the late nineteenth century to the Second World War, as authors like Alirio Díaz Guerra, Conrado Espinosa, Daniel Venegas, and Teodoro Torres, among many others, were demythologizing the American Dream and casting the Hispanic woman as the saintly repository of national values and symbol of the homeland, Hispanic women assumed intellectual, creative, and activist roles, at first within the areas assigned to women in publishing enterprises and later in their own newspapers, magazines, and books.[1] They were never as numerous as the thousands of males who wrote and published and who took for granted their access to and domination of the means of intellectual and artistic production. Many of their names are lost to history because of the anonymity or pseudonymity that was part of their strategy for gaining access; other names are only now being recovered, even though these women published side by side, on the same pages and in the same periodicals, with male transmigrant authors who have garnered attention now for decades. There are ample texts available today to affirm that women wrote from the same three positions outlined in chapter 2: as natives, as migrants, and as exiles. In the past two decades the extensive works of such native authors as María Amparo Ruiz de Burton, Jovita González, Cleofas Jaramillo, Nina Otero Warren, and various others have shown how each in her own way sought to preserve a Hispanic past in the Southwest and even challenge the imposition of American culture and its political hegemony. If they did not directly contest American national myths, they did construct equally valid—and equally fantastic and flawed—Hispanic myths of priority, civilized European roots, and racial background. But these native authors are not the subject of my exploration of the literature of transmigrants. Among the transmigrant women authors can be found a nascent Hispanic feminism that began to challenge stereotypes about the docility and submissiveness of *hispanas* or *latinas*. More directly related to the literature of transmigrant women, however, are the documents created by women political exiles and their immigrant sisters of both working-class and upper-class backgrounds. Taken as a whole, these documents demonstrate that their authors were able to create a space within the receptor country from which to evaluate and challenge gender roles and develop a concept of feminist theory and praxis for the Hispanic world.

WOMEN AND MILITANCY

Among the most militant women to have graced American soil were the anarcho-syndicalists who participated in laying the foundations for the Mexican Revolution of 1910. Accompanying the male leaders of the insurrection into exile and participating in the founding and promoting of the Partido Liberal Mexicano (Mexican Liberal Party, or PLM), Andrea and Teresa Villarreal, Sara Estela Ramírez, Blanca de Moncaleano, and Leonor Villegas de Magnón, to name just a few, created a space—what Emma Pérez calls third-space feminism—for women in the articulation of the nation they were attempting to create through militant, revolutionary action: "Women as agents have always constructed their own spaces interstitially, within nationalisms, nationalisms that often miss women's subtle interventions" (Pérez 33). These women were not food preparers and clothes washers for the revolutionaries whom Mexico celebrates today as its founding fathers: they were thinkers, speech-makers, even frontline, gun-wielding fighters. More important, each of those mentioned above wrote. They complemented their activism with a powerful record of journalism and, in the case of Villegas de Magnón, detailed memoirs of women's revolutionary activities. Pérez writes, "The revolution, then, created a kind of renaissance during which women wrote essays and edited their own magazines, newspapers, and journals. Many of these women who sought political exile in the southwestern United States wrote prolifically, criticizing the dictator Porfirio Díaz and championing the revolution for women" (56).

Like her sister Teresa and most of the other female revolutionists mentioned above, Andrea Villarreal was a teacher in Mexican normal schools, and she placed her education and writing talent at the service of the PLM. When the PLM men were imprisoned, she and Teresa traveled the Southwest to organize protests that sought their release. Both she and Teresa published essays and articles in the party's primary forum, *Regeneración*, in Los Angeles and went on to found and operate their own newspapers in San Antonio: Andrea's *La Mujer Moderna* (1909, The modern woman) and Teresa's *El Obrero* (The worker). In these publications they continued to espouse anarchism in support of labor organizing. In an essay signed by both sisters entitled "¿Qué hacéis aquí hombres? Volad, volad al campo de batalla" (What are you doing here, men? Fly off, fly off to the battlefield), published in *Regeneración* on 21 January 1911, they base their call to arms to men in the United States and Mexico alike on their mettle as women who do not

fear violence and death: "Mujeres somos, pero no hemos sentido fla-
quezas que nos empujen a abandoner la pelea. Mientras más punzante
el dolor que nos hería, más se acrecentaba el cariño que profesamos a
la causa de la libertad" (*En otra voz* 463) (We are women, but we are not
so weak as to abandon the fight. However throbbing the pain of the
wounds we suffered, we have felt even more the love for the cause of
liberty that we profess). This militant enunciation from a place of supposed weakness is typical of what Pérez calls a "dialectics of doubling,"
in the sense that Homi Bhabha uses the concept,[2] as referenced earlier,
whereby women openly supported the "nationalist cause of the revolution, but they intervened interstitially with their own rhetoric about
their place and meaning in the revolution" (59). While the women supported and even mimicked the male ideologues, they also "advocated
their own agenda, they wrote and spoke third-space feminism" (68).

Another practitioner of third-space feminism, one who, as a fer-
vent anarchist, did not subscribe to nationalist projects and did not believe social classes or borders should exist but nevertheless joined the
PLM, was the Colombian Blanca de Moncaleano.[3] Active in Bogotá,
where she and her husband, Juan Francisco Moncaleano, an anarchist
leader, ran the Casa del Obrero (Worker's house), she taught school and
published articles in periodicals such as *El Revachol* (the name of a
famous martyred anarchist). After her husband was jailed and released
in 1911, the couple and their four children fled to Mexico to participate
in the Revolution. In Mexico City Blanca and Juan Francisco established an anarchist society and school, La Casa del Obrero Mundial
(Workers of the world house) and the newspaper *Luz* (Light) in order
"to prepare a firm ideological base for the reconstruction of Mexican
society."[4] The first victorious faction under Francisco Madero exiled
them to Cuba, where Blanca continued to publish in such newspapers
as *Tierra* (Land). By 1913 Blanca had joined the PLM in Los Angeles,
where she and her husband ran the Casa del Obrero International (The
international workers' house), and she edited the women's anarchist
newspaper *Pluma Roja* (Red pen), which was known for its virile writing style.[5] The newspaper positioned women's liberation as central to
any social change. For *Pluma Roja*, according to Clara Lomas, "unques-
tioned patriarchal authority, upheld by religion and the state, was the
target of the red pen" ("Articulation" 305). Beyond attacking patriarchal society, the state, and the Church, Moncaleano was severely critical of revolutionary men who were not conscious of their suppression
and enslavement of women ("Articulation" 306). Moncaleano sought to

break down the nationalist ideological linking of woman to home and family and to procreating the nation. In the edition of *Regeneración* for June 13, 1914, she wrote, "Do not forget that a woman has rights equal to those of a man. She is not on this earth only to procreate, to wash dishes, and to wash clothes" (cited in Pérez, 69). Unlike the leaders of the PLM, Ricardo and Enrique Flores Magón, among others, who believed, as the Villarreal article cited above did, that it was women's "'feminine duty'—to coddle men, nurture them, and dare them to become revolutionaries"; Moncaleano, "by contrast, ordered women from their prescribed functions entirely" (Pérez 69).

Laredo, as a border crossing and rail terminus for Mexico, became an important center of revolutionary and feminist organizing. Another PLM member who articulated gender and labor issues in her speeches and writing was Sara Estela Ramírez, who had immigrated to Laredo from Saltillo in 1898 at the age of seventeen to teach school. She soon became an intellectual leader in the border town, helping to prepare the way for the Revolution. Through her reading of her own poetry and her eloquent, moving speeches, Ramírez promoted labor unions and addressed political issues at community meetings and labor rallies. She published articles in two of Laredo's newspapers, *La Crónica* (The chronicle) and *El Demócrata Fronterizo* (The border democrat), and in 1910 began publishing her own newspaper, *La Corregidora*, named in honor of a heroine of Mexican independence. In 1910 also she founded a short-lived literary magazine, *Aurora*. She died that same year, probably of tuberculosis.[6]

It was another PLM coconspirator in Laredo, however, who became the personification of writing and militancy, the women's version of the "pen and the sword": Leonor Villegas de Magnón. Villegas was born in Nuevo Laredo, Mexico, but from the age of five lived in Laredo, where her father administered his ranching, import-export, and other businesses. The bilingual Villegas obtained a college education in New York in 1895, moved back to Laredo, and in 1901 married Adolfo Magnón and lived for nine years in a turbulent Mexico City. There, she became associated with Ricardo Flores Magón and the PLM in preparing the way for the coming revolution. When the revolution broke out in 1910, Villegas was back in Laredo, teaching school, organizing revolutionary groups, founding and running the Unión, Progreso y Caridad (Unity, progress, and charity), giving refuge to political exiles, and proselytizing through articles she published in *La Crónica*, *El Progreso*, and *El Radical*. Within a couple of years, she recruited Texas Anglo and

Mexican women for her nursing corps, the Cruz Blanca (White cross), which worked on the battlefields as part of Venustiano Carranza's Constitutionalist Army. Serving often at Carranza's side, she was like a general to her nurses and often to the female spies and fighters (*soldaderas*) who rendered service as well. Ever cognizant of the historic role she and her nurses were playing, Villegas hired a photographer to document the Cruz Blanca's activities. When the major hostilities were over and men began taking account of and writing the history of the Revolution, Villegas became aware that the important role women had played was being forgotten. She wrote a memoir, *La rebelde*, to correct the record and celebrate the leadership and contributions of women. Despite all the connections she and her family had in the political and business spheres in Mexico, no one would publish her story. She then decided to rewrite, not translate, the story in English as *The Rebel* and met a similar fate with publishers in the United States. Villegas continued her feminist and political activism in Laredo throughout her life, but her manuscripts, extensive correspondence, and photographs remained in a trunk passed down to her granddaughter, Leonor Smith, who eventually worked with the researcher Clara Lomas to get both documents published by the Recovering the U.S. Hispanic Literary Heritage Project at the University of Houston in 1994 and 2007, respectively. According to Lomas, "These narratives stand as one of the few perspectives written by women in the early 1900s on the Mexican Revolution. They document the pivotal role of border activism that in effect erases geopolitical boundaries" (*Greenwood Encyclopedia* vol. 3). More important, they serve as a sterling example of women working within the interstices, the third spaces assigned to their gender, such as nursing, to expand their assigned role in public life. Even though her books were not published in her lifetime, they are an example of a feminism that transcended borders, both of gender and of geopolitics.

By far the most productive anarchist writer was Luisa Capetillo, who was not a political exile or a participant in armed insurrection but a transmigrant who worked as a labor organizer in the islands of the Caribbean, Tampa, Florida, and Long Island, New York. Unlike Villegas and her cohort of teachers, Capetillo was largely self-educated and belonged to the working class that the aforementioned women intellectuals aspired to liberate. Perhaps this partially explains her more radical embrace of anarchism's antinationalist program and its goal of creating a classless society in which there was absolute equality of the sexes. Capetillo was born in Puerto Rico of self-educated, unwed working-class parents who worked at numerous jobs, including domestic and migrant work, and who studied the revolutionary ideas of the late nineteenth century. Capetillo was politicized from a young age, especially by her mother, who participated in literary and study groups, often as the only female in attendance (Valle 44–45). She received her primary education from her parents and attended a private girls' school for a few years. When Puerto Rico came under U.S. dominance, Capetillo became active in the island's major labor union and began publishing articles in newspapers such as *Unión Obrera* (Worker unity) (Matos xv). She herself became a purveyor of working-class ideologies when she joined the ranks of the most important institution of worker self-education as a *lector*. Lectores, who were almost exclusively male, worked in cigar factories on the island and the continent and would spend one half of the day reading newspapers to the workers and the other half reading, for example, the works of Pëtr Kropotkin, Mikhail Bakunin, and other theorists of anarchism and socialism.

Her mission, namely, to educate workers as to their human rights and as to participation in the social revolution that would remake world culture, was not limited to the factory readings but eventually extended to articles she wrote for Spanish-language newspapers everywhere she worked, whether on the islands or in the continental United States. It also extended to writing plays and poetry to be performed in labor halls; after the performances she led discussions and answered questions about her artistic framing of the principles of anarchism and women's liberation. After years of writing articles and giving speeches, Capetillo was able to rewrite, compile, and self-publish a number of books of essays, plays, and poetry, all aimed at educating workers. Her books include *Ensayos libertarios* (Libertarian essays, 1909), in which she details her anarchist ideology; *La humanidad en el futuro* (1910), which she published to raise funds for her magazine; *Mi opinión sobre las libertades, derechos y deberes de la mujer* (My opinion on the liberties, rights, and duties of women, 1911), in which she details her feminism and argues for the education of women; and *Influencia de las ideas modernas* (1916), which includes many of her more literary works, including theatrical pieces performed in union halls. All of these books were published before Puerto Ricans became citizens of the United States in 1917, and most of her activism on continental soil was undertaken while she was an economic refugee. In her eyes her work lay more in organizing and proselytizing than in laboring as a lector in the factories. She also founded and edited a magazine entitled

La Mujer (Woman). In her personal life as in her writing, Capetillo was iconoclastic, not recognizing the authority of males, the Church, or the state; deconstructing and criticizing patriotism;[7] working for women's suffrage; advocating free love; having two children out of wedlock; and even cross-dressing, for which she was expelled from Cuba, where she had been organizing cigar workers.

Capetillo illustrated in her plays how marriage was a form of bondage or prostitution for women, and she openly advocated the benefits of free love and its relationship to a classless society. In most of her plays women were the most dynamic characters, driving the plot and delivering Capetillo's theses. Despite her creation of aggressive female protagonists, Capetillo's art did not separate the genders. As Lara Walker has shown, "Capetillo's feminist practice and class equality propose places of contact, alliances between women and men of heterogeneous backgrounds, which in turn are corollary to her keen observation of the oppressive effects of social difference. Capetillo consistently creates characters who incorporate her political ideals and utopian visions, forging female working-class subjectivities that are leaders and instruments for change and equality" (xviii).

Her modus operandi for concretizing her ideology for worker audiences was to take a theatrical genre with which they were all familiar, Spanish nineteenth-century melodrama, shorten and simplify the plot structure involving well-worn character types that represented the social classes, and subvert these structures in a sort of early *verfremdungseffekt* (that is, making something strange out of the familiar) long before Bertolt Brecht had made it famous. As Walker explains,

> Capetillo's writing, like other texts of working-class literature, employs bourgeois literary conventions and elements, subverting not only elite culture, but also anarchism's and anarcho-syndicalism's phalolo-gocentrism and orthodox Marxism. In this sense Capetillo's "literature of resistance" in this context signifies writing directed not only against dominant culture, but also against restrictive elements within a sub-culture—in this instance, the working-class and union organizing. (xi)

Capetillo was a militant anarcho-feminist, and it is in her *Influencia de las ideas modernas*, especially the plays, where many of her ideas received full treatment. She demonstrates how history, societies, political systems, classes, and genders are constructed. Walker believes Capetillo was employing what Stuart Hall would much later call a "politics of representation" and "the designs and desires for cultural resistance" that today's cultural critics, such as bell hooks and Gloria Anzaldúa, among others, have proposed (xxx). Capetillo devoted her life and her writing to radical resistance as far as permitted by the limits imposed on people by traditions and institutions: "She crosses spatial boundaries and borders in order to blur, disrupt and resist them. In doing so, she crafts other spaces and interstices, or finds access to spaces that attempt to deny her and all women in general. Thus, woman is the catalyst to create a utopian society of equality and progress in which, 'woman will always be a woman' (*Influencias* 85), an instigator of social change, radical possibility, and revolution" (Walker xxxiv).

By assuming positions of power as a lectora, union organizer, speechmaker, public performer, writer, and intellectual leader among working-class Hispanic immigrants, Capetillo went well beyond creating from the interstices and third spaces of a patriarchal society mentioned by theorists above. However, there was probably no economic or political segment of the continental United States and the Hispanophone Caribbean as marginalized as these transmigrant workers and their communities. Where Capetillo presumably impacted her communities significantly, especially in raising the level of consciousness about workers' rights and needs around the world and the imperative for absolute equality of the sexes—which must have helped women gain access to public spaces and the workplace as well as furthered the unionizing efforts in certain industries—Capetillo's words lay dormant and inaccessible to those national imaginaries until now. Scholars are finally disinterring and translating those words as part of the effort to create new histories and genealogies that go beyond borders, genders, races, and social classes. According to Lisa Sánchez González, "A radical anarcho-feminist may be the most apt foundational figure for a colonial diaspora's literary history. Indeed, Capetillo's intransigent rejection of geopolitical, gendered, erotic, philosophical, and generic borders as obsolete concepts suggests the kind of socially, ethically, sensually, and aesthetically engaged hermeneutics relevant to a community barred wealth and sociosymbolic status, in transit from one stifling national context to another" (76).

WOMEN CREATING SPACES WITHIN THE PATRIARCHY

Whereas the preceding writers found their voice and activism mainly by writing from within and for working-class transmigrant communities, another generation of women writers created from the interstices to be found in the overwhelmingly patriarchal community of conservative exiles who took up political refuge in the United States when the dictatorial regime of Porfirio Díaz was deposed in 1910. As I mentioned in chapter 2, many of the members of this generation of political refugees, who arrived with resources and ascended to the business and cultural leadership in the urban centers that received the brunt of the Mexican diaspora, became the publishers, editors, and writers that formed a market for their intellectual products, among not only fellow political refugees but also the vastly larger community of economic refugees. It was this sector that formulated and disseminated through all cultural venues—newspapers and periodicals, the theater, the Church, and mutual aid societies—the ideology of exile that eventually came to be known as *El México de Afuera*. A group of women writers associated with the publishers of periodicals and constituting the very rare female voices to resound on the pages of these male-dominated periodicals have been seen as a cohort of "conservative feminists." They believed that women were defined by maternity, but they nevertheless called for fundamental rights, such as education; they continued to affirm that women were the procreators and symbol of the nation, but they also created an activist role for women, who could legitimately enter public spaces to advocate for their education and freedom of thought (Villarroel, 5–8). They advanced their program through participation in the feminist debates raging in the United States and Mexico: "Si bien es cierto que ellas lo hacían desde una posicionalidad conservadora como lo era el México de Afuera, su escritura reflejaba un intento por escribir desde *su* lugar, escribir como mujer, lo que las llevó a participar, desde diversas perspectivas, en el debate político y femenino que se estaba llevando a cabo en Estados Unidos y México" (Villarroel 23).[8]

Such writers as Sara Estela Ramírez, Angelina Elizondo, Hortensia Elizondo, and Dolores Bolio, among a few others in this small community, sustained a discourse of woman as the "Angel del Hogar" (Angel of the Hearth/Home), all the while proposing a program of small reforms in the name of the common good related to woman's education:

Así que por un lado defendían la naturaleza maternal y abnegada de la mujer mexicana, por otro postulaban la necesidad de que la mujer mexicana se preparara intelectualmente para cumplir mejor su rol de educadora y protectora de la cultura. Esto introducía un cambio en el

concepto de la Mujer Mexicana, un cambio enunciado desde una per-
spectiva propia y femenina que en el nivel discursivo significaba de-
mandar el poder de dicha enunciación.[9] (23)

The condition of exile brought their ideological stance to a critical head. They found themselves confronted with the advances Anglo-
American feminists were making, including gaining the vote in 1920,
and had to defend their position before more radical feminists from
the Hispanic world, such as those discussed above. This stance was
especially difficult to articulate, given the nationalist ideology promoted in the exile community, whose overriding thrust was battling
the effects of the Revolution and reinstalling itself in the homeland.
These women, too, had to engage in doubling and writing from a third
space and even to resort to writing as men.

The poet, novelist, and *cronista* María Luisa Garza made San
Antonio her home after being uprooted by the Mexican Revolution.
From the Alamo City, she contributed articles and columns to a number of periodicals in Texas, such as *El Demócrata Fronterizo* in Laredo,
and was the editor of *La Epoca* (The epoch). But her renown came in
the form of her weekly column, entitled "Crónicas Femeninas," which
she published in San Antonio, first in *El imparcial de Texas* and later
in *La Prensa*, the most important Spanish-language newspaper in the
Southwest. Writing under the pseudonym of Loreley, Garza dispensed
advice on customs and the appropriate role of women, often addressing
her audience as *mis lectorcitas* (my little readers). Her apparent mission in these crónicas was to reinforce the exile philosophy of México
de Afuera that the male power structure at these papers promoted—
including the publishers and editors, such as Ignacio Lozano, Teodoro
Torres, and Nemesio García Naranjo (see chapter 2)—with all of its
implications for female domesticity, religiosity, and nation building.
If she did not invent the concept of Angel del Hogar, Garza was one of
its most ardent elaborators and promoters. Although she subscribed
to ideological principles similar to those of Julio Arce and other male
cronistas (see chapter 6), unlike them she never resorted to censure
or satire of *agringadas* and *renegadas* in seeking to educate women as
to their proper roles regarding the United States and the homeland.
She did, however, take American and British feminists to task, always
contrasting their selfish and frivolous movements with the grand role
for the nation and humanity of La Mujer Mexicana. She warned her
readers, "¡Abominemos el feminismo! ¡Seáis hija, esposa, y madre!

¡Seáis femenil!" (Let us abominate feminism! Be a daughter, a wife and a mother! Be feminine!). She thought the only rights women are entitled to are "amor, deber y piedad" (love, duty and piety) (*El Imparcial*, September 2, 1920). Always serious and cultivating an elevated, highly stylized modernist diction, Garza offered her columns as an escape from the sad exile in which her readers supposedly found themselves: "Las que como yo, añoráis entristecidas la patria enferma y acaso por enferma más amada, como lenitivo a esos quebrantos, venid conmigo después de haber visitado esos infiernos de comercialismo brutal, hacia la Gloria imperecedora del arte" (*El Imparcial*, November 16, 1920).[10]

She offered her art as an antidote to the materialism of American society, a common theme in the literature of immigration. According to Loreley, exile leveled the social classes among Mexicans in U.S. exile, and this allowed her, privileged by education, not only to speak to them informally, but as a sister using the familiar second-person *tú* in Spanish. And despite her elite stance as a woman privileged by education and social class, one who ironically sought to connect through what she presented as a dialog with her lectorcitas and *amiguitas*, Garza nevertheless saw herself as defending Mexican women and educating them for their survival as immigrants and exiles. Gabriela Baeza Ventura evaluates Garza's mission as follows:

> A pesar de que Loreley abogue por la emancipación femenina que permite a las mujeres obtener más derechos, su arraigo en la tradición y su ubicación en el "México de afuera" no le permiten aceptar que la mujer se "americanice", lo cual se identifica con un feminismo perverso, antifemenino. La mujer puede adquirir derechos, siempre y cuando no interfieran con su condición de mujer "Mexicana", donde la definición de "Mexicana" enfatiza la tradición. Además, sus recomendaciones son necesarias, por ser mujer. Como Ulica, reconoce que la mujer es más débil y más vulnerable a la americanización que los hombres.[11] (74)

Despite serving as a voice for maintaining the status quo, or because of it, Garza developed a following large enough that the entrepreneurs who ran *La Prensa* and the Librería de Quiroga publishing house in San Antonio decided to publish her first book, *La novia de Nervo* (1922, Nervo's betrothed). Luziris Pineda has discovered that notwithstanding Garza's conservative stance in her crónicas, she too was able to create agency for herself in her subsequent books, all of which, apparently, were self-published, Garza having declared her independence from the patriarchal publishing world in San Antonio and, later, in northern Mexico.[12] Purportedly, Garza was able to assume a more progressive interpretation of women and their relationship to the nation in those publications, which include the novels *Los amores de Gaona, Apuntes realistas por Loreley* (1922, Gaona's loves, realistic notes by Loreley) and *Tentáculos de fuego* (1930, Tentacles of fire); the collection of short stories *Hojas dispersas* (Dispersed leaves); and a collection of poems, *Escucha* (1928, Listen). Nevertheless, in 1923 radical feminists in Mexico did not allow Garza to attend a conference of women and their organizations because of her conservatism, despite the fact that she had been designated as the delegate from the state of Nuevo León (Villarroel 107). Pineda asserts that Garza led a life of activism in protecting children and families by working in temperance crusades and making antialcoholism a theme in her novels, by participating in such international forums as the Pan American Round Table, and by taking on other social roles.

Somewhat more progressive and more in the realm of art than the productions of the women discussed above are the writings of Dolores Bolio, who sought to insert herself into a world reserved for men by publishing her book *Aroma tropical* under the pseudonym Luis Avellaneda.[13] Making use of the rights and privileges of an upper-class family and education in the Yucatan, Bolio traveled extensively in Europe and the United States before taking up political refugee status during the Revolution. The prologue to this collection of stories, legends, and poems, which Bolio did write under her real name, elucidates her feminist thought, as she deconstructs male intellectual and literary dominance (Villarroel 72). Bolio's prologue, a marvelously ingenious challenge to patriarchal power in the literary world, revisits literary history as far back as classical times and serves notice that the days when women were consigned to the silent role of muse and when their literary work was not taken seriously by men are over. The prologue develops into a Socratic dialog in which the differences between male and female literary esthetics are debated; it ends with a forceful declaration: "La musa toma la palabra y deja su carácter simbólico para transformarse en la escritora" (75) (The muse speaks and abandons her symbolic nature to transform herself into a writer). The intent is to retrieve women from the shadows of literature and art and to empower them to act on their own and produce works not mediated by men serving as patrons and critics. The last lines of the introduction firmly plant Bolio as a transmigrant in New York, one who misses the homeland—but ironically one who is able to enunciate the changes in women's artistic agency: "Por la vidriera viene a acecharme un crepúsculo melancólico. Hay una mortaja de nieve sobre Nueva York. ¡Qué nostalgia!" (13) (I'm faced with a melancholic dawn through the window. There's a shroud of snow over New York. What nostalgia!) And this prologue sets the stage for the texts that follow, which demonstrate the problems of women who are not free to act. The longest story, "Aromas de antaño" (Aromas from the past), is narrated not by Avellaneda but by an old woman who tells it to him. This tale of a father arranging a marriage for his daughter, Catalina, who wishes to enter the convent instead, contrasts with Capetillo's dramas, in which women rebel outright against paternal decisions over daughters. Bolio's purpose is to protest: she shows the generations of women—grandmother, mother, daughter—who have faced similar patriarchal imperatives and implies that forcing women like Catalina into undesirable situations only leads to tragedy, in this case to the suicide of the man she was forced to wed. Ultimately, Catalina is able to join the convent and pursue not only the religious life but also a life devoted to study. The story underlines the importance of education in developing women's intelligence as a Mujer Mexicana, the inheritor of Sor Juana Inés de la Cruz, who serves Bolio as the historical model for this brand of conservative feminism.[14] In general the tales in the book illustrate the abuse, neglect, and undervaluing of women before and during marriage: abandoned women, women treated as trophies, women kept from educating themselves even to be able to earn enough to feed their children, women treated like little girls, women treated as possessions of men, and so forth. In this way, Bolio is subverting the nationalist project on which the Mexican family is built: the woman at home and the man in public, the woman as generator and educator of future citizens, all based on the differences between the sexes and the superiority of males. Bolio demonstrates her keen awareness of the prescribed role of women in nationalist projects when she references the Revolution and the important role women played in it, only to be consigned after the hostilities have ended once again to the private sphere: "La mujer hubo prestado servicios a las revoluciones; servicios que entrañaron *mucho* en los períodos álgidos, en tiempos de paz significaron casi nada" (202) (Women had lent their services to the revolutions; services that were deeply needed during the peak periods but in peacetime meant almost nothing).

Villarroel summarizes Bolio's method and mission as follows:

Bolio no sólo presenta su época política tumultuosa, sino también toma el rol de denunciante, de deconstructora de un sistema hegemónico opresor que discrimina y desfavorece a la mujer. Bolio aboga por una reconstrucción de la sociedad a través de las esperanzas de sus protagonistas, convirtiéndose en un antecedente literario del Ateneo Mexicano de Mujeres, del cual posteriormente formará parte y que entre sus preceptos promoverá la superación de la mujer y la creación de una mujer nueva.[15] (94)

Hortensia Elizondo, a much younger woman than Bolio, went to San Antonio initially because her family was in exile there, but she was raised as an immigrant in the United States. Because her family was financially well-off she acquired part of her education in Canada and Europe. Practically nurtured on the conservative México de Afuera and Mujer Mexicana ideology of her sister, Angelina, and her brother-in-law, García Naranjo, at that time the editor of *La Revista Mexicana* (The Mexican review), the most insistent promoter and one of the primary forums of those ideological stances, Hortensia nevertheless moved beyond their explicit nationalism and articulated a vision of the "mujer moderna" (modern woman). Although she was the author of a book of short stories, it was through her weekly column, "La Mujer Moderna," published weekly in El Paso's *El Continental* in the mid-1930s, that she elaborated this vision.[16] Consciously reinvigorating the concept of the modern woman as initially promoted at the beginning of the century by the Mexican radical Hermila Galindo, Elizondo went on to assimilate the teachings and experiences of feminists in the United States, Canada, and Europe and to attempt to influence her readers to move the project of Latina liberation forward.[17] In writing for a border newspaper, she also hoped her ideas would be carried into interior Mexico, where *El Continental* had a wide circulation, especially in northern cities. To Elizondo, writing in the 1930s, as opposed to her forebears of the late 1910s and early 1920s, the difference between the United States and Mexico was glaring: women had won the vote over a decade earlier north of the border, while they were still disenfranchised in the homeland. Thus the nationalist project of the Mexican Woman as part of the Revolution and its remaking of society could no longer win her allegiance or creative imagination.

The unique contribution Elizondo made in her column, according to Villarroel (129), was to distance women from the patriarchy and its control of symbolic discourse; she promoted the idea that women should take responsibility for their own education, shuck off traditional ideas of women's inferiority, and develop careers. Elizondo openly indicted sexism and rejected the male canon, insisting that women formulate their own language, style, themes, in short, their own discursive space, a counterculture (Villarroel 130–131). She further shows in her column that history is constructed by the patriarchy and molders of the nation and that women can contest this social construction, proposing and defending their own alternative construction. She warned that no man had the right or the capacity to write convincingly either about women or in their name (at this time there were thousands of periodical articles and books by Latino males purporting to do precisely that): "Aquel autor que haya escrito un libro sobre la psicología femenina, por más observador que sea, tiene forzosamente que estar trunco y falso. Sólo lo que se vive es verídico." (June 16, 1935) (Any [male] author who has written a book on feminine psychology, no matter how observant he is, that book will be incomplete and false. Only what is lived is truthful). In spite of her status as an intellectual with a privileged upbringing, Elizondo was striving for a goal similar to that of the working-class Capetillo, that is, a future society of absolute equality of the sexes, because she understood that women's liberation also meant the liberation of men.

Another intriguing figure to emerge from the disruption and displacement resulting from the Revolution was Elena Arizmendi, an upper-class woman of singular resolve and commitment to the cause of women. Although born into a family that achieved great wealth in the late nineteenth century under Díaz's regime, Arizmendi became an iconoclast where men were concerned.[18]

From her base in New York City, Arizmendi entered the fray of women's rights, participating in such organizations as the Pan American Conference on Women, held in Baltimore in 1922, a conference sponsored by the National League of Women Voters and the Pan American Union. According to Villarroel, Arizmendi became incensed at the comments of Anglo women at the conference, who openly expressed their belief that Hispanic American women were backward (99). The experience turned out to be a primary motive for Arizmendi to attempt to develop a Hispanic feminism and to create what in December 1922 became the first journal of Hispanic feminism, *Feminismo Internacional: Revista Mensual Ilustrada Dedicada al Mejoramiento Moral, Cultural y Económico de la Mujer. Organo de la Liga de Mujeres Ibéricas e*

Hispanoamericanas (International feminism: Illustrated monthly review dedicated to the moral, cultural, and economic improvement of women. Organ of the League of Iberian and Spanish American Women). Arizmendi began her activist role as part of the nation-building project of the Revolution, but in New York she found her way to a broader, international sisterhood that did not recognize borders and cultural differences in the Hispanic world. For one year *Feminismo Internacional* published literature and essays by some of the leading women intellectuals and writers of Spain, Spanish America, and the Hispanic United States, along with editorials, book reviews, and news dealing with the advance of women and feminism in the Hispanic world.

Five years after founding *Feminismo Internacional*, Arizmendi published a short novel of immigration in New York: *Vida incompleta: Ligeros apuntes sobre mujeres en la vida real* (1927) (Incomplete life: Quick notes on women in real life), a work that explores the cultural and gender differences between Anglo-American and Hispanic societies. The work is highly autobiographical in that it features two Latina protagonists, one married to an Anglo-American and the other involved in an adulterous relationship. The novel, like her essays and editorials in *Feminismo Internacional*, serves as a forum for Arizmendi's feminist ideas. Villarroel considers *Vida incompleta* to be the first Hispanic feminist novel (121); nevertheless, it is still rather conservative in emphasizing the home and the important role of women in educating the future citizens of their countries. Throughout the novel, as in much immigration literature, there is a binary of comparison between the Anglo and Hispanic worlds, especially in various dialogs that compare women's upbringing and worldview. The novel takes on a polemic tone in defending Latinas against stereotypes and advocating a Hispanic feminism that continues to recognize maternal instincts and women's duty to their children and family. Responding to stereotypical Anglo views, Arizmendi deconstructs Anglo family life as follows: "El hogar considerado por la mayoría como un hotel, un lugar de tránsito; segundo, porque la servidumbre es muy difícil de conseguir, retener, y de pagar . . . tercero, porque las mujeres o no pueden o no quieren dedicarse única y exclusivamente a trabajos caseros; y cuarto, porque los propietarios . . . exigen precios exorbitantes por el alquiler de las casas" (23).[19]

In addition to an indictment of American womanhood, the novel is a latent criticism of capitalism and modernity, a characteristic of much literature of immigration. It is precisely the issue of parenthood that brings to an end the marriage of the protagonist Elsa: her husband, a businessman, refuses to have a child for economic reasons, while Elsa, who is all spirit and art and study, wants to fulfill her creative nature by raising children as well as educating herself and advancing intellectually. Thus the common criticism of American materialism and modernity—along with a good dose of censure for American popular culture as found in movies, jazz, and the obsession with sports—is united with the Hispanic feminist's prescribed role for women and their fulfillment. Elsa divorces her husband.

The plotline involving Alicia, the other protagonist and Elsa's best friend, allows Arizmendi to deconstruct the traditional Hispanic marriage in that Alicia's lover, Ricardo, is trapped in a loveless matrimony, the product of an economic arrangement in which a woman is protected by a husband. Both Elsa and Alicia, who leaves Ricardo and takes refuge in New York, are treated as widows in the novel, brought together by the scandals of divorce and an adulterous affair. The two women finally agree on the differences in culture and education, language and intelligence that have broken the relationships with their consorts, and Alicia concludes in a set speech that women do not really need men: "¡Te bastas a ti sola!" (94) (You yourself is all that is needed). As Villarroel concludes, "Esta independencia femenina aseguraría lo que reafirma Alicia en la obra: la independencia económica y social de la mujer. Al mismo tiempo en un gesto simbólico le resta importancia al nombre masculino, un nombre que tradicionalmente es el encargado de dar prestigio social y honor a la mujer. Consecuentemente Alicia impulsa a Elsa a hacerse cargo de su individualidad y de su propio nombre" (119).[20]

By the end of the novel, the two newly independent women dedicate themselves to "chastity," read here "celibacy," and to helping less fortunate women. Alicia dies, and the omniscient narrator imagines her communicating with Elsa from what Villarroel calls a "feminist heaven": "—Soy dichosa. Aquí no hay hombres ni mujeres. No hay sexos, todos somos iguales por lo tanto no hay celos, odios u otras malas pasiones. En esta vida, es donde Dios, el Dios de todos: católicos, judíos, protestantes; latinos, sajones y asiáticos, recompensa las intenciones buenas y los sacrificios nobles" (117).[21]

Villarroel concludes that Arizmendi is important because her writings represent the first attempt to create a Hispanic sisterhood, the first community of feminists in the Hispanic world, regardless of borders and the geographic limitations of the nation-states, a community that would develop a feminist ideology and praxis adjusted to their own respective cultures and capable of withstanding the imperialistically aggressive feminism of Anglo-American women seeking to impose their standards on Latinas (123).

Not of the working class, like Capetillo, or a political exile, like the Villarreal sisters, or an economic refugee, Clotilde Betances de Jaeger was the niece of Ramón Emeterio Betances, an important ideologue of Puerto Rican independence from Spain, a celebrated national hero whose last name commanded respect everywhere on the island. Of middle-class upbringing, Clotilde's family had the resources to pay for her education at Cornell University, where she received her degree in natural sciences in 1916, and later to earn a master's degree in religious studies at Butler College in Indianapolis in 1949. After receiving her Bachelor of Science degree and returning to Puerto Rico, Betances began her career as a schoolteacher and columnist for periodicals in San Juan and extended it to Spanish-language newspapers and magazines when she relocated to New York City in 1923.[22] She would spend the rest of her life in the city, teaching and producing an important body of feminist thought as well as religious writing in a broad range of periodicals published not only in the city but also in Spanish America and Spain.[23]

According to María Teresa Vera-Rojas in *El género de la charlas* . . . (The genre of chats . . .), Betances, who was bilingual and married to a German-American, Frank Jaeger, had begun her career as a columnist in Puerto Rico in 1921, writing for an audience of middle- and upper-class women in the women's page of *El Heraldo de Puerto Rico*. Betances used the women's fashion and beauty beat to gain a foothold in the male-dominated media, a foothold that subsequently, in New York publications, would become a space for the exploration of feminist issues. She published in many periodicals, but especially in *Gráfico* in New York, which became a primary forum for her more than fifty columns written in 1929 and 1930 (Vera-Rojas 48). Along with other women who wrote for *Gráfico*'s "Charlas Femeninas," Betances was able to transform a journalistic space dedicated to traditional domestic feminine interests into one of pointedly public and political implications: "Poniendo en práctica las tretas con las que el débil desafía el discurso hegemónico, condujeron las discusiones acerca del feminismo y la feminidad al espacio público, y desde allí se erigieron como 'consejeras' e 'informantes' de un sector femenino de la inmigración" (Vera-Rojas 62).[24]

These women, with Betances in the lead, constructed themselves as subjects in an overwhelmingly male-dominated public medium in a genre, the newspaper crónica, that had often been used by males to belittle and demean women and prod them into conforming to Hispanic nationalist projects created by the patriarchy. As was true of many of the authors discussed above, Betances and the others went beyond their ethnic-national origins to create through these "charlas" a dialog with all Latinas living in the Metropolis.[25] In other, later publications Betances would address audiences beyond New York City and environs.

It is ironic that Betances and her group were able to accomplish so much in the entirely male-run and -dominated, at times even misogynistic, *Gráfico*, which announced its Pan-Hispanic mission as defending the international family constituted by those who were far from their beloved *patrias*.[26] In her weekly columns Betances took on such issues as the new role of women in society, especially exploring the implications of women's having won the vote in the United States; the growth and importance of the number of women in the workplace and the significance of receiving professional training; the need to free women from the bonds of marriage and move them toward economic independence and even free love; her control over her body, even to the extent of family planning, the use of contraceptives, and abortion; as well as such political topics as the poor quality of the schools, racism in the United States and Puerto Rico, the Church, American imperialism, and the colonial status of Puerto Rico and other Latin American countries. In general, in the construction of a *mujer nueva* (new woman), Betances encouraged women to participate in the economy and in politics both nationally and internationally. In her columns, she commented on city and national politics, presidential campaigns, international affairs, and war, which she denounced repeatedly. In her column of June 15, 1929, she analyzed how women's liberation was intimately linked to the economy and noted that in a time of crisis, like the onset of the Depression, it was incumbent on women to educate themselves and become consciously involved in the economy: "Mujer de corazón, mujer de mentalidad, mujer nueva, la economía es tu problema inminente y tienes que resolverlo. La economía del hogar entra en tu jurisdicción, la economía del mundo es tu herencia" (Woman of the heart, woman of the mind, new woman, the economy is your imminent problem and you have to solve it. The economy of the home is part of your jurisdiction; the economy of the world is your heritage). As Vera-Rojas states,

Clotilde Betances Jaeger pretendía dar impulso a una nueva forma de ser mujer encauzada en una lucha feminista que hacía visible la importancia de la mujer en la vida económica de las naciones, al tiempo que destacaba el valor de la economía en la independencia de las mujeres. Para la nueva mujer su independencia económica debía ser uno de sus intereses fundamentales, sobre todo, porque su sumisión y subordinación social y subjetiva habían sido regidas durante siglos por el dominio económico que el hombre ejercía sobre las mujeres. Sin duda alguna, Clotilde Betances entendía que la relación entre los sexos era una relación de poder, en la que para poseer derechos de igualdad el voto no era suficiente, la mujer debía poseer derechos económicos. La mujer nueva era, de hecho, una revolución.[27] (185)

Rather than look for foremothers in the past, as other Latina feminists had in Sor Juan Inés de la Cruz, Betances sought out contemporary role models of women who were seeking to free their sisters from economic subjugation and the fiction of the nation. She wrote about Spanish, Cuban, and Puerto Rican authors, among others, and reviewed their books as points of departure for her essays. While she advocated Puerto Rican independence from the United States, in the main she considered the question of women beyond the constraints of national projects and thus chose her models from throughout the Hispanic world. While at times employing the binaries of immigrant literature, contrasting American and Latino cultures and their construction of womanhood, she did not further a discourse of conflict between the two. Neither did she cultivate other themes of immigrant literature, such as U.S. materialism and modernity compared with the wholesomeness of the homeland, racial and ethnic discrimination (although she did come out against it), or the demythologizing of the American Dream and the melting pot.[28] If there was any demythologizing to do, it was directed at the male construction of the home, the society, and the place of women within its constrictions. And she was not beyond satirizing and ridiculing this construction, as in her charla of January 20, 1929, entitled "Matrimonio y Mortaja del Cielo Bajan" (Marriage and a shroud descend from heaven):

Bajo la presente status quo, la mujer es la depositora del honor de la familia. ¡Responsabilidad enorme para una esclava! Ella debe dirigir las mentes de los hijos en la verdadera religión, guiar sus pasos en la vida y llevar siempre el sambenito infamamente. . . . Es decir que el cielo se

complace en unir las vidas de una mujer y un hombre para que ella en-
vilecida y prostituida . . . tenga la obligación de recibir sus caricias porque sí, porque ella es su cosa.[29]

Betances's educational mission was to reveal the constructedness
of gender in the Hispanic world and to encourage the development in
her audience of an alternative construction for a new woman. As Vera-
Rojas states, "Sus textos reflejaron su preocupación por lo que significaba ser mujer en tanto sujetos libres, poseedores de autonomía y conciencia para decidir acciones. Antes que definirse como inmigrantes, se
definieron como mujeres a partir de lo que significaba el concepto de
libertad" (207) (Their texts reflected their preoccupation with the significance of being a woman as a free subject, possessing an autonomy
and conscience with which to decide on actions. Before defining themselves as immigrants, they defined themselves as women parting from
what the concept of liberty meant). This is a statement that arguably
can be made about most of the writers discussed.

CHAPTER 6

IMMIGRATION AND GENDER:
MALE PERSPECTIVES

Si los hombres casados quieren ser menos felices, . . . no deben
venir, con sus consortes, a los Estados Unidos. Pueden cruzar
la frontera solos, dejando a sus respectivas mitades allende el
Bravo, lo más "allende" que puedan, a muy respetuosa distancia.
Porque aquí andan las cosas muy mal y el género masculino va
perdiendo, a pasos agigantados, "sus sagradas prerrogativas y
sus inalienables derechos.
—JORGE ULICA, "INACIO Y MENGILDA,"
FROM "CRÓNICAS DIABÓLICAS"

AS WE SAW IN chapters 3 and 4, the genre of the novel served male
authors well in their efforts to deconstruct American society and its
myths while writing their version of their own nation and, in most
cases, defining the role of women in that imaginary. As I demonstrated
in chapter 5, the few women who gained access to the printed word
were able to create interstices and develop strategies from which to
write themselves into the public sphere, the nation, the world. Some
were able to go beyond male-directed nationalist projects in order to
construct a world not divided by class, nation, and gender, at times
attempting even to establish an international sisterhood of Hispanic
women. Male authors were more concerned with the themes and
issues discussed in this book by manipulating the image of the female,
whom they consistently elevated as the symbol of the nation and the
homeland and, because of that, foisted upon her the traditional role of
generating the nation from within the domestic sphere. From there,
they were assigned to preserve national values and history and pass
them on to their children, who would grow up to duplicate the gender
roles of their parents as the bulwark of the imagined community.

THE IMAGE OF WOMEN PROMOTED BY THE *CRONISTAS*

Owing to limited publishing resources, including scarce financial investment as well as the problems associated with distributing foreign-language works within the United States, the novel among Hispanic transmigrants was very limited in its reach. Very few publishing houses and bookstores served immigrant communities—as is the case even today—and most novelists relied on other means of employ to make a living. Laborers, however, when they did have access to fiction between two covers, often had it read to them by more literate companions. In the early twentieth century the medium with the most reach in transmigrant communities was the newspaper; its pages included a broad variety of genres and writing styles, including entire novels, usually published in serialized versions. Robert Park (51–52) in his study of the immigrant press (1922) and Benedict Anderson's analysis of print capitalism in *Imaginary Communities* (46–49) emphasized the role of newspapers in constructing the nation because of their standardization of language and their wide distribution and economic accessibility. Among the various types of writing published in newspapers was a genre traditionally identified with and central to Hispanic newspapers everywhere and essential in forming and reinforcing community attitudes, imagining the community, as it were. I am referring to the *crónica*, or chronicle, a short, weekly column that through humor and satire commented on current topics and social habits. Rife with local color and inspired by the oral lore of the immigrants, the crónica had its origins in Joseph Addison and Richard Steele in England and arrived in Spain via France, where the *flâneur* also became part of its optical view of society. The leading *costumbristas*, or chroniclers of customs, were Ramón de Mesonero Romanos and José Mariano de Larra in Spain; costumbristas and cronistas existed in Mexico since the writings of Joaquín Fernández de Lizardi in the early nineteenth century.[1] In Mexico, the crónica was cultivated extensively and evolved further. The crónica helped to define and develop Mexican identity over the course of the nineteenth century. According to Carlos Monsiváis,

> De principios del siglo XX hasta casi nuestros días, a la crónica mexicana se le encomienda verificar o consagrar cambios y maneras sociales y describir lo cotidiano elevándolo al rango de lo ideosincrático (aquello sin lo cual los mexicanos serían, por ejemplo, paraguayos). En el tránsito de la mentalidad colonial a la independiente . . . una colec-

tividad pequeña, insegura de sus logros, incierta en su nacionalismo, ve en la crónica el espejo refulgente (ideal) de sus transformaciones y fijaciones.

Escribir es forjar. Durante un período prolongado el detallismo exhaustivo de los cronistas sirve a un propósito central: contribuir a la forja de la nación, describiéndola y, si se puede, moralizándola. Los escritores del siglo XIX van a la crónica a documentar y lo que les importa más, promover un estilo de vida, aquél que va a la reiteración de las costumbres el verdadero ritual cívico. Los cronistas son nacionalistas acérrimos porque desean la independencia y la grandeza de una colectividad . . . porque anhelan el sello de identidad que los ampare, los singularice, los despoje de sujeciones y elimine sus ansiedades y su terror más profundo: ser testigos privilegiados de lo que no tiene ninguna importancia, narrar el proceso formativo de esta sociedad que nadie contemple. Se necesita fortalecer la Nación infundiéndole y aclarándole sus orgullos locales y regionales, recreando literariamente las formas de vida más ostensiblemente "mexicanas" y subrayando el desdén por la imitación de lo francés y la nostalgia servil de lo hispánico.[2] (26–27)

In the Hispanic immigrant communities of the United States, the crónica came to serve purposes never imagined in Mexico or Spain. From Los Angeles to San Antonio, Chicago, and New York, Hispanic moralists assumed pseudonyms (in keeping with the tradition of the crónica) and, from this masked perspective, commented satirically in the first person. As flâneurs who traveled the city streets and witnessed the customs and behavior of the colony whose very existence was seen as threatened by the dominant Anglo-Saxon culture, they were influenced by popular jokes, anecdotes, and speech, and in general their columns became a mirror of the surrounding social environment. It was the cronista's job to fan the flames of nationalism and to enforce the ideology of *México de Afuera* or other, similar ideologies for Cubans, Puerto Ricans, and Spanish immigrants, for Latinos in general. Cronistas had to battle the influence of Anglo-Saxon immorality and Protestantism and to protect against the erosion of the Spanish language and Hispanic culture with equally religious fervor. But they did so not from the bully pulpit but through sly humor and a burlesque of fictional characters who represented general ignorance and naiveté or who were adopting Anglo ways because they considered them superior to those of the Hispanics. Using such pseudonyms as El Malcriado (The

Brat, pseudonym of Daniel Venegas), Kaskabel (Rattlesnake, pseudonym for Benjamín Padilla), Loreley (María Luisa Garza), Ofa (Alberto O'Farrill), Miquis Tiquis (Jesús Colón), Az.T.K. (The Aztec, real identity unknown), and Chicote (The Whip, real identity unknown), the cronistas were literally whipping and stinging the community into conformity, commenting on and poking fun at the common folks' mixing of Spanish and English (seen as contaminating the purity of Cervantes's beautiful language) and becoming overly impressed with Yankee ingenuity and technology. By developing the binary I have cited in previous chapters, they identified the two ways of life as being in direct conflict, even down to the food that was consumed, the clothes that were worn, and the furniture placed in the home. As noted earlier, the worst transgressors were labeled with the epithets of *agringados, ayancados, pitiyanquis*, and *renegados*, that is, Americanized renegades, traitors who had rejected the nation.

Among the cultural elites who disseminated the ideology of México de Afuera was one political refugee who, by publishing a newspaper and writing a widely syndicated crónica, became immensely influential. Julio G. Arce was a newspaper publisher from Guadalajara who was not only disillusioned with the Revolution but had to flee for the his safety and that of his family after he had attacked in print the triumphant forces of Francisco I. Madero.[3] As noted earlier, he went into exile in San Francisco, vowing never to return to Mexico. In San Francisco, Arce first worked as a laborer for the American Can Company but soon became associated with *La Crónica*, an immigrant newspaper published by the Spaniard J. C. Castro. In 1919 Arce bought *La Crónica* and rebaptized it *Hispano América*, giving it the motto "Por la Patria y Por la Raza" (For our fatherland and for our culture).[4]

While writing for *La Crónica* in 1918, Arce had resuscitated the pseudonym Jorge Ulica, which he had used in Guadalajara, and launched a weekly column he would continue in *Hispano América*. Eventually Ulica's column, entitled "Crónicas Diabólicas," became the most widely syndicated crónica in the Southwest. Ulica's unerring ability to reflect life in the Mexican immigrant community made it highly popular. As was the convention in such local color columns, his pseudonymous alter ego would report weekly on his adventures and observations in San Francisco, often satirizing humorously the errant customs that were becoming all too common in the *colonia*, such as Mexicans remembering they are Mexicans only during the celebration of Mexican Independence Day and Mexicans calling themselves Spaniards in order to assume greater social prestige and to avoid the barbs of discrimination. By and large, Ulica assumed the elite stance of observer of the human comedy, moralist, and satirist, that is, a self-appointed conscience for the Mexican immigrant community. As a purveyor of the ideology of México de Afuera, like many other educated cronistas, he revealed his upper-class, bourgeois resentment of working-class Mexican immigrants who, on the one hand, were fascinated by Yankee technology, know-how, and economic power and, on the other, were poor, ignorant representatives of the Mexican nation, all of which he forcefully illustrated in his crónicas. Ulica's particular talents lay in caricature, in emulating the colloquialisms and popular culture of the working-class immigrant and in satirizing the culture conflict and mis-understandings encountered by greenhorn immigrants from the provinces in Mexico. While his message was rarely subtle, his language and imagery were so richly reflective of common immigrant humor and folk anecdotes that they are worthy of study as literature, a literature that arises directly out of the immigrant experience and its folklore.

By far, Ulica's favorite and probably most popular target was the poor, greenhorn Mexican woman who had emigrated from the interior provinces, such as the imaginary "Palos Bonchis" (Bunch of sticks) in his story "Por No Hablar 'English'" (Because of not speaking English). The poor, uneducated female consistently received the brunt of Ulica's attempts to stem the tide of acculturation and support the survival of the Hispanic family and its culture in an alien environment. In his story "Inacio y Mengilda" (country bumpkin names truncated into common rural dialect), Ulica warned Mexican men not to bring their wives to the United States: "Si los hombres casados quieren ser menos felices, . . . no deben venir, con sus consortes a los Estados Unidos. . . . Porque aquí andan las cosas muy mal y el género masculino va perdiendo, a pasos agigantados . . . sus sagradas prerrogativas y sus inalienables derechos. . . . Me duele en el alma ver a los pobres 'maridos' sujetos a una perra vida, a un porvenir parecido y a un fin trágico" (89).[5]

After this introduction slightly satirizing the U.S. Declaration of Independence, Ulica goes on to narrate the apocryphal tale of a Mexican immigrant woman who defenestrated her husband and was acquitted by the courts. Ulica has her testifying in court, utilizing the most provincial and uneducated Spanish, explaining that she was so frustrated that her husband was "encevelizado" (uncivilized) and "impropio" (an Anglicism meaning "improper"). According to her testimony, Mengilda went to great lengths to dress and eat stylishly, as is called for here in the United States, but her husband resisted tooth and nail. He committed such sins as taking off his shoes on arriving home and going barefoot; he wouldn't get his hair cut in "ese rape aristocrático que se usa por acá" (that aristocratic razor-cut style that is used here); and he would consume only "cosas inominiosas" ("ignominious things," mispronounced as a sign of her incorrect use of big words in putting on airs). Included in the "iniminius things" were such "low-class" Mexican foods as "chicharrones, chorizos, sopes, tostadas, frijoles, menudo y pozole." It was just impossible to get him to eat clam chowder, bacon, liver and onions, beef stew, or hot dogs—supposedly high-class American fare.[6]

It turns out that Inacio came home one Saturday with his fingernails so dirty and ragged (he was a working stiff, after all) that she insisted on hiring a girl to give him a manicure. But he locked himself in his room and refused to cooperate. Mengilda became so frustrated and enraged that she threw him out the window and then, as if that wasn't enough, threw a monkey wrench at him, splitting his skull. The poor man expired on the street below. After an eloquent defense by her lawyer, who insisted that she was just a poor foreigner struggling to better herself and become cultured in the United States, she was exonerated by unanimous decision.

After this, the narrator Ulica breaks in to emphasize to the reader that this is just one of a legion of incidents that happen every day in the United States. As soon as compatriot women arrive they find out they are the bosses here, and their husbands must remain shy of heart, short on words, and with still hands (meaning they cannot beat their wives anymore). Ulica concludes that that is why it is so common to see the husband carrying the baby in public, along with packages from the store and grocery bags, ambling along sad, meditative, crestfallen, depressed, as if he feared possible sentencing to San Quentin or execution for rebelling against his wife. This unselfconscious role reversal of genders is a recurrent stratagem of Ulica's to create a humorous reaction in his readers and to reinforce women's rightful status of inferiority to Mexican males;[7] it also obliquely indicts American males as effeminate, and the whole project is integral to the binary opposition of Mexican and U.S. national cultures.

It seems that no matter where Ulica turns his gaze he encounters the deflated remains of what were once proud, independent Mexican men. A general of the Revolution, now a waiter in a third-rate restaurant, bemoans his fate to Ulica: "En este país las mujeres hacen lo que les da la real gana. La mía, que era tan obediente, tan fiel y tan mosquita muerta en Ojinaga, aquí se ha vuelto 'de cohetería', no me hace caso, se encierra con sus amigos a jugar 'bridge' y no sé qué cosas más, y, cuando reclamo, me echa de la mama. En mi tierra, podía haberle tumbado los dientes a manazos; pero aquí si hace eso, lo cuelgan en San Quintín" (145).[8]

In "Arriba las Faldas" (Up with the skirts—Ulica uses "skirts" ambiguously to mean "women" and to suggest what is under skirts), after presenting the gender role reversal that women wear the pants in the United States, Ulica attests that, contrary to what happens in other countries, after dinner here it is the wife who tells the husband, "Hijito, voy al cine; lava los platos, acuesta los niños y dale un limón al W.C. Después, si tú quieres, te acuestas" (Baby, I'm going to the movies; so wash the plates, put the children to sleep, and clean the toilet. After that, you can go to bed, if you want). He states that with some technological advance men will also be able to bear children: "No sería raro que por métodos perfeccionados, tenga los hijos y los críe" (147) (It won't be unusual that through some perfected method he'll bear children and raise them). In "Como Hacer Surprise Parties" (How to give surprise parties), Doña Lola Flores is another uneducated denizen of the colonia who is enamored of everything American. She, too, attempts to adopt all of the customs of her adopted country and rid herself of the trappings of the homeland. Doña Lola Flores and her daughters even go to the extreme of changing their names: she from Dolores Flores to Pains Flowers; her daughters Esperanza and Eva to Hope and Ivy; she changes her husband's from Ambrosio to Hungrious Flowers; even their dog Violeta has been rebaptized Vay-o-let.

One of the customs most attractive to Mrs. Pains Flowers is that of the surprise party, and so she plots with her daughters and their Anglo boyfriends to arrange for one on Pains's saint's day; they prepare even for the exact minute when everyone should surprise her by yelling, "Olé, Hurrah, Hello!" The mother, daughters, and boyfriends spend the whole day decorating and making sandwiches and punch, and finally Hungrious shows up full of moonshine. However, he is lucid enough to inform her that there is no reason to party because it is not her saint's day. To which she replies that yes, indeed, it is Viernes de Dolores— Saint Dolores's Friday. But Hungrious is quick to have the last word when he reminds her that she is Mrs. Pains Flowers now, not Dolores!

No matter how hard he looks at the American calendar, he cannot find any date called Pains's Friday. The episode ends with Pains dragging Hungrious into the bathroom to give him a sound beating.

If these women are so anxious to shuck off their Hispanic culture, their loyalty to the mother tongue is even more suspect, as Ulica ably demonstrates in the types of letters he receives at the newspaper from the likes of Mrs. Pellejón, who changed her name to "Skinny-hon" (a play on the negative word *pellejo* for "skin" and possibly meaning changing the color of one's skin). The letter is replete with Anglicisms, malapropisms, regionalisms, poor grammar, misspellings, and so on. And when it comes to the entry of women into the workplace, more specifically the office domain of men, Ulica is even more agitated. In "La Estenógrafa" (The stenographer) he is not only scandalized but titillated by the Mexican or Mexican-American flapper whom he employs as a stenographer. Ulica relates that he had the misfortune of employing Miss Pink, a comely young lady who not only Anglicized her last name (Rosa) but insists that she is Spanish. Despite having graduated from "grammar school," "high school," and "Spanish class," Miss Pink makes horribly embarrassing typing errors. But the main problem for Ulica is that even after Miss Pink has found out that Ulica is married, she compromises his modesty. She removes her hose in front of him and changes out of her street shoes, leaving the hose and shoes in back of his chair. She tells him that she hopes he is not like other bosses she has had who like to pick up her stockings and smell and kiss them. Eventually, Ulica becomes so intrigued and tempted that he does just that in one of the few examples of self-deprecating humor to be found in Arce's crónicas. When Ulica confronts the stenographer about her typing errors, she quits, complaining that he is the worst boss she has ever had because the married Ulica never even invited her to a show or to dinner. Here is a clear case of ambivalence: Ulica censures the Americanized stenographer but is sexually attracted to her. More intriguing, Ulica unselfconsciously confesses his feminization in this process as a result of Miss Pink's misspelling of a word in his dictation and a letter she sent out: she misspelled *agotado*, meaning "tired," as when Ulica stated, "I am tired"; instead she typed *ajotado* with a *j*, changing the meaning to "I have become a fag." Ulica subsequently receives an angry response from the recipient of the letter, who takes it to be a sexual advance from the by now truly exhausted Ulica, who has lost face and become dishonored as a male among his colleagues.

This gender-identification anxiety in Ulica is completely consonant

with his interpretation of the Mexican immigrant woman as a symbol of the collectivity, the nation: in Mexico, men can be real men and
women real women in their inferiority and subservience to males; in
the United States, the roles are reversed: women become masculine
and men effeminate. As Nira Yuval-Davis understands these gender
relations,

> Hegemonic cultures present a specific view about the meaning of the
> world and the nature of social order. The relationships between women
> and men are crucial for such a perspective, and therefore in most soci-
> eties also the control of women by men. Women are often constructed
> as the cultural symbols of the collectivity, of its boundaries, as carriers
> of the collectivity's "honour" and its intergenerational producers of
> culture. Specific codes and regulations are usually developed, defining
> who/what is a "proper man" and a "proper woman," which are central
> to the identities of collectivity members. Feelings of disempowerment
> which result from processes of colonization and subjugation have
> often been interpreted by the colonized men as processes of emascu-
> lation and/or feminization. The (re)construction of men's—and often
> even more importantly women's—roles in the processes of resistance
> and liberation has been central in most such struggles. (66)

It can be argued, even within the humor and satire of Ulica's crónicas, that Arce is on a mission to resist the overwhelming pressures to
assimilate to American culture and erase Latino identity, most directly
by transforming gender and familial relations. Ulica raises the specter
among his male readers that they lack masculine fortitude if they do
not join the struggle to resist, a struggle that in many of his apparently
misogynistic crónicas involves violently repressing women, a violence
over their bodies that is identified with male prerogatives in the homeland. Ulica not only becomes the border guard defining and separating
what is and is not Mexican, but also the guardian of sexual identity.[9]
In another of Ulica's crónicas, "Repatriación Gratuita" (Free repatriation), it becomes clear that one of the main motives for the
efforts to control and isolate Mexican and Hispanic women is the fear
of exogamy. Marrying outside the group is a subtheme present also
in the "Como Hacer Surprise Parties" column, in which Ulica created
Anglo boyfriends for Mrs. Pains Flowers's daughters, and in "Arriba
las Faldas," where Ulica expresses anxiety over losing Mexican immigrant women to Anglos because of the women's advantaged position

in American society. In this outrageous "repatriation" story, however, Ulica creates a Mexican woman who has just married a blond, blue-eyed Anglo, Mr. Blackberry, after having divorced her Mexican husband, Sr. Mora (which means "blackberry" as well as "Moor" in Spanish, obliquely indicating his dark racial heritage), because he refused to wash his face with gasoline in order to whiten it: "Lo dejé por prieto, por viejo y porque no tenía olor en los dientes como los americanos 'fines'" (I left him because he was dark, old, and his teeth didn't smell nice like those refined Americans). In this anecdote, greater freedom for women, higher class aspirations through association with the white race, and American materialism come together to entice the vain, ambitious Mexican woman to abandon both her ethnic culture and her husband. According to Gabriela Baeza Ventura's analysis, the crónica in Ulica's hands

> va a hacer una crítica severa de la inmigrante mexicana que haya optado por seguir prácticas que distan de las mexicanas. Pues al seguir costumbres y desear libertades y derechos que no son tradicionales, como el ser mujeres independientes, éstas están en peligro de ser exógamas. Si esto sucede, la comunidad mexicana en Estados Unidos estará en camino a la extinción y se perderá la comunidad y con ella la nación.[10] (59–60)

Eleuteria Hernández, in her article "La Representación de la Mujer Mexicana," has rightly attributed Ulica's attack on Mexican women to an attempt to preserve the family in an alien environment (34), but she attributes his attack primarily to Ulica's desire to stem the feminist advances made by women both in the United States and Mexico. While I agree that Ulica is antifeminist, I would add that his fears of cultural annihilation led him to place that burden on women as the center of the family. And making poor, uneducated women the target of his barbs in no way served as a direct and clear reaction to the feminist movements alluded to in Hernández's article. On the particular burden Ulica was requiring of Latinas, it too is part of the national imaginary created by him and the other male writers of immigrant literature. As Yuval-Davis states, "Women especially are often required to carry this 'burden of representation,' as they are constructed as the symbolic bearers of the collectivity's identity and honour, both personally and collectively" (45). For Ulica and the others, it is through the gendered family that women enter into and come to represent the nation. As Ida Blom summarizes it, "Identifying the nation with the family—a timeless and global unity of loyalty, evoking sentiments as well as hierarchies of gender and age—facilitated the construction of national identities and national loyalties. This symbolism also served as a guarantee for the continuation of traditional bonds between individuals as the process of nation building widened the understanding of loyalty to include the national community" (8).

While Ulica was without doubt expressing a bourgeois sensibility in censuring working-class Mexican women for their disloyalty to the nation, his point of view was by no means exclusive to his social class. Another immigrant journalist and creative writer, one who identified himself as a working-class Mexican immigrant, Daniel Venegas, expressed similar views in his weekly satirical newspaper *El Malcriado* and also, as we have seen, in his picaresque novel of immigration *Las aventuras de Don Chipote, o Cuando los pericos mamen* (*The Adventures of Don Chipote, or When Parrots Breast Feed* (see introduction and chapter 3). Venegas's humor-filled novel displays little sympathy for Mexican women in the United States, depicting them almost exclusively as prostitutes, gold-digging flappers, and vaudeville actresses of low morality. The one exception is Don Chipote's wife, who typically represents home and hearth and the nuclear family; she has no name, other than Doña Chipota, an extension of her husband's identity. Doña Chipota serves to restore order in bringing the novel to its resolution by rescuing her errant husband, who has been beguiled by the incarnation of gringo corruption of Mexican femininity: the flapper.

It is striking that Venegas, who so identified with the working-class immigrant, would not make common cause with working-class women. This aversion is amply seen in *El Malcriado*, which he singlehandedly wrote, illustrated, and typeset. In the edition for April 17, 1927, for instance, Venegas drew a caricature of a poor waitress with her toe protruding from her *huarache* and satirized waitresses delivering food orders, trafficking up and down Main Street in Los Angeles in dirty, broken-down shoes, smelling up the sidewalk to the extent of overcoming the fragrance of the food on their trays. On the front page of the same issue of this tabloid, Venegas drew a scene of two flirtatious Mexican flappers getting their hair bobbed in a men's barbershop under the banner headline "¡Cómo Gozan los Barberos Rapando las Guapetonas!/Se Pasan los Días Enteros Papachando a las Pelonas" (The barbers love to cut the hair of these beauties!/They spend the entire day caressing flappers). Beneath the cartoon, Venegas placed the following satirical verse:

Al arreglarse la coca dos pelonas
Fueron al "Barber Shop" de Don Simón,
Pues iban esa noche las gallonas
A darle vuelo y duro al vacilón.

—Acabe pronto en mí, —decía Julieta,
Mientras le razuraban el pescuezo,
Para que suba luego Enriqueta;
Y acabando a las dos le doy un beso.

Trabajó el peluquero
Que acabó en un momento.
Mas no le dieron de lo prometido,
Ni después que acabó con Enriqueta.[11]

Venegas satirizes the qualities that repeatedly stereotype the flapper in the literature of Hispanic immigration: transgressing into a masculine space and dressing or cutting hair in a masculine style; loose morality with men, even if it is only in flirting with the promised kiss; frivolousness and the constant desire to have a good time, especially in dancing and nightclubbing.[12] What is also implicit in their portrayal is the author-artist's attraction to these *guapetonas*, a titillation that is not always as open as in Ulica's smelling and caressing Miss Pink's nylons. Venegas frames the illustration of the barbershop with tall radio antennas on each side; men and flappers (indiscreetly) climb and shimmy up the antennas, easily readable as phallic symbols. No explanation of the antennas on the cover and in the pages of this issue of *El Malcriado* is given; they are obviously meant as a decorative frame that unselfconsciously betrays Venegas's phallocentric disposition.

One would think that for a change a crónica featuring a female transmigrant would occasionally present a somewhat different perspective on Mexican women. In 1928 Quezigno Gazavic, an anagrammatic pseudonym of the author's name, Ignacio G. Vásquez, published a novel-length series of rhymed crónicas that spun the sad tale of a woman who abandons her husband in Mexico because he cannot feed and clothe her and goes north to look for a blue-eyed giant ("grandotote

FIGURE 6.1. Cover of *El Malcriado*.

y colorao y de cabello muy güero" [large and red-faced and very blond])
who can take care of her. The plot of the weekly serial, entitled "Tanasio
y Ramona: Narración Continuada y en Verso de las Pintorescas Aventuras de Dos Sujetos 'de Allá en Casa'" (Tanasio and Ramona: Continuous narration in verse about the picturesque adventures of two subjects

"from back home"), published in San Antonio in *El Heraldo Mexicano*, consisted of the misadventures of Ramona and her husband, Tanasio (folkspeak for Atanasio), who hits the road in order to find her and bring her back home. Not only does this vehicle give Vásquez the pretext of attacking the materialistic values of American society and deconstructing the American Dream, but it fully indicts the frivolity and perfidy of women who are traitors to the family and the nation. As one would expect, during the course of the serialized narrative Ramona becomes a flapper and hooks up with her American Johnny, who, by Mexican standards, seems to be weak and effeminate. At one point, gloating over her success, she sends her poor Tanasio a photo documenting her complete makeover into an indecent and pretentious flapper:

> no sólo está pelona,
> sino que exhibe sus zancas
> "hast'onde llegan las ligas"
> usa choclos, tiene perro,
> y numerosas amigas
> "que l'acompañan al tiatro"
> y hasta un Fotingo muy feo
> modelo mil novecientos en el que
> sale a paseo.[13] *(January 22, 1928)*

Despite the active role played by Ramona, the reader never gets to see her directly, as her activities are related by Tanasio, often as he reads letters from her, or by the narrator Gazavic, who becomes a character in the story by accompanying Tanasio on his quest, intercepting her letters and reporting the story through this crónica as it currently unfolds in real time (Baeza, 84). Thus the woman herself never really gets to tell her own story and contradict the two male narrators as to her status as a *renegada* and *exógama*. For Gazavic, states Baeza, "por naturaleza, la mujer es un ser egoísta que sólo ambiciona y no piensa en el prójimo. El único remedio es controlarla y manternerla lejos de la influencia anglosajona" (85) (by nature woman is a selfish being that only thinks of herself and not of others. The only recourse is to control her and keep her far from Anglo-Saxon influence).

In this exchange of the usual character roles of immigrant literature, where the man usually leaves home to go north, it is Tanasio, the male, not his wife, who comes to represent Mexican national culture, the homeland with all of its values intact: he is simple, honest, and faithful and will not abandon his *patria*, except to bring home his beloved. Poor Tanasio, the greenhorn innocent, provides the humor and the bathos as his attempts to track her down become frustrated and he becomes a drunk. In an ironic departure, Tanasio comes across his photo and the articles that Gazavic has written in newspapers and begins to become famous, greeted by reporters and admirers in all the cities they visit. So renowned has he become, in fact, that he gets hired as a travel writer to document the cities he visits as a *verde*. Apparently he begins to forget about Ramona and soon gets fleeced repeatedly by fast women, a further indictment of the amoral and materialistic United States. By the end of the tale, Tanasio is dreaming of home, and it is understood that he will return.

Mexican immigrant writers were by no means the only Latinos to satirize the dangers of assimilation, cultural annihilation, and exogamy or to construct the flapper as the personification of supposedly liberated women in the United States. Hispanic immigrant newspapers in New York, catering to a diverse community of Cubans, Puerto Ricans, Dominicans, Spaniards, and others, also utilized the crónicas much like the Southwest papers did.[14] But while the ideas expressed in these crónicas and their host newspapers did not coalesce into as strong an ideology as the México de Afuera was, *Gráfico*, like many other Hispanic newspapers of New York, promoted a pan-Hispanism that united the Hispanics in the metropolis with all of Latin America. Home-country nationalism could not develop as strongly in an environment of such diverse Hispanic ethnicity. But standing on their Hispanic cultural background, the predominantly male journalists and cronistas quite often did attempt to encourage the community to tighten the already tight reins on Hispanic women.

THE HISPANIC MALE'S GAZE

Gráfico, the same newspaper in which Clotilde Betances de Jaeger and other Latinas conducted their enlightened conversations on Latina feminism, was published by a consortium of tobacco workers, writers, and theatrical artists. It was first edited by Alberto O'Farrill, an Afro-Cuban actor and playwright who was very popular for depicting the stereotyped Cuban farce role of *Negrito* (Blackie) in blackface. In addition to editing *Gráfico*, he served as its chief illustrator and as a frequent cronista who used the pseudonyms Ofa and Gabitofa in writing in the first person as a type of mulatto *flâneur* whose main preoccupation was finding work and keeping life and limb together. Almost every issue during the first year of publication of *Gráfico* displayed on the cover a full tabloid-page caricature drawn by O'Farrill to satirize American flappers. But more than the satire and censure, the cartoons made apparent the sexual attraction Latino men felt for these women of supposedly looser morals than Latin women. Almost all are displayed with flesh peeking out of lingerie or from under their short dresses because the seated flappers have raised their legs too high. At least two of the caricatures have purposefully ambiguous legends with double entendres to titillate. In one, from July 3, 1927, a flapper is reclined in an unladylike position on an overstuffed chair and holds a basket of flowers in her lap; the legend reads, "Lector ¿No te da el olor?" (Reader, doesn't the smell hit you?). One is left wondering whether the fragrance alluded to is coming from the flowers or the woman. In another, from March 27, 1927, a flapper raises the skirt of her dress as she peers over the hood of a stalled car, while a man holding a cigarette lighter is bent over at her feet. The legend reads, "Buscando el Fallo" (Looking for the problem). But the man is looking under the woman's dress, not at the car engine.

O'Farrill published a series of signed and unsigned columns in *Gráfico*. In the "Pegas Suaves" (Easy jobs) crónicas, which he signed "Ofa," he developed the running story of the mulatto immigrant trying to survive in the big city. In the unsigned ones, O'Farrill poked fun at local customs, which more often than not dealt with the relationship of *viejos verdes* (dirty old men), machos, and flappers. Above the unsigned ones he usually placed an illustration of the crónica that followed. Again, flappers were a frequent preoccupation in these whimsical pieces. In "El Misterio de Washinbay" (Mystery on Washinbay; June 5, 1927), O'Farrill depicts three American flappers who abandon their customary Broadway cabarets in an attempt to attract publicity and rich husbands by establishing a three-woman colony of abstention and deprivation in a rural location. In "El Emboque" (The maw; May 8, 1927), O'Farrill goes on at length about how Latin men position themselves strategically at the street-level entrance down to the subway in order to ogle the flappers as they descend to their trains: "contemplando las líneas curvas que más derecho entran por su vista" (observing the curves that come straight into their view). The sight of two flappers, whom the narrator compares to merchant ships, is depicted as so enticing that even the *Gráfico* photographer who supposedly provided the accompanying illustration could not steady his hands because he

Lector ¿no te dá el olor?

FIGURE 6.2. Cover of *Gráfico* with Alberto O'Farrill illustration "Lector, ¿No Te Da el Olor?"

was so jealous of the two oglers. O'Farrill states that ogling has become so popular that it has become a true plague, and he closes the column with a warning to potential oglers that the police have on occasion used their blackjacks on them.

A much more serious note on the subject of Hispanic women adapt-

Buscando el Fallo.

FIGURE 6.3. Cover of *Gráfico* with Alberto O'Farrill illustration "Buscando el Fallo."

FIGURE 6.4. Alberto O'Farrill.

ing the American flapper dress and personality was sounded by Jesús Colón, for more than fifty years one of the most important Hispanic columnists and intellectuals in the New York Hispanic community. Colón began his writing career as a cronista for a variety of Spanish-language newspapers in the area, including for the labor union newspaper *Justicia* in the 1920s, *Gráfico* (1926–1931), *Pueblos Hispanos* (1943–1944), *Liberación* (1946–1949), *The Daily Worker* (1924–1958), and various others. A self-taught cigar worker and one of the most politicized members of the community of cultural workers and union organizers, Colón made the transition to writing in English and in the mid-1950s became the first Puerto Rican columnist for the *The Daily Worker*, the newspaper published by the Communist Party of America. Colón was a lifelong progressive thinker and later in his career, in the 1950s, wrote feminist-type essays long before such thinking became politically correct. However, upon assuming the convention of cronista and taking on the moralistic persona of his pseudonym Miquis

Tiquis,[15] which he used in *Gráfico* in 1927 and 1928, Colón nevertheless joined his colleagues in attacking Hispanic women for assimilating to the loose morality of American women represented by the flapper in "¡A la bullanga latina le gusta el brillo!":[16]

> Si quieres ver lector la caricatura de una flapper no tienes nada más que mirar a una latina que aspira a serlo. La flapper yanqui siempre busca que su conjunto de exageraciones tenga una apariencia de chic, como se dice en alemán. Además poseen esa divina joya de la frialdad bien imitada. Ese arquear desdeñoso de ojos que al cruzar las piernas casi desde . . . desde . . . parecen no importarle que las miren. *Seeming frigidity, that's the phrase. La would-be flapper* Latina le gusta que la miren y para conseguirlo se pinta con una mascarita. Dos chapotas mal puestas en cada buche y cuatro bien pronunciadas montañas de rouge en los labios. Critican primero los nuevos fads; después los adaptan, llevándolo hasta la exageración.[17] (September 25, 1927)

Colón's further preoccupation with the flapper is also seen in a poem, "La Flapper" (*Lo que el pueblo . . .* 63), which he published in *Gráfico* (September 25, 1927) under his own name:

> *Como una niña Chole que fuera neoyorquina,*
> *rasga el aire la "flapper" contoneándose toda.*
> *Su traje, un futurismo de la última moda,*
> *hace mil sugerencias con seda divina.*
> *Que la miren los hombres mientras ella camina*
> *es su supremo anhelo. Si hay quien le hable de boda,*
> *contesta con alguna carcajada que poda*
> *la ilusión más sublime. ¡Carcajada asesina!*
> *Reina experta del último salto mortal bailable,*
> *Niña pintarrajeada, superficial, variable,*
> *Como el liberto esclavo al probar nueva vida.*
> *Por contraste me hacen recordar a mi abuela,*
> *Que hilando me contaba del gigante que vuela,*
> *Con su voz temblorosa cual plegaria perdida.*[18]

Both of these pieces are fine examples of the Hispanic man's gaze on what for him is a transgressor of gender roles who tests the limits of a freedom recently conceded by access to the vote. That in the poem Colón would compare her to the excesses enjoyed by recently freed

FIGURE 6.5. Jesús Colón in his home library.

slaves is ambiguous and ambivalent in that it may or may not celebrate the winning of that freedom, but it also may be an indirect link
to Colón's biography: he was the grandson of slaves, although in his
early writings he never made mention of his African and slave heritage.
The reference to "liberto esclavo," however, may be the direct link to
his saintly grandmother mentioned in the next line, who contrasts directly with this frivolous, ostentatious, loud ("carcajada") sexual tease
of a woman who is covering her inner essence with facial paint and
a flourish of garments. Dancing life away, single, and disdaining the
sacrament and social foundation of marriage in favor of unbridled independence, she is the opposite of his industrious, aged grandmother
sewing, praying, and helping to raise children and educating them by
spinning tales, continuing traditions. That any Latina, referenced in the

prior quote, would attempt to imitate this personification of American liberties/libertinage would be anathema, the equivalent of a mask on a mask, the "caricature" and "imitation" Colón uses as indictments. In both cases, the Anglo flapper's and the Latina's, the performance is meant to attract the male gaze, if not ogling, as in O'Farrill. In both works, Colón is blaming the women for male sexual attraction to them and their performance. In "A la bullanga latina," like the cover illustrations of *Gráfico*, it is in the Latino male imagination that the flapper's short skirt serves to provoke men's lust; and with the hesitation of *desde . . . desde . . .* , it becomes apparent that Colón does ogle. While condemning the Latina for practicing such a performance of freedom, Colón also directly indicts the society that makes the performance possible through its emphasis on the conspicuous consumption of material goods.[19] Silk dresses and the frivolities of the jazz age have taken the place of the pure, wholesome pursuits of women like his grandmother in the homeland, who produced their own clothes (*hilando*), remained true to their faith (*plegaria*), and maintained the home by raising children—even if they had recently been freed from slavery.

GENDER AND NATION BUILDING IN IMMIGRANT LITERATURE

The graphic and written records published in newspapers by community moralists and satirists, *flâneurs* and *pícaros*, and observers of the human comedy alike not only amply illustrate the nation-building aspirations of the cronistas, but also show how those published attitudes applied pressure on families to conform to old gender roles and resist the social changes that the new American host culture was making imminent. The pressure placed on women in this conflict of cultural roles and mores was probably greater than that ever felt in the homeland. These commentators perceived greater competition for Latinas in the United States than back home, there being fewer of them in the immigrant community. More important, the writers also perceived that American women enjoyed greater freedom of movement and self-determination, which would lure their own women away from establishing good Latin families and progeny. While the roaring twenties[20] saw the liberalization of women's roles and women's massive entrance into the workplace in the United States, it was also a period of massive Hispanic immigration of very conservative segments, especially of the Mexican population—as many as a million economic and political refugees from Mexico alone entered the United States before 1930. The first reaction of the immigrant writers was not to liberalize but to resist the liberal influence and example by tightening men's control over women. Hispanic male writers on the East Coast, while not as severe as the Mexican writers in the Southwest, also censured women for Americanizing and, perhaps less moralistically, allowed themselves to be titillated by the perceptibly freer American sex roles. They openly displayed this behavior in their illustrations and crónicas. In both groups, the Mexicans in the Southwest and the Latinos in the Northeast, Hispanic women were seen as the center of the family and the key to survival of the group, the language, and the culture. It was men doing the gazing and the moralizing, and they controlled the media: publishing houses, newspapers, theaters, and so on. It was these very men who saw themselves as the self-appointed conscience of the community in the crónicas that were so popular in the immigrant communities. That despite the stringent economic and editorial controls exerted by men in these media, women were able to articulate and evolve a feminist discourse is deserving of recognition and tribute. It is a tale that merits recovery and dissemination not only for the dispelling of stereotypes, but also for filling the gaps in the cultural history of the United States and the Americas.

AFTERWORD: LIFE ON THE SUPPOSED HYPHEN

The myths that once grounded our identity have become bankrupt.
—GUILLERMO GÓMEZ-PEÑA, "DANGER ZONE: CULTURAL RELATIONS
BETWEEN CHICANOS AND MEXICANS AT THE END OF THE CENTURY,"
IN KANELLOS, *HERENCIA*

IN THE COURSE of this book it has become apparent that the impulse to erase borders, to create a transnational and transcultural community is not new to the literature created by Latinos living in the United States. One might say that this tendency springs from the very nature of living in a figurative space between two linguistic-cultural regions in the Americas, where national histories and myths (but national histories are myths) collide. Today, numerous theorists referenced in this book and artists, such as Guillermo Gómez Peña and Eduardo González-Viaña and others, look upon globalization as a recent phenomenon that is eradicating borders and national-cultural distinctions. They see the world as a postmodern hodgepodge of ethnocultural characteristics resulting from the long age of European colonization of the rest of the world and the imperial rise of the United States, with its powerful technology, communications, and corporate power, which have produced and continue to produce great migrations into the industrial world. As seen from the vantage point of New York, Paris, or London, much of the third world now resides within the borders of the first world, and much of the first world has penetrated the national cultures of the third. A transmigrant born in Mexico who received his university education in California, the performance artist and writer Gómez-Peña has become the most outspoken advocate of hybridization as a solution to current national, ethnic, and racial conflicts. Acknowledging we people have always led hybrid lives of multiple social identities, Gómez-Peña uses satire, humor, and shock to force readers and spectators to identify and embrace all the borders they cross in daily life and to understand their multiple identities. While grounded in the Mexican-Chicano bilingual-bicultural experience, Gómez Peña's vision goes far beyond the nation-building or rejecting motives that we have seen in the transmigrant texts represented in this book. As Maria Antonia Oliver-Rotger characterizes his work, "It forces us to look straight in the face at the most unsettling dimension of chauvinism, nationalism, to question the stability and security of our identity, and to reflect upon how much of the other, as we imagine it, fear it and desire it, we have in ourselves" (241). Many Latino writers and artists today, both transmigrant and native, use their position in the interstices of nationhood and cultures to produce similar esthetic visions.

As far as Latino culture in the United States is concerned, chapter 1, in particular, provided a schema for understanding how Latinos across time have created texts from, at times, contrary positionalities relating to the home and receptor cultures. But the transmigrant texts written in Spanish presented in this book make amply clear how the concepts of homeland and alien receptor environment have survived to this day in much of this literature. The desire to debunk the American Dream has survived also, while dreaming of return to the homeland, to an Eden, a Golden Age, from captivity in Babylon and torture and death in the North American Inferno, where true love, family, and spirituality are greeted only by hypocrisy, cupidity, and discrimination. It is true that some anarchist and feminist transmigrants rejected the dream of nationhood and that other writers, such as Cotto-Thorner, dreamt of integration through internal colonial hybridity. Other transmigrant authors, such as Torres, even dreamed of utopias far from the oppositional binaries of cultures in conflict. And González-Viaña's messianic vision of a Latinized United States was proposed as a final resolution to the binary that has dominated this literature. Gustavo Pérez Firmat calls it not a binary or an opposition but an "apposition" with his use of the metaphor of "life on the hyphen," specifically when referring to his generation of Cubans who went into American exile as children and grew up and were educated in the United States.

In his *Life on the Hyphen: The Cuban-American Way* (1994), Pérez Firmat posited three existential alternatives for Cuban transmigrants in the wake of the diaspora initiated after the Communist takeover of the island: (1) live as an exile preserving pre-Castro Cuban culture, (2) acculturate to American culture after being born or raised (or both) in the United States, (3) live a dual/ambivalent existence of relating to both cultures equally, although selectively, the latter interpreted as "life on the hyphen" both separating and uniting the identity terms of Cuban and American. He further argues that only those people of his "1.5" generation, who came to the United States as children, are capable of this Janus-like existence, translating the cultures to each other, identifying with both but really being of neither: "The 1.5 individual is unique in that, unlike younger and older compatriots, he or she may actually find it possible to circulate within and through both the old and the new cultures" (4). In the course of writing this book, on occasion I have considered what could be regarded as texts generated by a possible 1.5 generation, such as those of Dolores Bolio in chapter 5. But in the main my book has been about texts written exclusively in Spanish by transmigrants, regardless of their self-designated status as political refugee or immigrant; what has been important is the actual stance of the author or narrator in the text itself as a transmigrant or for a transmigrant audience. As I say in the introduction, part of my mission has been to distinguish immigrant writing from American ethnic autobiography, as represented by such English-language texts as those written by Julia Alvarez, Sandra Cisneros, Cristina García, Edward Rivera, Richard Rodriguez, Piri Thomas, Victor Villaseñor, and many others.

Despite the generally verifiable distinctions I have made between immigrant and native texts, Pérez Firmat's thesis and praxis, as we shall see below, problematizes my schema and analysis in various ways. First of all, as a "one-and-a-halfer" he demonstrates a fluency in both Spanish and English to such an extent that he writes and publishes in both languages. Even in his poetry his command of the linguistic and cultural signs and meanings of both languages reaches the level of virtuosity in its code switching.[1] But he chooses to write most of his works in English. He first writes his memoir, *Next Year in Cuba*, in English and then rewrites it in Spanish and publishes both in separate editions. It would be hard to conceive of Pérez Firmat achieving this sophistication and artistry had he not been a college English major and later received a doctorate in Spanish American literature and lived a bilingual life in Miami. As a literary theorist, memoirist, poet, and novelist, Pérez Firmat is not alone. Other writers, both transmigrants and natives, including Lucha Corpi, Roberto Fernández, Rolando Hinojosa, and Tomás Rivera, have produced similar bilingual-bicultural textual histories, writing some books in one language and others in the other. Nevertheless, despite Pérez Firmat's familiarity with and study of Latino writers and memoirists in his *Life on the Hyphen*, in *Tongue Ties: Logo Eroticism in Anglo-Hispanic Literature* (2003) and elsewhere Pérez Firmat forswears a Latino identity and unequivocally considers himself a Cuban exile:[2]

> Puesto que Cuba es mi pasado, es también mi presente y mi futuro. Vivir como exiliado en Estados Unidos puede ser una bendición o una maldición, pero no es una elección. La asimilación es una alternativa sólo para aquéllos que ya están asimilados. . . . Soy demasiado cubano para ser americano pero demasiado americano para ser otra cosa. Para gente como yo, dividida y multiplicada a la vez, la verdad siempre se reviste de paradojas: que nuestro exilio ya ha terminado, y que nuestro exilio nunca terminará; que no hay exilio que dure cien años, y que no hay exiliado que lo resista. A veces me jacto de esta duplicidad, otras veces me harto de ella, pero así soy: yo y *you* y tú y *two*. (*El año que viene* 197)[3]

Pérez Firmat further problematizes the schema in arguing against the concept of hybridity: "Mi vida no es síntesis sino vaivén" (201) ("My life is less a synthesis than a seesaw") [*Next Year* 212]). Perhaps we can accommodate this author's autobiographical and theoretical postulations as to not being either an immigrant or a native and exclusively understand his work as the product of exile—the political exile that was forced upon him by wealthy parents fleeing a Communist regime when he was twelve years old—for we can readily understand that his American experience was the product not of his choice but dictated by his parents and by the political receptivity of his adopted country. But, I would argue, in no way can one accept the language, themes, and positionality of his texts as exilic.[4] Rather, I would place them all on the continuum of immigrant to U.S. native literature as a hybrid product born in the interstices of competing national identities that ultimately lead Pérez Firmat to deny his status as an immigrant but, nevertheless, to embrace the American national myths; after all, he is a perfect example of living the American Dream: according to his autobiography, he has had a successful, remunerative career in elite American universities, has been a successful author of texts written in English and published by mainstream houses[5] (his Spanish and out-of-print works issued by minority Latino presses), has married the personification of America in a *gringa*, and fathered two of what he calls 100 percent

American children born to his previous Cuban-American wife. All of this is documented in his memoir and reflected as well in his novel *Anything but Love* (2000).

Perhaps Pérez Firmat chooses to distance himself from the type of ethnic autobiography he references as "immigrant autobiography" in *Life on the Hyphen* (71)—the works of Richard Rodriguez, Edward Rivera, and Oscar Hijuelos—preferring to identify himself more with the autobiography of the untutored Desi Arnaz, *A Book*, with which he finds common cause because of its concordance with his 1.5 generational thesis and Arnaz's spectacular rise to success in capturing the American Dream. Whether Pérez Firmat wishes to recognize it or not, all of these books, *and his* as well, support this national myth and acknowledge the status of their authors as Americans. Pérez Firmat's own *El año que viene estamos en Cuba/Next Year in Cuba* explicitly supports the national myth in identifying more with an American space, Miami more than a Havana or a Cuba, to which there is no return. Cuba belongs to his late childhood and adolescence, but he is an American as an adult: "El niño cubano es el padre del hombre americano" (*El año* 25); "The Cuban child is the father of the American man" (*Next Year* 25). Casting himself as a New Adam in the third part of his memoir, "Vida Nueva," he leaves Miami and comes to terms with his American identity: "Cuando abandoné Miami empecé a ser otra persona" (*El año* 150); "Once I moved away from Miami, I began to become a different man from what I had been up to then" (*Next Year* 146); earlier in the text he even envisioned leaving Havana on the ferry as the real beginning of his life (*El año* 25). In "Vida Nueva," he decides he is more a child of exiled parents than an exile himself and settles for a "legado espiritual" (spiritual legacy, *El año* 177) of exile, his particular dark night of the soul he has had to overcome to fully participate in American society. Not only has he experienced success as a writer and intellectual, he has engendered American children, and this investment, more than anything, makes him American, albeit without abandoning his past as a Cuban: "A través de mis hijos he aprendido que el exilio puede ser una fatalidad, pero no tiene que ser un destino" (*El año* 185); "Although they don't know it, David and Miriam have given me the opportunity and the incentive to reach this place that I call 'after exile'" (*Next Year* 197). Finally, his move to the larger American world outside of Miami was the first step in his successful development or *bildung* as a truly American success story: "Aunque Miami es la única Cuba que conozco bien, me cuesta trabajo imaginar cómo hubiera sido mi vida si nunca hubiera partido. Me temo de haberme quedado en Miami seguiría estancado en el pasado, igual que mi padre" (*El año* 198); "If I still lived in Little Havana, I'm afraid I would be trapped by memory, the way my father is" (*Next Year* 209). Ultimately, he has found the true way and is no longer disoriented: "despistado en su propio país" (*El año* 185); "didn't feel at home in their own home" (*Next Year* 195).

If one deconstructs his memoir as a potential work of immigrant literature, however, the following characteristics rise to the surface. His dream of return to a Cuba he hardly remembers ("fui desprendiéndome de esa parte de mi biografía que había transcurrido en Cuba" [*El año* 25]; "I was quickly losing touch with that part of my biography that unfolded in Cuba" [*Next year* 25]) is displaced by a feeling that Miami is his true home, and any dream of return is to this place that has become purer and more authentic than Cuba:

> La comunidad de exiliados no sólo emulaba La Habana, sino que la completaba. . . . el exiliado que se complace en creer que él no abandonó la patria, sino que la patria lo abandonó a él. . . . Desde la perspectiva del guajiro—que aquí hace vocero del exiliado—La Revolución ha desvirtuado la ciudad [La Habana], haciéndola menos cubana. . . . Para nosotros La Pequeña Habana estaba más cerca del corazón de Cuba que La Habana misma. *Ser* no es *estar*—una forma de vida no se reduce a un lugar de residencia (*El año* 60–62).[6]

This is basically the same attitude developed in the México de Afuera ideology of exile and the deterritorialized nation that underpinned much of the immigrant literature of the early twentieth century. And what is nationality for him is being a part of the Miami exile community: "Me parecía que mi nacionalidad derivaba de mi condición de exiliado" (*El año* 25); "It seemed to me that my national origin derived from my exile status" (*Next Year* 25).

When he does go off to teach and live in the North, his nostalgia for the homeland is for Miami: "Cuando me mudé de Miami en 1973, me convencí de que me exiliaba por segunda vez. . . . Quería regresar a Miami—mi paraíso cálido y verde" (*El año* 91); "When I moved from Miami in 1973, I convinced myself that I was going into exile a second time. . . . I wanted to go back to Miami, my cozy, green exilic cocoon" (*Next Year* 67).

In both *El año/Next year* and *Anything but Love*, Pérez Firmat maintains the tension of two worlds in conflict and contrast, ever comparing Cuban (perhaps *Latino* would be a better term) and American (perhaps *Anglo-American*) cultures, especially how they define and treat genders, often expressing attitudes similar to those expressed by male transmigrant writers throughout the twentieth century. The truest and most authentic values of the nation are incarnate in his mother, who has made the refuge in Miami the real nation (119–132). In spite of his respect for his mother and other Cuban and Cuban-American women who represent the national culture and his identity, he fixes his gaze[7] on *las americanas* and, as it did for his model Arnaz, conquering *la americana* becomes a main indicator of making it in U.S. society: "Nuestra misión: alcanzar el *American Dream*—o sea, ligar con las americanas de nuestros sueños" (*El año* 49); (my translation: "Our mission: achieve the American Dream—that is, hook up with the *americanas* of our dreams" [not literally in the English original]). In *Anything but Love*, a novel written in English and not translated by Pérez Firmat, the overriding motivation of the first half is the conquest and marriage of the Cuban-American protagonist to Catherine, impelled by a deep psychological force "buried inside" (*Anything* 14) the protagonist: "the allure of otherness, the tug of novelty, bicultural vibes" (*Anything* 18). His dreams are finally consummated: "There she was, the *americanita* of my dreams, my ideal date of 1968, the first woman I had truly loved, naked right in front of me" (*Anything* 25). After their first earth-shaking sexual encounter, Catherine confesses to him that ever since she was six years old and her parents had given her a mambo kit, she had been waiting for him (*Anything* 26). The obvious reference is to Desi Arnaz and Lucille Ball and the mambo craze of the fifties and sixties; it also implies that the Cuban and the American complement each other, make each other complete. But in the rest of the novel, Catherine (Cat) goes on to become just as inscrutable as Lucille was to Desi.

Pérez Firmat claims that Arnaz is a "tutelary spirit" who, in loving Lucy, renounces the regression or return—which, I might add, is so primary in immigrant literature—and the love of Lucy is a love for America: "As Ricky himself stated, to love Lucy is to embrace the unfamiliar in the form of an *americana* who stands, more generally, for Americana" (*Life on the Hyphen* 12). As Pérez Firmat's and Arnaz's autobiographies become intertwined and overlap as stories about Cuban-American adolescents who engaged in making it in America, both the tutor and his student see Americanization as a sexual encounter (in circular logic, Pérez claims this is natural because both of them are Cuban one-and-a-halfers):

For Arnaz, who came to this country as an adolescent, sexual matura-
tion and cultural adaptation are so tightly wound together that it may
be impossible to pry them apart. Gender identity merges with cultural
identity, as sex becomes a way of finding and defining one's place in
the new world. It may not be too much of an exaggeration to say that
Desi's womanizing was one way—perhaps his dominant way—of con-
versing with American culture. The *americana* incarnates Americana;
she is America in its most graspable form. (*Life on the Hyphen* 73)

While the gaze, if not the ogling, are evident in both authors, their
actions and words go far beyond what is present in most immigrant
literature written in Spanish: Gustavo and Desi actually consummate
their love affairs with the Americana/America. It is their stance vis-à-
vis American culture that codes their "ethnic" autobiographical experiences, in addition to their writing in English and all that that language
represents, no matter how broken Desi speaks and writes it nor how
eloquently and innovatively Gustavo articulates and translates it, his
adopted and schooled language. Whether in the English original or in
the loose translation, Pérez Firmat's *Next Year in Cuba* must be considered as part of the long line of American ethnic autobiography; it is
not a work of exile literature, in line with Heberto Padilla's memoirs,
for instance, and not a work of the Hispanic immigrant literature written in Spanish, even though he has taken pains to translate the memoir into Spanish. That there is deep Cuban/Cuban-American cultural
content in his work there is no doubt, and in this it may be more distinct and richer than other ethnic Hispanic or Latino memoirs or autobiographical novels. This is true especially because Pérez Firmat is so
intellectually and artistically fluent in Spanish and because he is much
closer to the ethnic enclave he writes about than other such authors he
references, such as Richard Rodriguez and even Desi Arnaz. Regardless
of his fluency, Pérez Firmat will have to resign himself to being considered as part of the ethnic curriculum, an insider, an American, unlike
the authors discussed in this book, who stuck to the Spanish language,
were not skilled enough to write in English or scale the barriers to
publication and distribution by American mainstream presses, fought
agringamiento, and often did return to their homelands.

NOTES

INTRODUCTION

1. Nevertheless, so influential a play as René Marqués's *La carreta*, produced in 1953 and subsequently published in multiple editions in Spanish, English, and French, is the epitome of immigrant literature. As we will see in the ensuing chapters, such folk songs as the "Lamento de un jíbaro," probably from the early 1960s, and plays performed in the 1970s in open theaters in East Harlem, the Bronx, and the Lower East Side and published during that decade—for example, Jaime Carrero's *Pipo Subway no sabe reír*—continue to promote traditional Hispanic immigrant values and to censure the Metropolis for its materialism, dehumanization, and violence against Hispanic minorities. The Nuyorican generation, however, went to great pains to distinguish itself from immigrants, claiming their cultural and linguistic rights as American citizens with the right to use either language or combine them both in one literary work.

2. As Paul White states from his reading of numerous immigrant novels in a variety of languages, "Amongst all the literature of immigration the highest proportion deals in some way with ideas of return, whether actualized or remaining imaginary" (14).

3. A few immigrant writers have written creative works in both English and Spanish. One such author has also explored the personal and individual language choices made by Spanish, Spanish American, and Latino writers, however, only cursorily exploring the nationalist and language-loyalty dimensions of these choices. See Pérez-Firmat, *Tongue Ties: Logo-Eroticism in Anglo-Hispanic Literature*. An extended study of language usage and choice in a number of first-generation and immigrant writers is Debra A. Castillo's *Redreaming America: Toward a Bilingual American Culture*.

4. I go into greater depth on this issue in "La literatura hispana en los EE.UU. y el género autobiográfico."

5. Cofer is also studied in a chapter entitled "Invention of the Ethnic Self in Latina Immigrant Fiction," of Christian's book *Show and Tell*. Christian provides an interesting general study of immigrant literary characteristics but conflates the concepts of ethnic and immigrant and undoes her argument for studying Cofer's *Line of the Sun* as an immigrant novel. Writing her prose always in English, the language in which she was educated in New Jersey, Cofer is a writer who expands the canon of ethnic autobiography and ethnic or postcolonial bildungsroman, and should be studied alongside the other Latino authors mentioned above who are struggling to expand the American canon.

6. Actually, Cisneros's mother was from a family that had lived in the United States for many generations; only her father was an immigrant.

7. Mexico does not seem to figure in Payant's and Rose's "North America," although Mexico has been a country that has received immigrants throughout its history and, indeed, does have a literature of immigration.

8. Another unfounded assertion by the editors is that "more female than male writers are writing on the immigrant experience" (xxii). Obviously, when one has

not conducted the necessary historical research nor completed a systematic survey of the field, there is a danger of arriving at such erroneous conclusions. As will be seen in the chapters that follow, Hispanic immigrant literature has been and continues to be dominated by male voices. Hispanic female immigrants never have had the same access to publication as males in the past or the present, for many reasons that are often shared by other immigrant groups. The first waves of immigration are overwhelmingly male, women have had less access to education than males in their home countries, patriarchal dominance of the media in immigrant communities is rampant, etc. That second- and third-generation Latinas who write about immigration are more accessible to professors and the public through mainstream, commercial publishing houses does not mean they are more productive writers or outnumber male writers. They are not and do not. As the publisher of such writers as Ana Castillo, Sandra Cisneros, Denise Chávez, Judith Ortiz Cofer, Helena María Viramontes, among others, I could offer a long, detailed discussion of these issues, but this would lead to too great a digression from the task at hand.

9. I could cite numerous works that not only do not account for the important role language plays in immigrant literature but that, without any intellectual reflection, only consider works written in English. Even an extensive bibliography like Anderson's *Immigrants in the United States in Fiction* does so, including not one work by a Hispanic author written in Spanish, other than the bilingual edition of Tomás Rivera's . . . *y no se lo tragó la tierra/And the Earth Did Not Devour Him*—but Rivera was a native-born Mexican-American, and at least one side of his family had resided in Texas for multiple generations.

10. One author who does study diasporic/immigrant communities and does justify the study of the literature created by the children of immigrants and exiles is Fatima Mujcinovic in *Postmodern Cross-Culturalism*; she writes, "The effects of physical displacement become manifested as crucial factors in an individual and, by extension, a socio-cultural development. Political immigrants' positioning in the new location is continuously disrupted by an unhealed trauma, which becomes intensified when political victimization intertwines with cultural repression and this trauma is passed on to new generations" (104). She refers to works by Helena María Viramontes (the daughter of Mexican-American parents, not political refugees), Cristina García, and Julia Alvarez.

11. Jesse Alemán plumbs the generational aspect of Cowart's book in more depth in his review-essay, "Barbarous Tongues."

CHAPTER ONE

". . . there is something that does not sink in a shipwreck, that is not shaken by earthquakes and does not burn in fires, and that immutable and eternal something is the soul of the Patria, which is always there to uplift the fallen, forgive the sinful, console the children who because they are absent cannot take refuge in their mother's lap." (318–319)

1. The Recovery project was founded in 1990 by scholars who recognized that a vast corpus of writing by U.S. Hispanics prior to 1960 remained virtually unknown and scattered across the United States and various homelands. Funded in the main

by American foundations, the project researches and preserves through microfilming the written culture of Latinos, makes it accessible through publications and online delivery, furthers its study through grants to researchers, conferences, and curriculum projects, and seeks to integrate it into all levels of education and popular culture. Centered at the University of Houston, its advisory board is made up of scholars, librarians, and archivists from across the United States, Mexico, the Caribbean, and Spain. For information: www.artepublicopress.com.

2. Recently, numerous scholars have characterized Hispanic or Latino immigration, or certain other migrations, as diasporic. Kalra et al., in *Diaspora and Hybridity*, one of the most extensive treatments of diasporic culture, relate *diaspora* in the classic sense to "forced movement, exile and a consequent sense of loss derived from the inability to return" (10). The classical referents are frequently the Jewish and African slave diasporas. The idea of forced exile, they state, would also apply to more contemporary migrations, especially if one interprets force to extend to economic and political conditions (10)—which, for instance, the Dominican-American essayist Silvio Torres-Saillant does in his book, *El retorno de las yolas* (see especially his "Epílogo: Contrapunteo de la diáspora y el Estado," 405–424). One then could be justified in applying the term to the diaspora of some million Mexicans displaced in the United States during the Mexican Revolution of 1910, even if the motive for displacement was more economic than political; and the Puerto Rican diaspora, which had economic and colonialist imperatives and intensified during the Second World War, reaching its height in the early 1950s; as well as the Cuban diaspora precipitated by the Cuban Revolution of 1959. But this conceptualization does not readily account for the people who found/find themselves within the United States because of the expansion of its empire and incorporation of their lands by conquest or purchase. In this category are the former Mexican subjects in the Southwest and West and the former Spanish subjects in the South and the island of Puerto Rico, which was forcefully incorporated and its peoples made citizens of the United States in 1917. Nor does it sufficiently account for the generations born to these incorporated "Americans," who to this day relate to the Spanish-speaking world and maintain ties with its peoples and countries. On the other hand, Kalra et al.'s book does help one understand such processes as hybridity and the destabilizing of the concepts of nation or nation-state and all that is attendant to the literature of immigration, such as the sense of loss, nostalgia for and the dream of return to the homeland, the binary of here and there that develops in the literature, etc. But so does the theory of transmigration that I apply in my text. To simplify things, I will refer to my subjects as transmigrants or immigrants or migrants, except in the cases where these literary authors themselves explore the concept of diaspora, which on occasion they do, for instance, as in the speeches of Nemesio García Naranjo, the essays of Silvio Torres-Saillant, and the novels of Teodoro Torres and Guillermo Cotto-Thorner. All of them compare the situation of their peoples, i.e., Mexican/Mexican American, Dominican, and Puerto Rican, to the Jewish diaspora related in the Old Testament.

3. While printing technology was not new to Spanish America, access to a free press, in fact, drew intellectuals and revolutionists to Philadelphia, Boston, and New York from the 1800s to the 1830s to write their respective nations and smuggle the resultant books back into Spanish America. See my article "Hispanic Intellectuals Publishing in the Nineteenth-Century United States."

4. See Poyo's study of the nation-building efforts of Cubans in the United States during the nineteenth century in *With All, and for the Good of All* . . . and Lazo's *Writing to Cuba*.

5. See my article "*El Clamor Público*: Resisting the American Empire," 15–16.

6. How individual authors see themselves and articulate their positionality always problematizes this type of general schema. One author, the Cuban-American Gustavo Pérez Firmat, who arrived with his political refugee family as a preteen but received all of his subsequent education in American schools and became completely bilingual, insists that his works are exilic, despite their having been predominantly written in English (see the afterword). Another, the Dominican-American essayist Silvio Torres-Saillant, who also came to the United States as a preteen with his family, who were economic refugees, writes from the Dominican "diaspora" and adopts many of the positions that are identified with political exile. In his *El retorno de las yolas*, Torres-Saillant censures internal politics on the island and condemns the oligarchy and Euro-white-identified business and governmental sector for having expelled the 20 percent of the population that lives as transmigrants in the United States and Puerto Rico. Further, he supports the thesis that the true Dominican nation can never be constructed on the island under this governmental-classist rule and its economic distortions: "El poder ha quedado en manos de los promotores de una visión excluyente, elitista y enajenante de lo que somos como pueblo" (381) (Power has remained in the hands of those who promote an exclusivist, elite, and alienating vision of who we are as a people). He advances the typical exile thesis (see chapter 4) that the trasnmigrant Dominican community and its intellectuals are more capable of writing the nation. Torres-Saillant nevertheless acknowledges that although the dream of return to the homeland is strong among Dominican transmigrants, such a return would be very difficult, if not impossible, for the majority of the expatriates, including himself. After careful analysis, I would situate Pérez Firmat in my schema as an American writer who furthers the well-worn genre of ethnic autobiography in such books as *Next Year in Cuba*, and I would treat Torres-Saillant's collection of essays as a work of exilic literature. Yet both works contain themes and attitudes commonly represented in immigrant texts.

7. See Luis Leal, "Adolfo Carrillo," *Dictionary of Literary Biography* 122:53–55 (1992).

8. Gray, "Francisco P. Ramírez. A Short Biography," 30–31.

9. As Bruce-Novoa has stated, "And when exiles cannot return, they dedicate themselves to justifying their existence in a dual manner: they manipulate the image and significance of their resistance outside their country by discrediting what the homeland has become; and two, they set about proving that they are the authentic bearers of the true tradition of the homeland and even of the ideals of the attempted revolution. . . . Eventually this exercise in self-justification leads to the claim that the homeland has actually moved with the exiles, that they have managed to bring it with them in some reduced form, and that if the opportunity should arise, they can take it back to replant it in the original garden of Eden. This explains how the Lozano group dared called themselves 'El México de Afuera.'" See "*La Prensa* and the Chicano Community," 153.

10. See Mirandé's chapter, "*Mi Casa Es Su Casa*: Displacement from the Land," in *Gringo Justice*, 27–49.

11. While many scholars believe that the great majority of Latinos write in English, they have not conducted the research that would conclude this. It is their observation of what is produced by publishers, not writers, that leads them to hold this belief, without reflecting on such market conditions as reviewing media, language preference of librarians and bookstore owners and managers, promotion and distribution systems, etc. A rough number of texts submitted to Arte Público Press in Spanish today would be 40 percent. Nevertheless, in the relative absence of reviewing and distribution systems for Spanish-language books today, Arte Público is forced to publish the majority of its adult literature in English.

12. See Leal's "Truth Telling Tongues" for historical antecedents of this bilingualism. Bakhtin has written extensively on hybridity in language and defines it not just as bilingualism but as a "double-accented, double-styled *hybrid construction*": "What we are calling a hybrid construction is an utterance that belongs, by its grammatical [syntactic] and compositional markers, to a single speaker, but that actually contains mixed within it two utterances, two speech manners, two styles, two 'languages,' two semantic and axiological belief systems. . . . the division of voices and languages takes place within the limits of a single syntactic whole, often within the limits of a single sentence" (304–305).

13. On code switching and linguistic heterogeneity, see Sánchez, "From Heterogeneity to Contradiction: Hinojosa's Novel."

14. What Kobena Mercer has said about black culture's dialogic tendencies can be readily applied to Alurista's *Spik in glyph?*: "The subversive force of the hybridizing tendency is most apparent at the level of language itself where creoles, patois and Black English decentre, destabilize and carnivalise the linguistic domination of 'English'" (57).

15. See Paredes' *Folkore and Culture on the Texas-Mexican Border*.

16. Alirio Díaz Guerra fully elaborates this theme, culminating with his characterization of the Statue of Liberty as the "Statue of Libertinism" (*Estatua del Libertinaje*) in *Lucas Guevara* (1914).

CHAPTER TWO

"In modern societies, newspapers represent the great effort for human progress. . . . They instruct, moralize, civilize and prepare men to be useful in the largest of labors in the never-ending struggles of life."

1. A vibrant native print culture has existed in Latino communities since the early nineteenth century, when the printing press was introduced to Louisiana, Florida, and Texas and later to New Mexico and California. When massive Hispanic immigration took place on all three coasts of the United States at the beginning of the twentieth century, the immigrant press tended to overwhelm the native press, the latter recovering only in the post–Second World War era. For a detailed study of both native and exile press cultures, see my *Hispanic Periodicals in the United States: A Brief History and Comprehensive Bibliography*.

2. I refer to the edition of 1970 issued by Greenwood Press of Westport, Connecticut, of Robert E. Park, *The Immigrant Press and Its Control* (New York: Harper and Brothers, 1922).

3. See *El Mercurio de Nueva York* (1829–1830) and *El Mensagero Semanal de Nueva York* (1828–1831).

4. Among these, I would include San Francisco's *Sud Americano* (1855), *El Eco del Pacífico* (1856), *La Voz de Méjico* (1862), and *El Nuevo Mundo* (1864).

5. Even Los Angeles's *El Clamor Público* (1855–1859), which was founded to protect the rights of the native Californios, became a defender of Hispanic immigrants, as did other native print efforts. See my article "*El Clamor Público*: Resisting the American Empire," *California History* 84.2 (winter 2006–2007): 10–18, 69–70.

6. See Mario T. García, *Desert Immigrants*, 35–36, for a discussion of the statistics on Mexican immigration.

7. See my *A History of Hispanic Theater in the United States*.

8. See my *Thirty Million Strong: Reclaiming the Hispanic Image in American History* for a review of the historical reasons for the predominance of working-class culture in Hispanic communities.

9. An autodidactic writer like Jesús Colón, during the late 1920s and the 1930s, had the option of publishing in a wide selection of worker-oriented newspapers; in fact, he published his *crónicas* in *Boletín de la Liga Puertorriqueña e Hispana*, *Gráfico*, *Vida Alegre*, *El Curioso*, *Pueblos Hispanos*, and *Liberación*. See Colón, *Lo que el pueblo me dice*.

10. In the Northeast, the large daily and weekly Spanish-language newspapers flourished and also published books, as did small, ephemeral presses. In 1913 José Campubrí founded *La Prensa* in New York City to serve the community of mostly Spanish and Cuban immigrants in and around Manhattan's Fourteenth Street (in 1962 it merged with *El Diario de Nueva York*). One of the main reasons *La Prensa* survived so long was that it was able to expand and adapt to the new Spanish-speaking nationalities that immigrated to the city, especially the Puerto Ricans who migrated from their island en masse during and after the Second World War and came to form the largest Hispanic group in the city. In 1948 *El Diario de Nueva York* was founded by the Dominican immigrant Porfirio Domenici, specifically appealing to the Puerto Rican community and giving *La Prensa* competition for this growing readership. *El Diario de Nueva York*'s slogan was "Champion of the Puerto Ricans." In 1962 O. Roy Chalk, the owner of *El Diario de Nueva York*, purchased *La Prensa* and merged the two journals. In 1981 the Gannett newspaper corporation bought *El Diario-La Prensa*; in 1989 it was sold to El Diario Associates, Inc., a corporation founded by Peter Davidson, a former Morgan Stanley specialist in the newspaper industry. In 1990 the Times Mirror Corporation purchased a 50 percent interest in Los Angeles's *La Opinión* (San Antonio's *La Prensa* had ceased to exist in 1963). In 1976 the *Miami Herald* founded *El Miami Herald*, which in 1987 was transformed into the new, improved *El Nuevo Herald*. Both the Spanish- and English-language Miami dailies are subsidiaries of the Knight-Ridder newspaper chain. Thus today, the three major Hispanic dailies are owned and controlled by American (non-Hispanic) multimedia corporations; how this has impacted their functioning in service of the immigrants has not as yet been assessed. There are, however, smaller Hispanic dailies publishing today in Chicago, Houston, San Antonio, and other cities.

11. The relationship of many of these newspapers to their transmigrant base was often a complicated affair. For instance, Jack Danciger, the owner and publisher of Kansas City's *El Cosmopolita* (The Cosmopolitan, 1914–1919), was an importer of

products from Mexico, including tequila, which he marketed in the Mexican community (Smith 74). He and his paper were fierce fighters for Mexican workers' rights and for a whole range of causes in the community. Further complicating the relationship was that Danciger received money from the Venustiano Carranza regime in Mexico to publish positive articles about the regime. Later, from the 1920s through the 1930s, Danciger was a pioneer in civil rights for Mexican Americans and was closely associated with such organizations as the League of United Latin American Citizens. Even the political exile columnist Julio Arce (see chapter 5) received fifty dollars a month from the Carranza regime in support of his newspaper (Richmond 190).

12. See Bruce-Novoa, "*La Prensa* and the Chicano Community," *Américas Review* 17/3–4 (winter 1989): 150–156.

13. And the fatherland lives. The United States should remember that some two-thirds century ago the Treaty of Guadalupe Hidalgo was signed and, nevertheless, Mexicans who live in Texas, New Mexico, Arizona, and California have not become Americanized. Our culture is persistent and, despite our hates and divisiveness, our character and homogeneity have been preserved. A country like that, which does not confuse itself among other peoples, which does with exceptions not mix with other peoples, which preserves its traditions and perpetuates its legends, which, in a word, maintains the always growing marvelous force of its genius, is not dominated through the occupation of three or four military forts, not even with the total incorporation of its territories.

Mexico, therefore, will not lose its nationality, even if it should be conquered. Our vitality, like Poland's and Ireland's, like Armenia's and Belgium's, survives beyond cataclysm.

14. Lozano, coming from a successful business family in northern Mexico, relocated to San Antonio in 1908 in search of business opportunities; there he opened a bookstore and gradually learned the newspaper business through on-the-job experiences while working first for San Antonio's *El Noticiero* and later for *El Imparcial de Texas* (DiStefano, 99–103).

15. Many of the publishing houses and weekly newspapers did not, in fact, survive through their publishing efforts alone; like Whitt Publishing and Artes Gráficas, they also had an extensive job printing business.

16. See my chapter "Labor," in *Hispanic Firsts: 500 Years of Extraordinary Achievement*, 133–150.

17. See F. Arturo Rosales, *Dictionary of Latino Civil Rights History*, for details on the various Hispanic labor-organizing efforts in the nineteenth and twentieth centuries.

18. The importance of the *lector* institution was summarized by Fornet: "El proletariado halló en la Lectura . . . la forma más democrática y eficaz de difusión cultural que hubo en su época. La transmisión oral, realizada en el mismo taller durante las horas laborables, era el mecanismo idóneo para satisfacer las necesidades intelectuales de una clase que había surgido pidiendo libros, pero que carecía de recursos, de tiempo y en muchos casos de escolaridad para leerlos. La Lectura fue el primer intento de hacer 'llegar' el libro a las masas con un propósito exclusivamente educativo y recreativo. Entre las clases privilegiadas el libro había sido siempre un objeto suntuoso y en última instancia un instrumento de dominio o de lucro; el proletari-

ado lo convirtió en un instrumento autodidáctico, empleándolo con el único fin de superarse ideológicamente y culturalmente" (185–186) (The proletariat encountered in The Reading . . . the most democratic and efficient means of acculturation that existed at the time. Oral transmission, effected in their own workplace during working hours, was the ideal mechanism for satisfying the intellectual needs of a class that had emerged wanting books, but not having the resources, the time, and in many cases the schooling to read them. The Reading was the first attempt at extending books to the masses for solely educational and recreational reasons. Among the privileged classes, the book had always been a sumptuous object and, ultimately, an instrument of domination or lucre; the proletariat converted it into an instrument of self-education, using it only to advance itself ideologically and culturally).

19. *La Aurora*, the first workers' newspaper in Cuba, was founded by the tobacco worker and poet Saturnino Martínez in 1865 and was highly identified with the *lector* tradition; in addition to publishing news of interest to workers, the newspaper pioneered schools for workers, encouraged workers to use libraries, and vigilantly protected the lector tradition from political repression (Fornet, 138–140).

20. *Ensayos Libertarios* (1907, Essays on liberty); *La escuela moderna* (1911, The modern school); *La humanidad en el futuro* (1910); *Influencia de las ideas modernas* (1916); *Mi opinión sobre las libertades, derechos y deberes de la mujer como compañera, madre y ser independiente* (1911, My opinion on the freedoms, rights, and duties of women as companion, mother and independent being). Also see *Amor y anarquía: Los escritos de Luisa Capetillo*, ed. Julio Ramos (Río Piedras: Ediciones Huracán, 1992); *A Nation of Women: An Early Feminist Speaks Out/Mi Opinión sobre las libertades, derechos y deberes de la mujer*, ed. Félix V. Matos Rodríguez (Houston: Arte Público Press, 2005); and *Absolute Equality: An Early Feminist Perspective/Influencias de las ideas modernas*, trans. and ed. Lara Walker (Houston: Arte Público Press, 2008).

21. While workers' periodicals obviously served the immigrant working class, Hispanic elites felt the need to reproduce the cultural refinement that was the product of their education and breeding in the homeland. Whether to remain connected to the cultural accomplishments of the greater international Hispanic community or to fill an intellectual void that existed in the foreign land, a number of high-quality periodicals were established in the Northeast and Southwest. Some of them, such as the New York monthlies *El Ateneo: Repertorio Ilustrado de Arte, Ciencia y Literatura* (The athenaeum: Illustrated repertoire of arts, science, and literature, 1874–1877), and *El Americano* (1892–?), retained the newspaper format but primarily published literature and commentary, with illustrations. Others looked much like the cultural magazines being published at the turn of the century, such as *Harper's Magazine* and *Cosmopolitan*. What was most distinctive about them was that they placed the Hispanic immigrant community of the United States on the international cultural map, for they drew their selections from essayists and writers of prose fiction and poetry from Spain and Spanish America as well as from the United States. Despite their elitism, these magazines felt they had to protect language, culture, and Hispanic interests just as the working-class Hispanic newspapers did. For more information, see Kanellos and Martell, *Hispanic Periodicals in the United States*, 64–73.

22. See ibid., 44—58; Carlos Monsiváis, *A ustedes les consta.* . . .

23. See Edwin Karli Padilla Aponte's "Introduction" to Jesús Colón, *Lo que el pueblo me dice . . . : Crónicas de la colonia puertorriqueña en Nueva York*, ed. Edwin Karli Padilla Aponte (Houston: Arte Público Press, 2001).

24. O'Farrill, who considered himself a mulatto, was a playwright and popular actor in Cuban farces, in which he donned blackface to play the stock *negrito* character.

25. Actually, according to the preface of his book, 5–6, he lost his job as a journalist for New York's *La Prensa* for political reasons or for not coming to terms with the newspaper's commercial mission.

26. Lucas Guevara does commit suicide in the end, a death that can be understood as the death of Hispanic identity in the Metropolis, one akin to the death of Luis in René Marqués's play of Puerto Rican immigration to New York: *La Carreta* (The oxcart, 1953).

27. Another novel which advocates an alternative solution is Guillermo Cotto-Thorner's *Trópico en Manhattan* (1951), which promotes the notion that Puerto Ricans should stay in New York and transform the city to reflect their culture (see chapter 4).

CHAPTER THREE

My translation: "Maybe it was my destiny / to come to foreign lands, / but someday I'll go return / to the mountains of Adjuntas / to deposit my mortal remains / in the care of her womb again." In *Herencia: The Anthology of Hispanic Literature of the United States*, 386.

1. My translation: Mexicans, whether they have or have not renounced the title, are always treated unjustly and negatively by judges, citizens, the powerful, and in general all of the children of this nation.

Therefore, no improvement will be achieved, and we are all convinced of that, why should we renounce the title of children of the Republic of Mexico . . . [given that] we shall always be foreigners in the United States and they will always consider us as such?

2. Chabram-Dernersesian discusses the various and changing meanings of the term in Octavio Paz, Arturo Madrid, and Américo Paredes, in "On the Social Construction of Whiteness within Selected Chicana/o Discourses," 144–146. On *pocho* and *agringado*, also see David G. Gutiérrez, *Walls and Mirrors: Mexican Americans, Mexican Immigrants, and the Politics of Ethnicity*, 62–65. (See chapters 5, 6).

3. See José Limón, "*Agringado* Joking in Texas Mexican Society," for a detailed definition and study of the usage of this term. "Ayancado" (Yankeefied) and "pitiyanqui" (a little Yankee) are also terms that appear in immigrant literature, especially in such works as José I. de Diego Padró's *En Babia* (see below).

4. In most of the literature of immigration created by Spanish speakers, the narrators and characters rarely see themselves as part of an overarching Hispanic or Latino identity; they always refer to themselves as members of a region or nationality, such as Cuban, Puerto Rican, Chicano, Mexican.In fact, in at least one novel,

En Babia (see below) there is a reaction against blurring nationality designation in favor of the Latino designation: "Son latinos, en el sentido estúpido que se da aquí a esa palabra. Es decir, hablan español." (77) (They're Latinos, in the stupid sense that applies here [in the United States]. They speak Spanish.)

5. The first novel written and published by a Puerto Rican author in New York, Juan Aboy Benítez's *Su primer amor, novela de costumbres* (1900, His first love, a novel of customs), treats the Cuban and Puerto Rican bourgeois community of New York as an integrated Hispanic community, and throughout the literature that follows there are mentions of Hispanics of varying ethnic and national backgrounds that work and live together. It is not until recently, however, in such novels as Roberto González Viaña's *El corrido de Dante* and Mario Bencastro's *Odisea del Norte*, that there is a real sense of camaraderie and community among the distinct Hispanic groups in the United States (see below). Aboy Benítez's novel, contrary to much of my argument, is also distinct from the other novels of immigration in Spanish in its embrace of the American Dream and its pursuit by the protagonist and his antagonists, parents of his beloved, of making a life for oneself and climbing upward in this society. There is never a mention of return to the homeland, and in fact the narrator hardly ever identifies himself, the protagonist, or the author as Puerto Rican; clearly, the author is not writing the nation, even if his work is written in Spanish and studies in detail the customs of Latinos in New York and New Jersey at the turn of the century.

6. For instance, see Paul S. Taylor, "Mexican Labor in the Calumet Region," in Lane and Escobar, *Forging a Community*, pp. 33-79, for a discussion of labor grades and ethnicity in the steel industry of Northwest Indiana.

7. See his "Discurso pronunciado en el banquete . . ." in *En otra voz*, 327.

8. Bruce-Novoa, "*La Prensa* and the Chicano Community," 153.

9. For a comprehensive study of *corridos* of immigration from 1848 to 1991, see Herrera-Sobek, *Northward Bound: The Mexican Immigrant Experience in Ballad and Song*, which analyzes some 150 song lyrics. Also see De la Garza's *Ni de aquí ni de allá: El emigrante en los corridos y en otras canciones populares*; Chew Sánchez's *Corridos in Migrant Memory*; and Alberto Ledesma's "Undocumented Crossings: Narratives of Mexican Immigration to the United States," in Maciel and Herrera-Sobek, *Culture across Borders*, 67-98.

10. Paredes (*Folklore and Culture* 14-15) cites "El corrido de Kiansis" from the 1860s as an early example of workers, in this case cowboys, herding cattle to a railhead in Kansas, traveling into the United States from Mexico; here, as in many later immigration *corridos*, the focus is on the long journey, the vicissitudes suffered en route, the strange sights seen by the workers, and the expectation of return to the homeland. Examples from the early twentieth century up to the Depression also focus on culture conflict, oppression of the migrants, and the discrimination they experience, as in such *corridos* as "La Pensilvania," "La discriminación," "Los enganchados," and "Los deportados" (15).

11. See Paredes' *Texas-Mexican Cancionero*, 53-55, for transcription and translations of two versions of this *corrido*.

12. Jeff Browitt, in "Sexual Anxiety in Alirio Díaz Guerra's *Lucas Guevara*." Rather than accepting the contrast between the pristine homeland, as represented by Santa Catalina, and an infernal New York City as representative of materialistic

and amoral society at the turn of the century, Browitt develops a case for Díaz Guerra's anxiety of modernity.

13. Whereas Díaz Guerra emphasizes American materialism and amorality in its women, José Martí blames these sins on the lack of "espíritu femenil" (feminine spirit) in the United States. See "Coney Island" (*En otra voz* 195). (See chapter 5 for a discussion of the role of women in immigrant literature.)

14. Brammer translation, 227: "His abandoned home was still far away; his affectionate mother mourned the absence of her loved one, now removed from the warmth of her embrace; his father's pale head was still bowed, not so much from the weight of the years as from the intense pain to which his gutless son had condemned him. The twilight of the homeland, once full of light and color, had presently disappeared in an impenetrable darkness; the dearest recollections of his childhood were almost completely forgotten; in the end, the entire sum of his memories from his first few years of life had long been shrouded in a sort of penumbra of indifference and despair, but they were struggling now to be resurrected from the depths of his being with all the elements of his happy childhood. There, all around him, stood the wild and treacherous city, an agglomeration of adverse conditions, of appalling realities, of people far from all noble sentiment. A boiling cauldron of hate spilled forth from his soul, now deaf to the virtuous voice of forgiveness, containing the bitterness of fighting in vain, the disillusionment of a conquered will, the night of utter dismay, and the specter of a frightening future without a glimmer of hope."

15. "Coney Island," in *En otra voz*, 195. Translated in *Herencia*, 338: "The fact is that never has a happier, a jollier, a better equipped, more compact, more jovial, and more frenzied multitude living anywhere on earth, while engaged in useful labors, created and enjoyed greater wealth, nor covered rivers and seas with more gaily dressed ships, nor overflown lovely shores, gigantic wharves, and brilliant, fantastic promenades with more bustling order, more childlike glee."

16. "Nueva York por dentro," in *En otra voz*, 200. Translated in *Herencia*, 342–343: "Its buildings, its portentous architectural works, its elevated railways fantastically crisscrossing through the air, its streets—broad arteries roamed by inexhaustible hordes from all countries of the world—, its parks,—austerely and aristocratically designed—, its steam engines, its powerful journalistic institutions, its treacherously beautiful women, its wonders, all instill, at first sight, a deep malaise on the foreigner, because it occurs to one that these large cities, deafening in their progress, are like the mouth of a horrible monster constantly busy simultaneously swallowing and vomiting human beings."

17. *Las aventuras de don Chipote*, 21.

18. Brammer translation, 44–45: "They thought they must have been dreaming on seeing such elegant houses and lavish houses, for the best home they had ever seen was the *hacienda* owner's house, which looked like a shack in comparison to the edifices that were so tall that they appeared to be lurking over them. They marveled at the smooth streets, all of the people dressed so swell, and, more than anything, so many big carts that ran without mules; all of these things simply could not fit into their imaginations and made them open their mouths to the point of drooling all over themselves."

19. The first such comparisons are seen in the poetry of Cuban exiles in the mid-nineteenth century. They compare their sojourn in the United States to the biblical

Babylonian captivity and see themselves writing with longing for a return to Zion. See the numerous poems in the first anthology of exile, *El laúd del desterrado*, published in Philadelphia in 1858.

20. "Mother, Borinquen calls me!/This is not my country!/Borinquen is pure heat!/And here I'm freezing to death." From his *Aromas del terruño: Versos criollos* (1916).

21. "To achieve a better future / I left my native home / and pitched my tent / in the middle of New York. / What I see all about me / is a sad panorama, / and my spirit calls to me, / wounded with deep nostalgia, / for my return to my homeland nest / *Mother, Borinquen beckons me!* / Where will I find her, / as in my Creole land / a plate of chicken and rice / and a real cup of coffee? / Where, where will I see / radiant beautifully dressed / lively lasses / with that blinding stare? / Here, eyes are not bright / *This country is not mine!* / If I hear a song here / one of those I learned at home, / or a *danza* by Tavárez, / Morel Campos or Dueño Colón, / my sensitive heart / becomes inflamed with patriotic fervor, / and the herald that faithfully proclaims / this saintly sentiment, / my eyes begin to tear / *Borinquen is pure heat!* / In my land, how blessed, / in the worst of winters / the trees are not denuded / every single hillside stays verdant, / gardens are full of flowers, / rivers, bubbling, continue flowing, / birds in the shade of forests / sing their random song / and, here, the snow is a shroud. / *Here, I'm freezing to death!*" (my translation). See the original at *Borinquen: Literatura del Edén* http://www.cuscatla.com/puerto_rico.htm.

22. Both Paul White and Homi Bhabha call this "doubling," but I prefer to characterize it as a binary because it establishes a rhythm the recurs throughout these works, a back and forth, as everything in the United States is compared with the homeland in accordance with a nationalist ideology which in most works prevails over the myth of the American Dream. In its simplest form, this binary rhythm contrasts homeland and receptor nation in song lyrics, but in its most complex form creates contrasting characters as well as ideologies and motivates the plots of novels. While this binary can account for ambivalence and ambiguity in some works, for the most part these are cleared up by the end of Hispanic narratives with the return to the homeland. Bhabha states, "Their metaphoric movement requires a kind of 'doubleness' in writing: a temporality of representation that moves between cultural formations and social processes without a 'centered' causal logic" (293). White states, "A common feature of many migrants and migrant culture is ambivalence. Ambivalence towards the past and the present as to whether things were better 'then' or 'now.' Ambivalence towards the future: whether to retain a 'myth of return' or to design a new project without furthering expected movement built in. Ambivalence towards the 'host' society: feelings of respect, dislike or uncertainty. Ambivalence towards standards of behavior: whether to cling to the old or to discard it, whether to compromise via symbolic events adhering to the new on an everyday basis" (3–4).

23. The narrator assures his readers that he invented the term *braquicéfalo* and that it means nothing: "Nada pretende significar" (14). However, the prefix brachio- in biology means having many arms or branches and cephal- refers to the head or brain. Thus the subtitle appropriately prepares the reader for the rambling structure of this novel that goes off on many extended digressions and covers numerous topics apparently extraneous to the plot.

24. . . . is the most dangerous of New York suburbs. You must take infinite care

and precaution when going there. In the Bowery there are numerous professional criminal gangs: con artists, pickpockets, killers, ex-convicts, bootleggers, drug traffickers, owners of gambling halls, extortionists, agents of white slavery. . . . In sum, all of the social detritus, all of the illegal flesh trade has made that zone the quarters for their machinations and illicit business.

25. The first thing I did on going outside was to raise the collar of my overcoat. Then I buried my hands in the pockets, leaving them nestled there like lizards in their burrow . . . and onward! It was very cold. A heavy snow was falling on New York, filling the air and wrapping the whole city in a grave and terrible sadness. The frowning sky, gray at the zenith, appeared injected with a dense red at the line of the mass of buildings, darkened in the distance and darkened on the lower horizon with grays and pale greens. The wind was blowing hard, swelled and intermittently rose to the cornices of the houses everywhere in furious revolving funnels of a fine, dry snow. . . . Gusts of wind whipped my face. My nose and chin lost all feeling; and my ears, if I can use a metaphor, were squealing, moaning, barking in pain.

26. I disagree with Rafael Falcón's statement, in his survey of the literature of Puerto Rican immigrants in New York, that Padró uses the Metropolis only as a backdrop for the interaction of the main characters and that the novel could have taken place in any large city. See *La emigración a Nueva York en la novela puertorriqueña*, 15.

27. The narrator softens this critique, noting that Guinard is a xenophobe and that one should not take him at his word or confuse his opinions with those of the author/narrator: "A decir la verdad, la estimación del autor por los Estados Unidos de Norteamérica no pasa de una tibia estimación. Pero no está tan obcecado que no sepa reconocer, aparte de los defectos, las innúmeras virtudes de los yanquis" (111) (In truth, the esteem the author has for the United States is lukewarm. But he is not so mindless as to not recognize, aside from the defects, the innumerable virtues of the Yankees).

28. "There you have them," he said to me ironically, "your coreligionists: the defenders and guardians of pragmatism, of common sense. There you have the professors of energy and selling stupidity wholesale. Ha, ha! That's how in the utilitarian motivation deeply ingrained in these people, even in their most idealized representatives (the soldier, the artist, the poet), can be perceived the characteristic stench of the clergy or the butcher. Schopenhauer states that the true character of the North Americans is vulgarity in all of its forms: moral, intellectual, esthetic, and social. An incontrovertible statement. Because, truly, there is nothing so bereft of ideological elegance as the North American brain. It is an empty drawer, an archive of pocketbook, routine, mediocre thought. The Yankees don't take one step forward unless it is calculated in a straight line as five times eight is forty. Everything is measured in dollars and cents: from the abstraction of time up to and including the most elevated accomplishments of human genius. For the Yankees, a man is evaluated and judged by what he produces in hard currency."

29. For a detailed analysis of the trilogy, see Alberto Ameal Pérez, "En Babia, una novela total," Ph.D. diss., University of Houston, 2007.

30. In the film version of *Paraíso Travel* (2009), directed by Simón Brand, the ending is changed: the last scene shows Marlon returning to Queens to pursue the romance with a young Colombian woman who had befriended him and fallen in

love with him. This Hollywood ending conflicts with the "immigrant narrative" formula of the novel and implies that there is a life to be made for the immigrant in the United States. See Tim Padgett's review in *Time*, "An Honest Look at Illegal Immigration," March 11, 2008. For a study of the treatment of Mexican immigrants in film, see Maciel and Acevedo, "Celluloid Immigrant: The Narrative Films of Mexican Immigration."

31. Brammer translation, 254: "How happy they were to be there, standing before the fatherland, right beside their country, on whose soil they could set foot by merely crossing that bridge. Mexico! In her arms once again, to once more face both good times and bad, but to share the same hard times and to experience the same joys as everyone else. Now he knew what it meant to be home, now he had learned to forgive his town's leaders and the leaders of his country. Of course, they were cruel, but they would be gone soon enough; they too were men, they too would succumb to an eternal rest; while she, that country, that blessed land, that brotherhood of man would go on forever. She would be free, she would be joyous, and with her all of her virtuous offspring, those who made noble efforts, those who had faith in the future, but worked in the present, showing respect and venerating the past" (*Under the Texas Sun* 254).

32. See Sisk's "Toward a Trans(national) Reading of Ramón 'Tianguis' Pérez's *Diario de un mojado*."

33. The native Hispanic writers' position will begin to predominate in the 1960s and beyond, as they proclaim their bilingual-bicultural identities and stake out "home" territories with accompanying mythologies for their nationhood, such as El Barrio (the same geocultural area as in Cotto-Thorner's narrative), Loisaida (Lower East Side), La Souhuesera (S.W. Miami, or Calle 8) and Aztlán, and proclaim themselves Nuyoricans, Chicanos, and other hybrid identities that stake a claim on American citizenship and rights. This is very different from Cotto-Thorner's transplant of island culture to New York, for it is a recognition of the type of hybridity that Cotto-Thorner and the other immigrant writers would scorn as not authentic but a distortion of the home cultures, employing such terms as *pocho, agringado, gringuito, renegado, pitiyanqui, ayancado,* and so forth. For the Nuyorican, Chicano, Cuban American, and other native writers and artists born or raised (or both) in the United States, who write in English and Spanish, sometimes mixing both languages in their texts and whose references may be Indo-Afro-Hispanic popular culture rather than the canonical Western European sources of mainstream American literature, there is no question of a return to a homeland; they are residing in their homeland, and their literary expression is American, even if they have been racialized as the other and even if their expression is articulated in a language other than English or demands through its English-Spanish code switching a bilingual audience. Their imperative is to be recognized as Americans and to be afforded the rights and privileges promised to American citizens; to see them as immigrants is, in many cases, to insult them and negate the rights they have won by suffering discrimination, ghettoization, and inferior education and employment and everything else that the United States reserves for its marginalized and oppressed ethnic and racial minorities. Cotto-Thorner treats them for the most part as immigrants whose aim is to benefit from American society.

34. The idea of loss of the homeland and contemplating it from a distance, always

awaiting a return, is metaphorized in much of the literature of exile and immigration as the Babylonian captivity of the Israelites. This is the first novel that actually inscribes the concept in its title, which is reinforced by the following lines in the book: "Nadie se juntaba, como los desterrados de Israel en la dura Babilonia a recordar a la patria perdida" (53) (No one got together to recall *the lost homeland*, like those exiled from Israel in cruel Babylon did).

35. Kansas seemed to him like all of the large cities of the United States, a city of steel, cold, noisy, and as hard as metal, molded from iron hammered out by a Cyclops. It was an immense forge that never stopped working in order to raise the Towers of Babel to the sky, these giant buildings, in order to manufacture the millions of cars that paraded down the crowded streets in an indistinguishable line; to supply the parts worn out by thousands of machines that operated everywhere to assist people in their most insignificant tasks, even in sweeping streets and in kitchen duties, as if to create more time for men and women to devote to business, work, and the insane pursuit of life and money.

36. It wasn't, it couldn't be a new *patria*, because *patrias*, like mothers, cannot be substituted for; but there in the solitude of the hacienda the country was taking on the enchantment of a virgin island, without noise from factories or the civilizing instinct of its indifferent and prideful cities; it provided, in addition, a place in which to live in peace and created an amiable silence around those two living beings who, dependent on each other's love, always awaited their return [home], without the mortal fears of the first days [in exile], instead with the stubborn illusion of those who never renounce their dream.

37. Do not forget it is our obligation to love Mexico above all else, to honor her, to live in a way that as we win respect for ourselves we win it for her. Let's benefit from this exilic adventure by being more Mexican than those who have never lived outside of Mexico. Let's learn the lessons of pain that exile has given us, with the awareness that there is no *patria* like ours, and with the hope that upon rejoining our paternal home we find more warmth and love. . . . Mexico will present itself to us with a new face when we return.

38. *Raquelo tiene un mensaje* (1970), by the Puerto Rican Jaime Carrero, does not rise to the ideological or epic level of *La patria perdida*. Carrero's novel, which chronicles the experiences of a Nuyorican returned to Puerto Rico to teach school, describes the difficulties he has in adjusting and the resistance he meets from the natives. Carrero, who returned home after years of studying art in the United States, incorporated the theme of return home in various of his plays and novels.

39. Alfaro experienced the first symptom of a malady that would make him very bitter during his trip: the fatal vision that ruins both the countries that allow their children to leave and the children who return after a prolonged absence, having acquired, without realizing it, foreign ways of living and thinking. The malady of comparison, inevitable, that always looks for contrasts and attempts to adjust to the measuring sticks of these two so distinct countries, Mexico and the United States.

40. It is the narrator himself, probably speaking for Torres, who actually envisions throughout the novel the large Mexican émigré community as a diaspora in the classical sense of a forced exile and migration with an inability to return; this diaspora is compared to the biblical one, much in the same way that Nemesio García Naranjo conceptualizes it, as mentioned previously in the text. For more analysis on

the various forms and conceptualizations of diaspora and their relationship to culture formation, see Kalra et al., *Diaspora and Hybridity*, chap. 1.

41. Here is where you should work and live. To multiply, to really multiply, is not what I am ordering because you will have only one daughter, but neither will you complain, I myself only had one son. If you remember, I'm the one who brought your wife and you out from Michoacán, you crossing through deserts on foot and Beatriz sequestered through a dark tunnel. Remember what I'm going to tell you: this is your land and the land of your daughter's children and of the children of your daughter's children. Don't ask me if you can return to Michoacán because I do not want to reveal that to you. . . . No, in your lifetime you will never again smell the fragrance of the piquant chili peppers or see the reddest cactus pears in the universe. You will earn your bread with the sweat from your brow and a pain in your soul and with nostalgia for your land, and at times it will be hard bread so different from the tamales of Michoacán. You will be happy with the companion I have given you, but you will rue having been so happy when you lose her and have to return her body back to Michoacán.

CHAPTER FOUR

"The homeland, that blessed land, / that fraternal people, was immortal. / It would be free, it would be happy, / and along with them so would their good children, / those who exerted their noble effort, / those who had faith in the future, / work in the present, / respect and veneration for the past."

1. Quoted in Worley, *The Third World*, 5.

2. Brammer translation, 220: "Because we are all Mexican . . . all of us Mexicans stand united, to demonstrate to those men [Americans] that we too are civilized people; we too know how to honor our motherland. We need for all of our children to nurse on the blessed milk of Mexico!"

3. Brammer translation, 222: "Oh, glorious times when men knew not of borders circumscribed by avarice and greed! Oh, happy, harmonious days when neither color nor languages had produced the differences between the sons of Adam, for we were all one and the same!

"Oh, golden age the time when valiant men exhausted their energies on the caring for and attending to the needy, for no other reason than a burning desire to spread goodness from their large, generous and loving hearts!

"Oh, happy men were those who knew not the yoke of cold, cruel governments, which are formed to exploit the masses, to divvy up the land and human beasts of burden, then jealously and suspiciously submit themselves to their profits!

* * * * *

"Oh, bright suns those that knew not the perverse progress of machine and vice! How much more leisurely the stroll along the country road than this dashing about shiny new highways, in carts, that, their images improved as Calivileño's magic, drive about in a fever of insatiable ambition and a writing of ever increasing agony . . ."

"What necessity, nay, what exigency would these simple men have had to abandon the mountains and plains of their homeland to go in search of the false riches of Egypt?"

4. "Who can tell me that this way of circumscribing nations and people would not be the best means for clashes of mutual penetration, for the fusion of interests, for the development of individual and personal virtues and for future amorous and prosperous unions?

"Why accuse the blond-haired men of being the calculating and cold-blooded executioners of dark-skinned people? They are guilty of having been the first to rob Providence of this, its power, this, its spirit, and this, its authority, to fully develop an era of capitalism, to put their own special stamp on civilization, to set afloat and facilitate the study and examination of a whole series of perilous virtues and nefarious vices.

"And the others, the dark-skinned men, are they guilty perhaps of their association with these men? Are they to blame for having been begotten of races created for the ages of heroic battles, for having lived epically, for having grand and sweeping enterprises? If they still maintain and still occupy their warm place in the sun, despite the fact that these times have worn away the fascination with fantasy and the sword, if they continue to so fervently cultivate the rites of honor and illusion, over there, their secret shall blossom tomorrow! Over there, the page that the finger of God has yet to turn will be shown to our eyes.

"Time will pass . . .

"Perhaps then . . ." (224)

5. Young, in *Colonial Desires*, however, would argue that every time hybridity is invoked it signifies biological mixing, i.e., race mixing: "To rethink hybridity in terms of biopolitics is to bring back to the fore the social contracts that govern the naturalization of differential relations between subjects, bodies, and the state, and that articulate race to nation" (7).

6. Lund defines the term in "The Mestizo State: Colonization and Indianization in Liberal Mexico": "In Mexican cultural politics, *mestizo* refers to an individual of mixed-race ancestry, generally assumed to be indigenous American and European. The presence of Africans in Mexico suffers from a profound historical erasure. . . . *Mestizo* also indicates the long-standing, favored racialization of national identity" (1431).

7. See his article, "The Mestizo State: Colonization and Indianization in Liberal Mexico," 1419.

8. Luis's humanitarian recognition of the suffering of the indigenes and *mestizos* is curious, given that the character separates himself and his social class, obviously identified with Spanish roots and heritage, from the way in which Americans think of Mexicans, i.e., as backward Indians, an impression which he has struggled to correct for himself and his adopted blond, blue-eyed son, who also finds it difficult to see his parents as Mexicans, given their European features and privileged social class (68–69). More important, Torres and his character Luis Alfaro were part of the Porfirio Díaz regime that not only persecuted the Yaquis and Tarahumaras but also enslaved them. As in *La patria perdida*, as easily observed in Luis's vision of history, the *porfirista* homage to the Amerindians is always to the pre-Columbian peoples that Mexican state ideology chooses to regard as a foundation for the nation as a land of *mestizos*, while erasing the masses of poor, oppressed Amerindians that surround them in daily life. The one reference to such an Amerindian is to Alfaro's servant, Gabriela, who, the narrator says, "tenía para él [the adopted Luisito] esa devoción

del indio para el blanco de ojos azules" (68) (had a devotion to him that Indians have for the blue-eyed white man). This attitude of the narrator, and author, I presume, is not just part of his general condescending, patronizing treatment of the *campesinos*, but is an ideological blindspot that destroys his utopian efforts in Bellavista and his desire for the Amerindians and their *mestizo* progeny to recover their lands and prosper some day. Maura L. Fuchs asserts about the *porfiristas* that "they developed a policy of exalting a mythical Aztec past of their own making while ignoring almost absolutely the problems of the Mexican contemporary Indians" (235). Of the *mestizos* imagined by such writers as Nemesio García Naranjo and Teodoro Torres, Fuchs states, "The particular mestizaje they celebrated privileged Mexico's Spanish legacy within it, and included only mythical Indians" (252). Héctor Pérez, in his *"La prensa, un periódico de San Antonio,"* has also noted this condescension and prejudice as well as an opposition to women's rights in Torres's novel and editorials. Castillo, in *Talking Back*, 13–15, specifically studies such icons of class and gender in Latin American literature as this indigenous *nana*.

9. They awaited, with the patience and sweetness of eternal things, the day that the long-suffering Indians would at last become the owners of their land, without shocks and losses, without commotions and revolts, without wars that take them from their homes, without the miseries that force them to wander the roads carrying on their backs the products of their poor industries, but settled solidly in the vast place that will accommodate and sustain them, not only the children of this country, but for entire humanities.

10. In the endless pilgrimage that began in the dark ages and continued in a very civilized fashion, but with the same fearful wandering toward refuge, in trains and automobiles on asphalt roads; it was the same pilgrimage he observed now linking together the grand events he had seen in his extended vision that night, with the scenes he had witnessed on the U.S. border, on the roads crowded with immigrants returning home defeated but still with hope, gone now the new Nuño de Guzmán [a possible allusion to contemporary revolutionary leaders, such as Pancho Villa] who had expelled them—hunger, discord—in search of peace, and the abundance they had been denied.

11. Here Torres may be subscribing to the ideas expounded in Ortega y Gassett's *The Revolt of the Masses* (1929), a work that was very popular among intellectuals of the time. In fact, Torres includes various sketches in his novel of what Ortega would call the *señorito satisfecho* (satisfied young man), the bourgeois educated person who takes advantage of and manipulates the ignorance of the masses to his own benefit. Torres depicts two mirror images of these *señoritos*, one in San Antonio and one in Mexico City: Pepe Sarmiento (156–164) and Licenciado Hernández de Alba (351–364), respectively.

12. In light of the technology, transportation, and communications available at the time Torres was writing, recognizing or propounding a deterritorialized nation, as conceived by García Canclini in *Culturas híbridas*, was not as possible as it is in today's globalized world. Nevertheless, the underlying psychological process in Luis's reasoning is similar to the psychology of transmigrants even in a postmodern age; as Mujcinovic states, "It is important to recognize the psychological basis of this process. The condition of displacement is always defined by the negotiation of multiple locations: uprootedness from one place invariably troubles settlement in

another place, and the self constituted in this process always seeks to remedy the dislocation. The often forgotten fact that territorial displacement dominantly signifies a forced departure—in the context of migrations from Latin America and other underdeveloped regions—intensifies the problematic of special detachment" (65).

13. The spectacle of a restless people without a sense of place and that lives in perpetual movement returned to Alfaro. The errant people, his people could be called for their not wanting or caring to establish themselves in one place, to a plan for living, to hold on to the family patrimony, exploit the land, the only salvation possible for this great desert country. . . . To emigrate? To move from one point to another with the inconformity of never feeling satisfied in any one place? Why, dear God? Why not return to the fields, to the towns, now that the danger had passed? Why have millions of Mexicans remained abroad and persisted as immigrants in spite of the painful conditions that those people have imposed on them in the neighboring country, who have invited them to leave in a thousand ways, and who despite everything the immigrants have stayed, some because of the absolute impossibility of returning and others because they have become part of the new nationality and cannot separate themselves from it?

14. The idea of creating a new and superior human being by bringing the races together was most famously expressed in José Vasconcelos's *La raza cósmica* (1925), which Torres undoubtedly read. Also there is an implicit messianism in Torres's novel, which in Vasconcelos's treatise is implicit. As Young interprets Vasconcelos's vision, "Mexico's history is *cosmic*, and that it *should have* considerable glory ahead of it" (111).

15. See Ernst Bloch, *Principles of Hope*, 197–223.

16. However original Torres's formulation may be as a utopia configured in a work of fiction, his ideas were common among the class of exiled Mexican intellectuals that wrote in the newspaper that he edited, *La Prensa*, and in the books issued from its affiliated publishing house, Casa Editorial Lozano. García, in his *Rise of the Mexican-American Middle Class*, summarizes these ideas as follows: "They argued for a new society that emphasized humanist philosophy and economic liberalism. They also wanted strong personal leadership, but a weak bureaucratic state; foreign investment in Mexico, but a 'new' patriotism; overall they called for 'national unity' via a new spirit of class cooperation. Most of all, they wanted an end to Mexico's self-destruction, because the revolution, they said, was a Judas: it destroyed and betrayed its own people. National salvation, they felt, could only be derived from economic production and material growth, not from political robbery, hate, and class murder. Even if the *ricos* had disliked Díaz's dictatorship, they longed for his economic programs, which had promoted national growth, his political programs, which engendered order, and his strong control of the state apparatus, which had brought stability. Specifically, the *ricos* believed that, in addition to economic production, the problems of Mexicans in Mexico and in the United States could be solved by a strong central government and a strong national culture; however, both depended on a highly educated and professional class of citizens" (230). Torres's fictive project, however, may have fulfilled the need of his social class to reassert itself after years of exile, precisely in the way outlined by Smith, in "The Nation: Invented, Imagined, Reconstructed?": "To resocialize uprooted populations and inculcate new values of order and hierarchy. Only by these means can the ruling classes reassert their con-

trol over the dangerous and dislocating processes of rapid industrialization and political mobilization which threaten to overturn the existing class order" (13). In the case of Torres and his cohorts, they struggled not to avert the overthrow, but to reestablish the leadership they once had, before the Revolution, by employing this invented history and redefining the nation.

17. Cotto's religious writings in Protestant periodicals were reprinted throughout the Spanish-speaking communities of the United States and Latin America. He also published numerous articles in nonsectarian Spanish-language newspapers around the United States. His first work, the full-length book *Camino de victoria* (1945, The road to victory), was also religious in nature. His next work, a pamphlet railing against the Catholic Church, *Conspiración romana contra la democracia* (1948, The Roman conspiracy against democracy), was published by the Baptist publishing house in El Paso for distribution throughout North and South America. Beyond his openly religious texts, Cotto-Thorner contributed cultural and political essays for such New York newspapers as *Liberación* and *Pueblos Hispanos* (Hispanic Peoples), in which he supported Puerto Rican independence and other liberal causes, basing himself on a Christian ethic and determinism. He firmly believed that Christianity promoted democracy, and he made this argument repeatedly in his books and articles. He also compared the colonial situation of Puerto Rico to the Roman enslavement of the Jews in biblical times.

18. If the description of the evangelical pastor, José Juan Quiñones, is indeed a self-portrait of Cotto-Thorner, then his career was not an easy one: "Muchacho brillante y bien preparado cuya única desgracia era ser demasiado liberal y progresista para su tiempo. Desde que salió del seminario, nunca fue pastor en propiedad de iglesia alguna. Siempre había sido 'pastor asociado', asociado de un ministro más viejo . . . y por lo tanto más conservador que él. Al ir a alguna iglesia a trabajar, por su simpatía, su honradez y su elocuencia, los filigreses lo aclamaban con regocijo y hasta le traían sus confidencias. Además participaba en acitividades y movimientos de redención social. Y todo esto, naturalmente, no les gustaba a los pastores en propiedad. Fueron muchas las veces que el joven pastor se vio atacado injustamente a causa de celos, envidias y cosas muy humanas que nada tienen que ver con el Reino de los Cielos. De ahí que Quiñones desde hacía dos años se dedicara a enseñar filosofía en una de las universidades de la ciudad, huyendo de las ingratitudes, pero conservando la fe" (175); (A brilliant and well prepared young man whose only pitfall was being too liberal and progressive for his times. Since leaving the seminary, he had never served as the pastor of his own church. He had always been an 'associate pastor,' the associate of a much older minister . . . and therefore more conservative than him. When going to work at some church, the members would regale him so much and even bring him their secrets because of his empathy, honor and eloquence. In addition, he even participated in social redemption movements. And all of this, naturally, was disapproved of by the church pastors. Many were the times that the young pastor was attacked unjustly out of jealousy, envy and human things that had nothing to do with the Kingdom of God. Thus Quiñones for some two years now had dedicated himself to teaching philosophy at city universities, fleeing from the ingratitude, but maintaining his faith.)

19. The metaphor continues, "Y así como hay diversidad de colores, y diseños y

matices, así somos nosotros; divididos pero también unidos" (242) (And as there is a diversity of colors and designs and shades, that's the way we are; divided but also united). For the most part Cotto-Thorner is silent on the diverse racial make-up of Puerto Ricans, only once mentioning that there is no discrimination on the island and generally not indicating any discrimination they suffer in New York because of color. This silence is especially hard to understand, given that the post-Second World War civil rights movement in the United States had begun when the book appeared. Cotto-Thorner's physiognomy and phenotype are unknown, but two contemporary authors of Afro-Puerto Rican heritage, Jesús Colón and Pura Belpré, similarly avoided the theme of African roots and color discrimination in most of their writings. Colón, who immigrated early in the century and, in fact, as a young *cronista* writing his newspaper column under the pseudonym of Tiquis Miquis, never revealed his Afro-Puerto Rican identity but instead attacked supposedly uncultured African habits in the lumpen that were giving the nascent Puerto Rican community in New York a bad name (see "A la Bullanga Latina le Gusta el Brillo," in *"Lo que el pueblo me dice . . . ,"* 9–11. On the other hand, in his later columns, written some three decades later in English for the *Daily Worker* and during the time Cotto-Thorner was publishing his works, Colón openly explored what it meant to be an African American and Afro-Puerto Rican. See *The Way It Was and Other Works*, by Colón. Colón's brother, Joaquín Colón López, however, made race a recurrent theme in his columns and speeches and in his book *Pioneros puertorriqueños en Nueva York, 1917–1947*. He attacked Puerto Ricans who denied their African roots and wanted to "whiten" themselves in American society and who otherwise discriminated against their darker brothers.

20. Another of Cotto's exemplary characters, Antonio, explains to the negative Lencho that Puerto Ricans in New York are learning how democracy works: "Hace falta, eso sí, mucha comprensión y tolerancia, de todas partes. Me parece que en los últimos años hemos aprendido una gran lección en este aspecto de la vida democrática" (101) (What's missing, that's right, is a lot of comprehension and tolerance from everyone. It seems to me that during these last few years we've learned a great lesson about this aspect of democratic life).

21. We are exploited not only economically, but also spiritually and intellectually. According to the owners and directors of the corporations, what are we? Well, instruments of production. And their idea is to produce more and more, amass large fortunes, at the expense of the unfortunate. And in social and cultural pursuits, what are we? Garbage. They think of us as barbarians, backward people, uneducated and almost savage. That's why, just as we have to struggle for our economic improvement, it's our duty to struggle to raise our cultural prestige in the eyes of the American people. . . . When the Americans finally respect us because of our culture, then we'll be on the road to solving our other important problems."

22. These attitudes are similar to those expressed in Pedro Juan Labarthe's memoir, *The Son of Two Nations: The Private Life of a Columbia Student* (1931), which similarly embraces the economic and political benefits of American society while trying to maintain a semblance of *puertorriqueñidad*. See Irizarry Rodríguez's "Early Puerto Rican Writing in the United States and the Search for a New Puertorriqueñidad," 35–36.

23. The northern people turned out quiet, orderly, thrifty, and good for mechanical things; they were blond and chaste, with their flesh a little undercooked as if the Maker was a poor chef, and he probably just didn't spice them up enough. But on making the southern people, he overdid the spice, and he made them intense, somewhat toasted in their complexion, partial to acting up and partying, intrepid, frenetic, and loving. Whenever you left them by themselves, they took advantage to grow and multiply themselves.

24. Perhaps all of the Latinos in the United States were making love at the same time, generating more life, trembling and brilliant from the natural steaminess of the passions which are twenty times hotter and more phosphorescent than those of the people from the cold regions of the world.

CHAPTER FIVE

"Times change. Women . . . are on the road to a complete emancipation, and if in another era the repression of female thought were excusable because of the absurd environment that existed back then, at present there is no right to prohibit women's intellectual development. Women must attain their rightful place."

1. For a more in-depth exposition of contemporary Chicanas and Latinas and the nation, see Kaplan, Alarcón and Moallem, eds. *Between Woman and Nation;* and for a broader view of contemporary transmigrant women, especially of Asian extraction, in the United States, see Grewal, *Transnational America.*

2. See Bhaba, *The Location of Culture,* 50–57.

3. On her death certificate, issued in Los Angeles and dated March 19, 1928, her place of birth is given as Scotland and her name at birth as Blanche Lawson. This certificate may not be an authentic record, and her grandson's memory may not be based on truth. The Moncaleanos were persecuted while in Los Angeles for their anarchist and revolutionary activities by both American and Mexican authorities. At some point, possibly soon after Juan Francisco's death in 1916, Blanca and her four children changed their surname to Lawson to escape persecution. To this day the grandchildren bear the Lawson name, despite knowing that their inherited patronym is Moncaleano. I am grateful to Lina DeVito for providing this information. She recovered papers from the Moncaleano grandson John Lawson in July 2009 and is writing her dissertation on the Moncaleanos at the University of Houston. Among the papers were textbooks for learning English, and it is evident from Blanca de Moncaleano's notebook, where she wrote poetry in English, that she was not a native English speaker.

4. See Catalina Castillón, "Moncaleano, Blanca de," in Kanellos, *Greenwood Encyclopedia of Latino Literature.*

5. See María de los Angeles Mendieta, *Carmen Serdán,* 33.

6. Inés Hernández Tovar, in her dissertation, "Sara Estea Ramírez: The Early Twentieth-Century Texas-Mexican Poet," provides a biography and the Spanish originals, accompanied by Hernández's translation, of most of the surviving texts of Ramírez.

7. See Sánchez González, "For the Sake of Love," 66–67.

8. It may be true that they were doing it [advancing their program] from a conservative positionality such as "El México de Afuera," but their literature reflected the intent to write from *their* place, to write as women, which led them to participate, from diverse perspectives, in the feminine and political debate that was raging in the United States and Mexico.

9. Thus on one hand they defended the maternal and abnegated nature of the Mexican woman and on the other they postulated the need for her to prepare herself intellectually so that she could fulfill the role of teacher and protector of the culture. This introduced a change in the concept of the Mexican Woman, a change enunciated from her own feminine perspective, which meant demanding the power of that enunciation.

10. You, who, like me, saddened, are missing the infirm fatherland, which because of that illness is even more beloved, like a remedy for those afflictions, come along with me after visiting those infernos of brute commercialism, toward the lasting Glory of art.

11. Despite Loreley's advocating of a feminine emancipation that would permit women to obtain more rights, her rootedness in tradition and her situation within "El México de Afuera" would not allow her to accept the Americanization of women, which would make it a perverse feminism, an antifeminism. Women may obtain rights as long as they do not interfere with her condition as a "Mexican" Woman, where "Mexican" emphasizes tradition. In addition, her recommendations are necessary because she is woman. Like Ulica [see below], she recognizes that women are weaker and more vulnerable to Americanization than men.

12. Luziris Pineda is currently writing her dissertation, "A Foremother of Latina Feminist Thought: The Crónicas, Novels and Social Activism of María Luisa Garza 'Loreley,'" at the University of Houston and is the first scholar to find and read the rest of Garza's oeuvre.

13. See Elaine Showalter's discussion of this dynamic in nineteenth-century American and British authors in "Feminism and Literature," 192.

14. Chicana feminists such as Alicia Gaspar de Alba, among many others, have also chosen Sor Juana as a foremother. Gaspar de Alba even radicalized her to the extent of seeing her as openly lesbian. See her *Sor Juana's Second Dream: A Novel* (Albuquerque: University of New Mexico Press, 1999).

15. Bolio not only represents her tumultuous political period, but also takes on the role of denouncer, of deconstructor, of the oppressive hegemonic economic system that discriminates against and works against women. Bolio advocates a reconstruction of society via the hopes of her protagonists, thus becoming a literary antecedent of the Mexican Atheneum of Women, in which she would later become a member and for which she would promote such precepts as the liberation of women and the creation of a new woman.

16. Her *Mi amigo azul* (1934), which was written before her column, possibly years before its publication, is a collection of stories which illustrate and support the "México de Afuera" ideology and contrast directly with what would be the substance of her weekly column.

17. See Emma Pérez's *The Decolonial Imaginary*, 43–44, for a discussion of Galindo. I somewhat disagree with Villarroel (128), who assigns much of the credit

for Elizondo's feminist advances to the Ateneo Mexicano de Mujeres, which counted among its members many of the same member writers, such as Dolores Bolio, who still sustained the nationalist project.

18. For a more detailed biography, see Villarroel, "La mujer ante el feminismo," 96–100.

19. The home considered by most of them a hotel, a place of transit; second, because servants are hard to find, keep, and pay . . . third, because the women cannot or do not want to dedicate themselves exclusively to work in the home; and fourth, because the property owners . . . demand exorbitant rent for houses.

20. This type of feminine independence ensures what Alicia reaffirms in the work: the economic and social independence of women. At the same time, as a symbolic gesture it devalues the importance of the man's last name, the name that traditionally provides social prestige and honor to the woman. As a consequence, Alicia motivates Elsa to take charge of her own self and her own name.

21. I am fortunate. Here, there are no men or women. There are no sexes, we are all equal and that's why there is no jealousy, hate, or other negative passions. In this life, where God is the God of everyone: Catholics, Jews, Protestants, Latinos, Anglo-Saxons, and Asians, where good intentions and noble sacrifices are rewarded.

22. In her "The Forgotten Migrant: Educated Puerto Rican Women in New York City, 1920–1940," Virginia Sánchez Korrol includes Betances Jaeger in a generation of Puerto Rican women intellectuals who contributed to the development of the community but who have not been adequately studied.

23. These biographical notes are provided by María Teresa Vera-Rojas's entry in Kanellos, *Greenwood Encyclopedia of Latino Literature.*

24. Putting into practice the strategies used by the weak to challenge hegemonic discourse, they conducted discussions about feminism and the feminine in a public space, and from there they promoted themselves as "counselors" and "informers" for the female sector of the immigrant community.

25. Vera-Rojas (93) prefers to see these "charlas" as what Mary Louise Pratt, in "'Don't Interrupt Me:' The Gender Essay as Conversation and Countercanon," has called the "gender essay" that Latin American women have used for two centuries to contest the disenfranchisement of women. Pratt states, "Historically, it can be read as the women's side of an ongoing negotiation as to what women's social and political entitlements are and ought to be in the postindependence era. Ideologically, its discussions of womanhood are eclectic, operating both within and against patriarchal gender ideologies" (16).

26. "El constante aumento de la colonia española e iberoamericana . . . nos ha impelido a editar este semanario . . . que . . . viene a cooperar a la defensa de todos los que forman la gran familia hispana. . . . Haremos una labor tendente a buscar la mayor compenetración y bienestar de los que ausentes de la patria amada debemos en suelo extraño agruparnos bajo una sola bandera: la de la fraternidad" (February 27, 1927) (The constant growth of the Spanish and Spanish American colony . . . has impelled us to publish this weekly . . . that . . . comes to participate in the defense of those who make up the grand Hispanic family. . . . We shall direct our labors to maximizing the integration and well-being of those far from the beloved *patria* who on this foreign soil should unite under one banner: that of brotherhood).

27. Clotilde Betances Jaeger was attempting to promote a new way of being a

woman involved in feminist struggle that would demonstrate the importance of women in the economic life of nations, at the same time that she emphasized the importance of the economy for the independence of women. For the new woman, her economic independence had to be of fundamental importance, especially because her social submission and subordination and subjugation had been determined for centuries by the economic dominance men exercised over women. Without a doubt, Clotilde Betances understood that the relationship between the sexes was one of power, in which in order to have rights it was not enough to have an equal vote; women needed to have economic rights. The new woman was, in fact, a revolution.

28. Among the few exceptions are her satirizing of an article she had read encouraging Puerto Ricans to migrate to the United States. In a biting tone in "Dejadlos Venir" (November 16, 1929, Let them come), she writes, "VENID a esta tierra extraña, pasad vergüenzas y pasad desprecios, VENID a luchar aquí, por el mal ganado pedazo de pan, y al ganarlo, olvidaréis con la lucha por la VIDA, la lucha por la libertad. VENID a fundiros en esta urbe, donde no somos nadie, VENID, hasta que no quede ni uno de nosotros en nuestra isla, VENID, hasta que el nombre de nuestra patria quede borrado, hasta que haya desaparecido, hasta que el puertorriqueño no exista más, fundido en las diferentes razas que inundan esta metropolis" (COME to this strange land, experience shame and contempt, COME here to fight to earn a crust of bread and, on earning it, you'll forget the fight for LIFE, the fight for liberty. COME in order to melt into this city where we are nobody, COME until not a single one of us is left on our island, COME until the name of our homeland is erased, until it has disappeared, until Puerto Ricans no longer exist, blended into the different races that inundate this metropolis).

29. Under the present status quo, the woman is the depository of family honor. An enormous responsibility for a slave! She must lead her children's minds to the true religion, guide their progress through life, and always humbly carry forward the stigma. . . . That is to say that the heavens are pleased to unite the lives of a woman and a man so that she, demeaned and prostituted . . . is obligated to receive his embrace just because, because she is his thing.

CHAPTER SIX

"If married men want to become less happy . . . they should not come accompanied by their opposite number to the United States. They can cross the border alone, leaving their respective other halves on the other side of the Bravo, as far away on the other side as possible, at a respectable distance. Because over here things are pretty bad, and the masculine gender is losing in giant steps 'its sacred prerogatives and inalienable rights.'"

1. For the evolution of *costumbrista* writing, see Susana Zanetti, *Costumbristas de América Latina: Antología*, 8–10.

2. From the beginning of the nineteenth century almost to the present, the role of the *crónica* was that of verifying or consecrating change and social habits and describing daily life, elevating it to the level of the idiosyncratic (without which Mexicans would be, for example, Paraguayans). In the transition from a colonial mentality to one of independence . . . a small collective, unsure of its accomplishments,

unsure of its nationalism, saw in the crónica the shining (ideal) mirror of its transformations and fixations. To write is to populate. Over a long period of time, the exhaustive details provided by the cronistas served a central purpose: to contribute to the forging of nationhood, describing it and, as much as possible, moralizing for it. . . . The writers of the nineteenth century wrote crónicas to document and, more important, to promote a lifestyle, one that repeated the customs of the authentic civic rituals. The cronistas are powerful nationalists because they desire independence and the greatness of the country as a whole . . . or because they wished for an identity that would help them, individualize them, liberate them, and eliminate the anxiety and their greatest fear: being the privileged witnesses of things of no importance, of narrating the process of formation of this society which no one was observing. . . . it is necessary to strengthen the nation, investing pride in her and describing her local and regional pride, representing in literature the most ostensibly "Mexican" ways of living and emphasizing their disdain for imitation of the French and nostalgia for the Hispanic.

3. See Jorge Ulica, "Treinta años de galeras . . . periodísticas, 1881-1911," undated manuscript in the Chicano Studies Collection, University of California, Berkeley, cited in Juan Rodríguez, Crónicas Diabólicas de "Jorge Ulica," 12.

4. This and other biographical information is provided by Juan Rodríguez in the introduction to Crónicas Diabólicas de "Jorge Ulica," 9–21.

5. All quotes are from the Rodríguez edition of Crónicas Diabólicas de "Jorge Ulica." If married men don't want to become less happy, . . . they should not come with their companions to the United States. . . . Because things are going very poorly here, as the masculine gender is losing in giant steps its "sacred prerogatives and inalienable rights," it sickens my soul to see unfortunate husbands subjected to a dog's life, to a dog's future and a tragic end.

6. Food is one of the essences of culture that becomes part of the Mexican versus American binary struggle in this literature. As Yuval-Davis has observed, "Because of the central importance of social reproduction to culture, gender relations often come to be seen as constituting the 'essence' of culture as ways of life to be passed from generation to generation. The construction of 'home' is of particular importance here, including relations between adults and children in the family, ways of cooking and eating. . . ." As can be seen in Ulica's "Por No Hablar English" and "Como Hacer Surprise Parties," these dynamics are in the forefront of his construction of the proper home and proper parents.

7. In popular entertainment, such as vaudeville, this gender role conflict was also played out with very similar results. However, beginning in the 1930s, some changes are manifested in such companies as La Chata Noloesca's and the Netty and Jesús Rodríguez comedy duo, which performed throughout the Southwest and even in New York Spanish-language vaudeville houses. La Chata Noloesca (stage name for Beatriz Escalona) ran her own company, featuring a streetwise maid (a *peladita* underdog character usually depicted by males) who often inverted conventional roles and challenged all types of borders. See Ybarra-Frausto, "La Chata Noloesca: Figura del Donaire"; Kanellos, *A History of Hispanic Theatre*, 93–95; and Arrizón, *Latina Performance: Traversing the Stage*. The vaudeville Rodríguezes often staged the conventional conflict of the *agringada* Netty being ridiculed or challenged by Jesús. Nevertheless, the strength and the charm of her liberated character on stage,

as in "Me Voy Pa' México" ("I'm Going to Mexico," in Kanellos, *En otra voz*, 308–311, and Kanellos, *Herencia*, 438–440), often gains more sympathy from the audience— and this can be heard on the 78 rpm records of performances—and overshadows the male role, making the male look machistic, especially when he references his right to beat his wife in Mexico. In "Cabrestea o Se Ahorca" (Move or get hanged) a vaudeville sketch preserved on 78 rpm recordings, there is a real role reversal: Netty censures Jesús, who has just arrived in Mexico from a long sojourn in Texas, for his gringo customs and his Spanglish. Representing the nation, Netty berates this *agringado* male and tells him in no uncertain terms that he is not needed or wanted in Mexico. See "The Strachwitz Frontera Collection of Mexican and Mexican American Recordings" for these two vaudeville sketches as well as others.

8. In this country women do as they damn well please. My wife, who used to be so obedient, so faithful, and such a little mouse in Ojinaga, has become "fireworks" here. She does not heed me, she locks herself up with male friends to play bridge and who knows what else, and when I call her on it she curses me out. Back home, I could knock her teeth out for less, but here, if you do that, they hang you in San Quentin.

9. "Border guard" is a term used by Arnold in *Nations before Nationalism*.

10. He will severely criticize the Mexican immigrant woman who decides to follow non-Mexican practices. Thus on taking up customs and aspiring to liberties and rights that are not traditional, such as becoming independent women, they are seen as becoming exogamous. If that were to happen, the Mexican community in the United States would be on the road to extinction, and the community would be lost, and with it the nation.

11. To get their hair done two flappers went to Don Simón's barbershop. That night both chickees were going out to party and have a good time. / "Please finish me in a hurry," said Julieta while her neck was shaved, "And then Enriqueta's turn will come, and I'll give you both a kiss." / The barber then worked so fast that he did Julieta before a minute passed, but he wasn't given what was promised to him, not even after finishing with Enriqueta.

12. Viki Ruiz dedicates a substantial part of her chapter "The Flapper and the Chaperone," in *From Out of the Shadows*, to examining the attraction of flapper dress and customs to transmigrant Mexican and Mexican-American young women, especially as promoted by popular culture; the resources she examines are an extensive body of oral histories, as well as some *corridos* and songs. See 51–57.

13. Not only is she shorn (*pelona*)/but she shows her legs/"up to where the elastics attach"/she wears clogs, has a dog,/and many girlfriends/"who 'company her to the theater"/and she even has an ugly Model T/from about 1900/in which she drives around.

14. Like the Mexican expatriates in the Southwest, other Hispanic authors did not limit their depiction of *agringadas* to the *crónica* genre but cultivated this image on the stage and in novels and essays. The plays of the Puerto Rican immigrant Gonzalo O'Neill all dealt with the subject of the Puerto Rican nation. In his *Bajo una sola bandera* (1934, Under one flag alone), set in New York City, O'Neill constructs the typical binary opposition of Puerto Rican versus American culture and personifies it in the choice a Puerto Rican teenage girl must make between two suitors, one an Anglo-American naval officer and the other a Puerto Rican *jíbaro*. The explicit

message favoring the *jíbaro*, however, is backgrounded by her father's tale of how an insect devoured the portion of the world map where Puerto Rico was located (33–34), implicitly invoking the threat that Puerto Ricans themselves were in danger of disappearing from the world, being so few and coming from such a small island. Thus, explicitly and implicitly the play warns against exogamy and trumpets the call for Puerto Rican women to continue the nation. Throughout the drama, the daughter's patriotic and romantic sentiments are contrasted with her mother's *agringado* materialism and admiration for American culture; in the mother's arguments in favor of her daughter's American suitor, she emphasizes the greater liberty Americans afford their women.

15. The pseudonym Miquis Tiquis, a Caribbean-Spanish phrase originating with the Latin *mihi* and *tibi*, indicated that the crónicas were intimate conversations "between you and me," from one Latino to another.

16. These quotes are taken from Padilla's collection *Lo que el pueblo me dice* of Colón's *crónicas*. (The Latin mob loves what glitters, 9).

17. Reader, if you would like to see the caricature of a flapper, you only have to look at a Latina who aspires to be one. The Yankee flapper always makes sure that her ensemble of exaggerations looks chic, as they say in German (*sic*). They also possess that divine jewel of finely imitated frigidity. That disdainful arching of their eyes that upon crossing their legs almost to . . . to . . . it seems not important to them that they are being watched. *Seeming frigidity, that's the phrase.* That *would-be* Latin *flapper* likes to be looked at, and to attract attention paints her face into a mask. Two poorly placed splotches of rouge on the cheeks and four really noticeable piles of lipstick on the lips. They criticize new fads; then they adapt them, to the extreme of exaggeration.

18. Like a Niña Chole (an erotically charged female character in Ramón del Valle-Inclán's novel *Sonata de estío*) but a New Yorker, the "flapper" agitates the air with her affected struts. Her dress, a futuristic version of the latest style, is a thousandfold suggestive with its divine silk. That men should look her over as she walks is her supreme desire. If someone should mention marriage, her answer is a loud laugh that cuts the most sublime illusion. Assassinating laugh! Expert queen of the latest dangerous dance step, covered in make-up, superficial, fickle girl, like a liberated slave entering a new life. In contrast she reminds me of my grandmother who, while knitting, would tell me stories of giants that flew in the air with her voice trembling as in a lost prayer.

19. In another *crónica* published under his own name, "Nuestras Señoritas Latinas" (Our Latin señoritas, 17), Colón censures the values that young Hispanic women are adopting in the United States: "Y el resultado siempre es el mismo cuando se buscan valores superficiales o valores inventados, o exigidos por una sociedad basada en principios corruptos, decadentes, y artificiosos" (And the result is always the same when one seeks superficial values, or invented values, or those demanded by a society based on corrupt, decadent, and artificial principles).

20. Although I have chosen to focus on early twentieth-century writing, by no means should it be understood that the attitudes about gender expressed by transmigrant males today differ all that much. As we have seen (see chapter 4), Jesús Franco's novel *Paraíso Travel* (2001) is somewhat reminiscent of Gazavic's *Tanasio y Ramona* in indicting the venality and materialism of the female who motivates the

protagonist's painful odyssey in the United States. Roberto Quezada's comic take on transmigrant gender, in *Never through Miami/Nunca Entres por Miami* (2002), has his forlorn hero come to the United States to earn enough money to bring his fiancée and future mother-in-law, only to have her dump him and marry the Cuban-American (therefore watered-down Latino) customs agent that gave him such a hard time when he tried to enter the United States. The horribly tragic ending of Jaime Carrero's play *Pipo Subway no sabe reír* (1972), signifies that the pure Puerto Rican values identified with the homeland are literally dashed to earth when Pipo pushes his pregnant mother down a flight of stairs; however, the mother is greatly at fault for embracing the materialistic and antifamily values that lead her son to his tragic action against his mother. In today's transmigrant Hispanic literature there are many examples (too numerous to cite here) of the female embodying the nation and its future and being punished when she does not.

CHAPTER SEVEN

1. In this code-switching virtuosity, Pérez Firmat is not alone, as native Latino literature is rife with such virtuous poets as Alurista, Sandra María Esteves, Tato Laviera, to a name just three. And in theater and fiction, Luis Valdez, and Rolando Hinojosa, respectively, to mention just two of the renowned representatives of this native literary style, have successfully cultivated the bilingual/code-switching text.

2. Curiously, in *Tongue Ties*, Pérez Firmat explores all aspects of the relationship of English and Spanish languages in a variety of Hispanic and Anglo authors but never gives any in-depth consideration to the relationship of language loyalty and nationalism, insisting on maintaining the focus on the linguistic decision being made by an individual artist. For example, see page 162.

3. Much more succinct in the original English, *Next Year in Cuba*, 209: "For people like me, the truth always comes gift-wrapped in fancy paradox; that our exile has already ended, and that our exile will never end; that no exile is forever, and that there is no after-exile. Sometimes I revel in the doubleness, sometimes I revile it, but the doubleness is me: I am *yo* and you and *tú* and two."

4. A transmigrant writer who, in fact, does legitimately assume the stance of exile is the Dominican-American essayist Silvio Torres-Saillant. A member of the Dominican "1.5" generation, one might say, for having accompanied his family, who were economic refugees, to the United States as a preteen, he nevertheless consciously writes from the "diaspora," and in so doing pitches the essays in his book *El retorno de las yolas* to a Dominican Republic readership, blatantly and profoundly criticizing regimes past and present as well as the social classes and business interests that he indicts for having expelled some twenty percent of Dominicans from their island home. Conscious of belonging to a transnational and deterritorialized community (24), Torres-Saillant writes from his base in a collectivity to express ideas that rarely penetrate the censorship in the island's media. Pérez Firmat, by contrast, writes as an individual, in the true tradition of American letters, and neither writes for a Cuban audience nor envisions reforming Cuba's governance and culture; rather, he writes in English for an audience that is broader than just Latinos in the United States or Cubans on the island. If there is a gaze, it is directed not toward Cuba but toward the Little Havana that once nurtured him but no longer exists.

5. In his book *Tongue Ties*, Pérez Firmat ponders his choice of English as follows: "Why I haven't tried to write more in Spanish is something that I've wondered about, something that I am wondering about right now, but that I don't entirely understand. I know the practical reasons for my use of English, but I also suspect that there may be other, more murky motives of which I am only half-aware: anger, fear of failure, maybe even a little self-hatred" (2). If indeed Pérez Firmat feels "self-hatred," it would place him squarely in the tradition of the American ethnic minority writing he has tried to resist.

6. "Our neighborhoods didn't just emulate Havana, they completed it. . . . In one respect this view of Cuban history testifies to the exile's capacity for comforting delusion. We console ourselves with the thought that, while we have remained the same, it's our homeland that has changed. We often feel that we haven't abandoned our country, but our country has abandoned us. From the guajiro's—that is, the exile's—perspective, the city that survived the revolution was a different place. . . . In some ways Miami was closer to the heart of Havana than Havana itself. In Spanish, there are two verbs of being: *ser*, which denotes existence, and *estar*, which denotes location. No matter how much geography may confine us, *ser* cannot be reduced to *estar*—a state of being cannot be reduced to a geographical place" (*Next Year* 56–58).

7. Even as a schoolboy in Miami he exhibits attitudes that, as I pointed out earlier, are present in such writers as Jesús Colón and Alberto O'Farrill: "Jocelyn era altiva e inaccessible—una *femme fatale* impúber. Parecía desdeñar a todos sus pretendientes, o por lo menos a mí. Era el tipo de muchacha que, años más tarde, daríamos en llamar 'una yegua americana', frase que manifestaba la reverencia y hasta pavor que sentíamos hacia esas americanitas quienes a menudo eran más altas que nosotros. Una de las características de las yeguas era su total indiferencia ante las payasadas más extravagantes de parte de sus pretendientes" (33) ("Jocelyn, with straight brown hair held in a pony tail that went down to her waist, was a pre-teen *femme fatale*: haughty, inaccessible, disdainful toward all suitors, or at least toward me. She was the kind of girl that a few years later my Cuban buddies would dub *una yegua americana*, an American mare, a term of reverence that probably originated in the fact that some of these girls were taller than we were. No matter what you did to get her attention, a *yegua americana* never gave you the time of day") (*Next Year* 33).

Acosta, Iván. *El super*. Miami: Ediciones Universal, 1982.

Alarcón, Alicia. *The Border Patrol Ate My Dust*. Translated by Ethriam Cash Brammer. Houston: Arte Público Press, 2004.

———. *La migra me hizo los mandados*. Houston: Arte Público Press, 2002.

Alemán, Jesse. "Barbarous Tongues: Immigrant Fiction and Ethnic Voices in Contemporary American Literature." *Modern Fiction Studies* 54.2 (summer 2008):398–404.

Almaguer, Tomás. *Racial Fault Lines: The Historical Legacy of White Supremacy in California*. Berkeley: University of California Press, 1994.

Anderson, Benedict. *Imagined Communities*. London: Verso, 1983.

Anonymous. *El laúd del desterrado*. Ed. Matías Montes Huidobro. Houston: Arte Público Press, 1995.

Arce, Julio G. *"Crónicas Diabólicas" de "Jorge Ulica."* Ed. Juan Rodríguez. San Diego: Maize Press, 1982.

Argudín, Yolanda. *Historia del periodismo en México desde el virreinato hasta nuestros días*. Mexico City: Panorama Editorial, 1997.

Arizmendi, Elena. *Vida incompleta: ligeros apuntes sobre las mujeres en la vida real*. New York: M. D. Dunon Printers, 1927.

Armstrong, John. *Nations before Nationalism*. Chapel Hill: University of North Carolina Press, 1982.

Arrizón, Alicia. *Latina Performance: Traversing the Stage*. Bloomington: Indiana University Press, 1999.

Avellaneda, Luis (pseud. of Dolores Bolio). *Aroma tropical*. New York: Neumann Brothers, 1917.

Baeza Ventura, Gabriela. *La imagen de la mujer en la crónica del "México de Afuera."* Ciudad Juárez: Universidad Autónoma de Ciudad Juárez, 2005.

Bakhtin, M. M. *The Dialogic Imagination: Four Essays*. Ed. Michael Holquist. Translated by Caryl Emerson and Michael Holquist. Austin: University of Texas Press, 1981.

Basch, Linda, Nina Glick Schiller, and Cristina Szanton Blanc. *Nations Unbound: Transnational Projects, Postcolonial Predicaments, and Deterritorialized Nation-States*. New York: Routledge, 1993.

Bencastro, Mario. *A Promise to Keep*. Translated by Susan Giersbach-Rascón. Houston: Arte Público Press, 2005.

———. *Odisea del norte*. Houston: Arte Público Press, 1999.

———. *Odyssey to the North*. Translated by Susan Giersbach-Rascón. Houston: Arte Público Press, 1998.

Bhabha, Homi K. "DissemiNation: Time, Narrative, and the Margins of the Modern Nation." In *Nation and Narration*, ed. Homi K. Bhabha, 291–322. London: Routledge, 1990.

———. *The Location of Culture*. New York: Routledge, 2004.

Bloch, Ernst. *Principles of Hope*. Translated by Neville Plaice, Stephen Plaice, and Paul Knight. Oxford: Basil Blackwell, 1986.

Blom, Ida. "Gender and Nation in International Comparison." In Blom et al., *Gendered Nations*, 3–26. Oxford: Berg, 2000.

Blom, Ida, Karen Hagemann, and Catherine Hall, eds. *Gendered Nations: Nationalisms and Gender Order in the Long Nineteenth Century*. Oxford: Berg, 2000.

Boelhower, William Q. "The Brave New World of Immigrant Autobiography." *MELUS* 9.2 (summer 1982): 5–23.

Browitt, Jeff. "Sexual Anxiety in Alirio Díaz Guerra's *Lucas Guevara*." *Hispania* 88.4 (2005): 477–86.

Bruce-Novoa, Juan. "*La Prensa* and the Chicano Community." *Américas Review* 17.3–4 (winter 1989): 150–156.

Capetillo, Luisa. *Absolute Equality: An Early Feminist Perspective / Influencias de las ideas modernas*. Ed. Lara Walker. Houston: Arte Público Press, 2009.

———. *A Nation of Women: An Early Feminist Speaks Out / Mi opinión sobre las libertades, derechos y deberes de la mujer*. Ed. Félix V. Matos Rodríguez. Translated by Alex West-Durán. Houston: Arte Público Press, 2004.

Carrasco Puente, Rafael. *La prensa en México: Datos históricos*. Mexico City: Universidad Nacional Autónoma de México, 1962.

Carrero, Jaime. "*Flag Inside,*" *Capitán F-4C, Pipo Subway No Sabe Reír, El Caballo de Ward*. Río Piedras, P.R.: Ediciones Puerto, 1973.

Castillo, Debra A. *Redreaming America: Toward a Bilingual American Culture*. Albany: State University of New York Press, 2005.

———. *Talking Back: Toward a Latin American Feminist Criticism*. Ithaca: Cornell University Press, 1992.

Castillón, Catalina. "Moncaleano, Blanca de." In *Greenwood Encyclopedia of Latino Literature*, ed. N. Kanellos, vol 2. Westport, Conn.: Greenwood Press, 2008.

Chabram-Dernersesian, Angie. "On the Social Construction of Whiteness within Selected Chicana/o Discourses." In *Displacing Whiteness: Essays in Social and Cultural Criticism*, ed. Ruth Falkenberg, 107–154. Durham: Duke University Press, 1997.

Chabrán, Rafael. "Spaniards." In *The Immigrant Labor Press in North America, 1840s–1970s*, 151–190. Westport, Conn.: Greenwood Press, 1987.

Chacón, Ramón D. "The Chicano Immigrant Press in Los Angeles: The Case of 'El Heraldo de México,' 1916–1920." *Journalism History* 4/2 (summer 1997): 48–50, 62–64.

Chew Sánchez, Martha I. *Corridos in Migrant Memory*. Albuquerque: University of New Mexico Press, 2006.

The Chris Strachwitz Frontera Collection of Mexican and Mexican American Recordings. *http://frontera.library.ucla.edu*.

Christian, Karen. *Show and Tell: Identity as Performance in U.S. Latina/o Fiction*. Albuquerque: University of New Mexico Press, 1997.

Cockroft, James D. *Intellectual Pioneers of the Mexican Revolution, 1900–1913*. Austin: University of Texas Press, 1968.

Colón, Jesús. *Lo que el pueblo me dice . . . : Crónicas de la colonia puertorriqueña en Nueva York*. Ed. Edwin Karli Padilla Aponte. Houston: Arte Público Pres, 2001.

———. *The Way It Was and Other Writings*. Houston: Arte Público Press, 1994.

———. *A Puerto Rican in New York and Other Sketches*. 2d ed. New York: International Publishers, 1982.

Colón López, Joaquín. *Pioneros puertorriqueños en Nueva York, 1917-1947*. Houston: Arte Público Press, 2002.

Concannon, Kevin, Francisco A. Lomelí, and Marc Priewe. *Imagined Transnationalism: U.S. Latino/a Literature, Culture, and Identity*. New York: Palgrave Macmillan, 2009.

Cowart, David. *Trailing Clouds: Immigrant Fiction in Contemporary America*. Ithaca: Cornell University Press, 2006.

———. "The Immigrant Novel as Genre." *MELUS* 8.1 (spring 1981): 3–13.

Craft, Linda J. "Mario Bencastro's Diaspora: Salvadorans and Transnational Identity." *MELUS* 30.1 (spring 2005): 149–167.

Debray, Regis. "Marxism and the National Question." *New Left Review* 105 (September/October 1977): n.p.

Díaz Guerra, Alirio. *Lucas Guevara*. Houston: Arte Públcio Press, 2001.

———. *Lucas Guevara*. Translated by Ethriam Cash Brammer. Houston: Arte Público Press, 2003.

Duany, Jorge. *Quisqueya on the Hudson: The Transnational Identity of Dominicans in Washington Heights*. Dominican Research Monographs. New York: CUNY Dominican Studies Institute, 1994.

Espinosa, Conrado. *Under the Texas Sun/El sol de Texas* (bilingual edition). Translated by Ethriam Cash Brammer. Houston: Arte Público Press, 2007.

Falcón, Rafael. *La emigración a Nueva York en la novela puertorriqueña*. Valencia-Chapel Hill: Ediciones Albatros Hispanófila, 1983.

Fitzpatrick, Joseph P. "The Puerto Rican Press." In *The Ethnic Press in the United States: A Historical Analysis and Handbook*, ed. Sally M. Miller, 303–314. Westport, Conn.: Greenwood Press, 1987.

Flores, Juan. *Divided Borders*. Houston: Arte Público Press, 1993.

Fornet, Ambrosio. *El libro en Cuba*. Havana: Editorial Letras Cubanas, 1994.

Franco, Jorge. *Paradise Travel*. Translated by Katherine Silver. New York: Picador, 2007.

———. *Paraíso travel*. Bogotá: Editorial Planeta Colombiana, 2001.

Fuchs, Maura L. *Revista Mexicana: Constructing the Conservative Mexican National in Exile*. Ph.D. diss., University of Houston, 2006.

Gallegos, Bernardo P. *Literacy, Society and Education in New Mexico, 1693-1821*. Albuquerque: University of New Mexico Press, 1992.

García, Mario T. *Desert Immigrants: The Mexicans of El Paso, 1880-1920*. New Haven: Yale University Press, 1981.

García, Richard A. *Rise of the Mexican American Middle Class. San Antonio, 1929-1941*. College Station: Texas A&M University Press, 1991.

García-Canclini, Nestor. *Culturas híbridas: Estrategias para entrar y salir de la modernidad*. Mexico City: Grijalbo, 1990.

García Naranjo, Nemesio. *Memorias de Nemesio García Naranjo*. 9 vols. Monterrey: Talleres de "El Porvenir," s.d.

Garza, María Luisa de la. *Ni de aquí ni de allá: El emigrante en los corridos y en otras canciones populares*. Cádiz, Spain: Fundación Municipal de la Cultura Excelentísimo Ayuntamiento de Cádiz, 2007.

Gómez-Peña, Guillermo. *A Binational Pilgrimage*. Manchester, Vt.: Cornerhouse, 1993.

————. *Warrior for Gringostroika; Essays, Performance Texts, and Poetry.* St. Paul: Graywolf Press, 1993.

————. *The New World Border: Prophecies, Poems and Loqueras for the End of the Century.* San Francisco: City Lights, 1996.

Gómez-Quiñones, Juan. *Sembradores, Ricardo Flores Magón y El Partido Liberal Mexicano; A Eulogy and a Critique.* Los Angeles: UCLA Chicano Studies Research Center, 1977.

González Viaña, Eduardo. *El corrido de Dante.* Houston: Arte Público Press, 2008.

————. *Dante's Ballad.* Translated by Susan Giersbach-Rascón. Houston: Arte Público Press, 2008.

Gray, Paul Bryan. "Francisco Ramírez. A Short Biography." *California History* 84.2 (2006–2007): 20–39.

Grewal, Inderpol. *Transnational American Feminisms, Diasporas, Neoliberalisms.* Durham: Duke University Press, 2005.

Griswold del Castillo, Richard. "The Mexican Revolution and the Spanish-Language Press in the Borderlands." *Journalism History* 4.2 (summer 1977): 42–47.

Grossman, Sari, and Joan Brodsky Schur, eds. *In a New Land: An Anthology of Immigrant Literature.* Lincolnwood, Ill.: National Textbook Company, 1994.

Gutiérrez, David G. *Walls and Mirrors: Mexican Americans, Mexican Immigrants, and the Politics of Ethnicity.* Berkeley: University of California Press, 1995.

Gutiérrez, Félix. "Spanish-Language Media in America: Background, Resources, History." *Journalism History* 4/2 (summer 1977): 34–41, 65–67.

Henderson, Ann L., and Gary R. Mormino. *Spanish Pathways in Florida.* Sarasota: Pineapple Press, 1991.

Hernández, Eleuteria. "La Representación de la Mujer Mexicana en los EE.UU. en las *Crónicas Diabólicas* de Jorge Ulica." *Mester* 12.2 (fall 1993): 31–38.

Hernández Tovar, Inés. *Sara Estela Ramírez: The Early Twentieth-Century Texas-Mexican Poet.* Diss., University of Houston, 1984.

Herrera-Sobek, María. *Northward Bound: The Mexican Immigrant Experience in Ballad and Song.* Bloomington: Indiana University Press, 1993.

Irizarry Rodríguez, José M. "Evolving Identities: Early Puerto Rican Writing in the United States and the Search for a New *Puertorriqueñidad.*" In *Writing Off the Hyphen,* ed. José L. Torres-Padilla and Carmen Haydée Rivera, 31–51. Austin: University of Texas Press, 1994.

Kalra, Virinder S., Raminder Kaur, and John Hutnyk. *Diaspora and Hybridity.* London: Sage Publications, 2005.

Kanellos, Nicolás. "*El Clamor Público*: Resisting the American Empire." *California History* 84.2 (winter 2006–2007): 10–18, 69–70.

————, ed. *Greenwood Encyclopedia of Latino Literature.* 3 vols. Westport, Conn.: Greenwood Press, 2008.

————, et al. *Herencia: The Anthology of Hispanic Literature of the United States.* New York: Oxford University Press, 2002.

————. *Hispanic Firsts: 500 Years of Extraordinary Achievement.* Detroit: Gale, 1997.

————. "Hispanic Intellectuals Publishing in the Nineteenth-Century United States: From Political Tracts in Support of Independence to Commercial Publishing Ventures." *Hispania* 88/4 (December 2005): 687–692.

———. *Hispanic Literature in the United States: A Comprehensive Reference.* Westport, Conn.: Greenwood Press, 2005.

———, with Helvetia Martell. *Hispanic Periodicals in the United States, Origins to 1960: A Brief History and Comprehensive Bibliography.* Houston: Arte Público Press, 2000.

———. *A History of Hispanic Theatre in the United States: Origins to 1940.* Austin: University of Texas Press, 1990.

———. "La literatura hispana en los EE.UU. y el género autobiográfico." In *Hispanos en los Estados Unidos*, ed. Rodolfo J. Cortina and Alberto Moncada, 211–18. Madrid: Ediciones de Cultura Hispánica, 1988.

———. *Thirty Million Strong: Reclaiming the Hispanic Image in American Culture.* Golden, Colo.: Fulcrum, 1998.

Kaplan, Caren, Norma Alarcón, and Minoo Moallem, eds. *Between Woman and Nation: Nationalisms, Transnational Feminisms, and the State.* Durham: Duke University Press, 1999.

Knippling, Alpana Sharma, ed. *New Immigrant Literatures in the United States: A Sourcebook to Our Multicultural Literary Heritage.* Westport, Conn.: Greenwood Press, 1996.

Kohn, Hans. *Nationalism: Its Meaning and History.* New York: Van Nostrand, 1965.

Lane, James B., and Edward J. Escobar, eds. *Forging a Community: The Latino Experience in Northwest Indiana, 1919–1965.* Chicago: Cattails Press, 1987.

Lau, Ana, and Carmen Ramos, eds. *Mujeres y revolución, 1900–1917.* Mexico, D.F.: Instituto Nacional de Estudios Históricos de la Revolución Mexicana, 1993.

Lazo, Rodrigo. *Writing to Cuba: Filibustering and Cuban Exiles in the United States.* Raleigh: University of North Carolina Press, 2005.

Leal, Luis. "Truth Telling Tongues: Early Chicano Poetry." In *Recovering the U.S. Hispanic Literary Heritage*, ed. Ramón Gutiérrez and Genaro Padilla, 91–105. Houston: Arte Público Press, 1993.

Ledesma, Alberto. "Undocumented Crossings: Narratives of Mexican Immigration to the United States." In *Culture across Borders*, ed. David R. Maciel and María Herrera-Sobek, 67–98. Tucson: University of Arizona Press, 1998.

Lerner Sigal, Victoria. "Algunas hipótesis generales a partir del caso de los mexicanos exilados por la Revolución Mexicana (1906–1920)." *University of Chicago Center for Latin American Studies Mexican Studies Program.* Working Papers Series no. 7, 2000.

———. *Mexicanos en Estados Unidos: su actitud hacia México, sus líderes y su situación. (1915–1930).* El Paso: Center for Inter-American and Border Studies no. 12, June 1994.

Limón, José. "*Agringado* Joking in Texas Mexican Society." *Perspectives in Mexican American Studies* 1 (1988): 109–128.

Lomas, Clara. "The Articulation of Gender in the Mexican Borderlands, 1900–1915." In *Recovering the U.S. Hispanic Literary Heritage*, ed. Ramón Gutiérrez and Genaro Padilla, 203–308. Houston: Arte Público Press, 1993.

———. "Introduction." *The Rebel.* Houston: Arte Público Press, 1994.

———. "Mexican Precursors of Chicana Feminist Writing." In *Multiethnic Literature of the United States: Critical Introductions and Classroom Resources*, ed. Cordelia Candelaria, 21–23. Boulder: University of Colorado at Boulder, 1989.

————. "Resistencia Cultural o Apropiación Ideológica: Visión de los Años 20 en los Cuadros Costumbristas de Jorge Ulica." *Revista Chicano-Riqueña* 6.4 (fall 1978): 44–49.
————. "Transborder Discourse: The Articulation of Gender in the Borderlands in the Early Twentieth Century." *Frontiers* 24 (2003): 51–74.
————. "Villegas de Magnón, Leonor." In *Greenwood Encyclopedia of Latino Literature*, ed. N. Kanellos, vol. 3. Westport, Conn.: Greenwood Press, 2008.
Lomas, Laura. *Translating Empire: José Martí, Migrant Latino Subjects, and American Modernities.* Durham: Duke University Press, 2008.
Lund, Joshua. *The Impure Imagination: Toward a Critical Hybridity in Latin American Writing.* Minneapolis: University of Minnesota Press, 2006.
————. "The Mestizo State: Colonization and Indianization in Liberal Mexico." *PMLA* 123.5 (October 2008): 1418–1433.
Maciel, David R., and María Herrera-Sobek, eds. *Culture across Borders: Mexican Immigration and Popular Culture.* Tucson: University of Arizona Press, 1998.
————, and María Rosa Acevedo. "Celluloid Immigrant: The Narrative Films of Mexican Immigration." In *Culture across Borders*, ed. David R. Maciel and María Herrera-Sobek, 149–202. Tucson: University of Arizona Press, 1998.
MacLachlan, Colin M. *Anarchism and the Mexican Revolution: The Political Trials of Ricardo Flores Magón in the United States.* Berkeley: University of California Press, 1991.
Marqués, René. *El puertorriqueño dócil: literatura y realidad psicológica.* San Juan: Editorial Antillana, 1967.
————. *The Docile Puerto Rican: Essays.* Philadelphia: Temple University Press, 1976.
Matos Rodríguez, Félix V. "Introduction." *A Nation of Women: An Early Feminist Speaks Out / Mi opinión sobre las libertades, derechos y deberes de la mujer.* Houston: Arte Público Press, 2005.
McClintock, Amir Mufti, and Ella Shohat, eds. *Dangerous Liaisons: Gender, Nation, and Postcolonial Perspectives.* Minneapolis: University of Minnesota Press, 1997.
Meléndez, Gabriel. *So All Is Not Lost: The Poetics of Print in Nuevo Mexicano Communities.* Albuquerque: University of New Mexico Press, 1997.
Mendieta, María de los Angeles. *Carmen Serdán.* Mexico City: Centro de Estudios Históricos de Puebla, 1971.
Mercer, Kobena. "Diaspora Culture and the Dialogic Imagination: The Aesthetics of Black Independent Film in Britain." In *Blackframes: Critical Perpsectives on Black Independent Cinema*, ed. Mbye B. Cham and Claire Andrade-Watkins, 50–61. Cambridge: MIT Press, 1988.
Meyer, Doris. *Speaking for Themselves: Neo-Mexicano Cultural Identity and the Spanish-Language Press, 1880–1920.* Albuquerque: University of New Mexico Press, 1996.
Miller, Sally M., ed. *The Ethnic Press in the United States: A Historical Analysis and Handbook.* Westport, Conn.: Greenwood Press, 1987.
Mirandé, Alfredo. *Gringo Justice.* Notre Dame: University of Notre Dame Press, 1987.
Monsiváis, Carlos. *A ustedes les consta: Antología de la crónica en México.* Mexico City: Ediciones Era, 1980.

Mujcinovic, Fatima. *Postmodern Cross-Culturalism in U.S. Latina Literature*. New York: Peter Lang, 2004.

Munguía, Rubén. "*La Prensa*: Memories of a Boy . . . Sixty Years Later." *Américas Review* 17.3–4 (fall-winter 1989): 130–135.

O'Neill, Gonzalo. *Bajo una sola bandera*. New York: Spanish American Printing, 1934.

Ochoa Campos, Moisés. *Reseña histórica del periodismo mexicano*. Mexico City: Editorial Porrúa, 1968.

Oliver-Rotger, Maria Antonia. "Performing the Fetichized Chicano: Guillermo Gómez-Peña's Work in the Context of the Latino Backlash and the Global Spectacle of Identity." In *Perspectivas transatlánticas en la literature chicana: Ensayos y creatividad*, ed. María Herrera-Sobek, Francisco Lomelí, and Juan Antonio Perles Rochel, 235–242. Málaga: Universidad de Málaga, 2004.

Ong, Walter J. *Orality and Literacy: The Technologizing of the Word*. London: Methuen, 1982.

Padgett, Tim. "An Honest Look at Illegal Immigration." *Time*, March 11, 2008. http://www.time.com.

Padilla, Benjamín. *Un puñado de artículos: filosofía barata*. 2d ed. Barcelona: Casa Editorial Maucci, s.d.

Padró, José I. de Diego. *En Babia (El manuscrito de un braquicéfalo)*. 2d ed. Mexico City: Gráfica Panamericana, 1961.

Paredes, Américo. *Folkore and Culture on the Texas-Mexican Border*. Austin: University of Texas Press, 1995.

———. *A Texas-Mexican Cancionero: Folksongs of the Lower Border*. Urbana: University of Illinois Press, 1976.

Park, Robert E. *The Immigrant Press and Its Control*. New York: Harper and Brothers, 1922.

Payant, Katherine B., and Toby Rose, eds. *The Immigrant Experience in North American Literature: Carving Out a Niche*. Westport, Conn.: Greenwood Press, 1999.

Pérez, Emma. *The Decolonial Imaginary: Writing Chicanas into History*. Bloomington: Indiana University Press, 1999.

Pérez, Héctor. "*La prensa*, un periódico de San Antonio." *http://www.angelfire.com*.

Pérez, Ramón ("Tianguis"). *Diario de un mojado*. Houston: Arte Público Press, 2003.

———. *Diary of an Undocumented Immigrant*. Houston: Arte Público Press, 1991.

Pérez-Firmat, Gustavo. *Anything but Love*. Houston: Arte Público Press, 2000.

———. *El año que viene estamos en Cuba*. Houston: Arte Público Press, 1997.

———. *Life on the Hyphen: The Cuban-American Way*. Austin: University of Texas Press, 1994.

———. *Next Year in Cuba*. Houston: Arte Público Press, 1995.

———. *Tongue Ties: Logo-Eroticism in Anglo-Hispanic Literature*. New York: Palgrave Macmillan, 2003.

Poyo, Gerald E. *With All, and for the Good of All: The Emergence of Popular Nationalism in the Cuban Communities of the United States, 1848–1898*. Durham: Duke University Press, 1989.

Pratt, Mary Louise. "'Don't Interrupt Me:' The Gender Essay as Conversation and Countercanon." In *Reinterpreting the Spanish-American Essay: Women Writers of the 19th and 20th Centuries*, ed. Doris Meyer, 10–26. Austin: University of Texas Press, 1995.

Quesada, Roberto. *The Big Banana*. Translated by Walter Krochmal. Houston: Arte Público Press, 1999.

———. *Never through Miami*. Translated by Patricia Duncan. Houston: Arte Público Press, 2002.

———. *Nunca Entres por Miami*. Barcelona: Mondadori, 2002.

Richmond, Douglas W. *Venustiano Carranza's Nationalist Struggle, 1893–1920*. Lincoln: University of Nebraska Press, 1983.

Rodríguez, Emilio Jorge. "Apuntes sobre la visión del emigrante en la narrativa puertorriqueña." In *Primer seminario sobre la situación de las comunidades negra, chicana, india y puertorriqueña en Estados Unidos*, 445–485. Havana: Editora Política, 1984.

Rodríguez, Juan. *Crónicas Diabólicas de "Jorge Ulica"/Julio B. Arce*. San Diego: Maize Press, 1982.

Ruiz, Viki L. *From Out of the Shadows: Mexican Women in Twentieth-Century America*. New York: Oxford University Press, 1999.

Sánchez-González, Lisa. "For the Sake of Love: Luisa Capetillo, Anarchy, and Boricua Literary History." In *Writing Off the Hyphen*, ed. José L. Torres-Padilla and Carmen Haydée Rivera, 52–80. Seattle: University of Washington Press, 2008.

Sánchez Korrol, Virginia. "The Forgotten Migrant: Educated Puerto Rican Women in New York City, 1920–1940." In *The Puerto Rican Woman, Perspectives on Culture, History and Society*, 2d ed., ed. Edna Acosta-Belén, 170–179. New York: Praeger, 1986.

———. *From Colonia to Community: The History of Puerto Ricans in New York City, 1917–1948*. Westport, Conn.: Greenwood Press, 1983.

Sánchez, Rosaura. "From Heterogeneity to Contradiction: Hinojosa's Novel." In *The Rolando Hinojosa Reader: Essays Historical and Critical*, ed. José David Saldívar, 76–100. Houston: Arte Público Press, 1985.

Shaffer, Kirwin. "The Radical Muse: Women and Anarchism in Early-Twentieth-Century Cuba." *Cuban Studies* 34 (2003): 130–153.

Showalter, Elaine. "Feminism and Literature." In *Literary Theory Today*, ed. Peter Collier and Helga Geye-Ryan, 179–202. Cambridge: Polity Press.

Sisk, Christina L. "Toward a Trans(national) Reading of Ramón 'Tianguis' Pérez's *Diario de un mojado*." *Aztlán: A Journal of Chicano Studies* 34.1 (spring 2009): 13–34.

Smith, Anthony D. "Culture, Community and Territory: The Politics of Ethnicity and Nationalism." *International Affairs* 72 (1996): 445–458.

———. "The Nation: Invented, Imagined, Reconstructed?" In *Reimagining the Nation*, ed. Marjorie Rincrose and Adam J. Lerner, 9–28. Buckingham, England: Open University Press, 1993.

Smith, Michael M. "The Mexican Immigrant Press beyond the Borderlands: The Case of *El Cosmopolita*, 1914–1919." *Great Plains Quarterly* 10 (spring 1990): 71–85.

Stefano, Onofre di. "Venimos a Luchar: A Brief History of *La Prensa*'s Founding." *Aztlán: A Journal of Chicano Studies*. 16/1–2 (1985): 95–118.

Tinnemeyer, Andrea. "Mediating the Desire of the Reader in Villegas de Magnón's

The Rebel." In *Recovering the U.S. Hispanic Literary Heritage*, ed. María Herrera-Sobek and Virginia Sánchez Korrol, 3:124–137. Houston: Arte Público Press, 2000.

Torres, María de los Angeles. "*Encuentros y encontronazos*: Homeland in the Politics and Identity of the Cuban Diaspora." *Diaspora: A Journal of Transnational Studies* 4.2 (1995): 211–238.

Torres, Teodoro. *La patria perdida: Novela mexicana.* Mexico City: Ediciones Botas, 1935.

Torres-Padilla, José L., and Carmen Haydée Rivera, eds. *Writing Off the Hyphen: New Critical Perspectives on the Literature of the Puerto Rican Diaspora.* Seattle: University of Washington Press, 2008.

Torres-Saillant, Silvio. *El retorno de las yolas: Ensayos sobre diáspora, democracia y dominicanidad.* Santo Domingo: Ediciones Librería Trinitaria y Editora Manatí, 1999.

Treviño, Roberto. *Becoming American: The Spanish-Language Press and Biculturation of California Elites, 1852–1870.* Palo Alto: Stanford University History Department Working Paper Series no. 27, 1989.

Valle Ferrer, Norma. *Luisa Capetillo: Historia de una mujer proscrita.* San Juan: Editorial Cultural, 1990.

Velasco Valdés, Miguel. *Historia del periodismo mexicano (apuntes).* México: Librería de Manuel Porrúa, s.d.

Venegas, Daniel. *Las aventuras de Don Chipote o, Cuando los pericos mamen.* Houston: Arte Público Press, 1999.

———. *The Adventures of Don Chipote, or When Parrots Breast Feed.* Translated by Ethriam Cash Brammer. Houston: Arte Público Press, 2002.

Vera-Rojas, María Teresa. "Betances Jaeger, Clotilde." In *Greenwood Encyclopedia of Latino Literature*, ed. N. Kanellos. Westport, Conn.: Greenwood Press, 2008.

———. "El género de las charlas y las charlas del género: ¿De qué hablaban las mujeres puertorriqueñas en Nueva York?" Diss., University of Houston, 2007.

Villarreal, Andrea, and Teresa Villarreal, "¿Qué hacéis aquí hombres?" In *En otra vo*, 462–464.

Villarroel, Carolina. "La mujer ante el feminismo: nación, clase y raza en la literatura femenina del destierro (1910–1940)." Diss., University of Houston, 2008.

Wegner, Phillip E. *Imaginary Communities: Utopia, the Nation, and the Spatial Histories of Modernity.* Berkeley: University of California Press, 2002.

White, Paul. "Geography, Literature and Migration." In *Writing across Worlds: Literature and Migration*, ed. Russell King, John Connell, and Paul White, 1–19. London: Routledge, 1995.

Worley, Peter. *The Third World.* Chicago: University of Chicago Press, 1964.

Wynar, Lubomyr R., and Anna T. Wynar. *Encyclopedic Directory of Ethnic Newspapers and Periodicals in the United States.* 2d ed. Littleton, Colo.: Libraries Unlimited, 1976.

Ybarra-Frausto, Tomás. "La Chata Noloesca: Figura del Donaire." In *Mexican American Theatre Then and Now*, ed. Nicolás Kanellos, 41–51. Houston: Arte Público Press, 1989.

Young, Robert J. C. *Colonial Desire: Hybridity in Theory, Culture and Race.* London: Routledge, 1995.

Yuval-Davis, Nira. *Gender and Nation.* London: Sage Publications, 1997.

Zamora, Emilio. "Sara Estela Ramírez: Una Rosa en el Movimiento." In *Mexican Women in the United States: Struggles Past and Present*, ed. Magdalena Mora and Adelaida R. del Castillo, 163–178. Los Angeles: UCLA Chicano Studies Research Center, 1980s.

Zanetti, Susana. *Costumbristas de América Latina: Antología*. Buenos Aires: s.d., 1973.

Aboy Benítez, Juan, 164n5
Acosta, Iván, 2, 9, 28, 31, 64, 81
Adam as a type, 9, 81, 91–96; "New
    Adam," 13, 52, 72, 78, 150
Adamic, Louis, 10
Addison, Joseph, 124
agringado, 4, 9, 23, 30, 53, 66, 72, 80,
    111, 125, 127–133, 153, 163n3, 168n33,
    180n6, 181n14
Alarcón, Alicia, 68
Alemán, Jesse, 156n11
Alemán Bolaños, Gustavo, 2, 9, 49
Alurista, 159n14, 183n1
Alvarez, Julia, 3, 10, 12, 13, 31, 148,
    156n10
Alvarez de Toledo, José, 32
ambivalence, 29, 130–131, 148–149,
    151–152, 166n2
American Dream, 3, 7, 11, 13, 15, 17,
    21, 24, 33, 35, 52, 55–57, 66–67, 72,
    91–96, 101, 136, 147, 149–153, 164n5,
    166n22
American values: amorality, 3, 62, 70,
    128, 137, 165n13; decadence, 182n19;
    democracy, 174n19; effeminate cul-
    ture, 56, 130–131, 136; individual-
    ism, 31, 33; inhumanity, 4, 50, 59,
    82; materialism, 3, 4, 31, 56–59,
    62–63, 67–68, 70–73, 81, 82, 112,
    118, 132, 136, 138, 147, 155n1, 165n13,
    181n14, 183n20; pragmatism, 62;
    technology, 3, 56–58, 63, 73, 81–84,
    125, 127, 146
anarchism, 26, 45, 47, 176n3
Anaya, Rudolfo, 31, 32
Anderson, Benedict, 82, 83, 124, 156n9
"Angel del Hogar," 110–113
Antin, Mary, 10
Anzaldúa, Gloria, 109
Arce, Julio G., 4, 8, 9, 25, 49, 51, 111, 112,
    123, 126–133, 177n11, 180n6
Arce, Miguel, 49

Arenas, Reinaldo, 32
Arizmendi, Elena, 115–119
Arnaz, Desi, 150–153
Arte Público Press, 159n11
Artes Gráficas, 43, 161n15
assimilation, 4, 7, 8, 16, 17, 19, 36, 52–
    53, 62, 131, 137, 142, 145, 147, 149,
    179n28
Ateneo Mexicano de Mujeres,
    177nn15,17
autobiography, 22, 23, 32, 48; bildungs-
    roman, 10, 23, 32, 150, 155n5; ethnic,
    3, 10, 12, 13, 16, 32–33, 148–153,
    155n5, 175n22, 184n5
Avellaneda, Luis. *See* Bolio, Dolores
"Az. T. K.," 48, 125
Aztlán, 23, 28–29, 168n33
Azuela, Mariano, 33

Babylon, 4, 6, 23, 25, 29, 58, 61, 73, 147,
    165n19, 168n34
Baeza Ventura, Gabriela, 112, 132, 136
Bakhtin, M. M., 159n12
Bakunin, Mikhail, 27, 107
Ball, Lucille, 152
Baptist Publishing House, 174n17
Barrio, El, 168n33
Belpré, Pura, 174n19
Bencastro, Mario, 2, 25, 33, 51, 68–69,
    81, 164n5
Betances, Ramón Emeterio, 119
Betances de Jaeger, Clotilde, 119–122,
    137, 178n22
Bhabha, Homi K., 12, 13, 15, 99–100,
    104, 166n22
Bible, 85, 96–99, 157n2
Bloch, Ernst, 90
Blom, Ida, 133
Boelhower, William, 11–12
Bolet Peraza, Nicanor, 7, 8
Bolio, Dolores, 110, 113–115, 148,
    177nn15,17

Bolívar, Simón, 29, 100
border literature, 28, 106
Border Patrol, 99
Brand, Simón, 167n30
braquicéfalo, 166n23
Brecht, Bertholt, 108
Browitt, Jeff, 164n12
Bruce-Novoa, Juan, 54, 158n9

Californios, 22
canons, 12, 13, 27, 31–34, 153, 158n6,
    168n33
Capetillo, Luisa, 26, 106–109, 114, 116,
    119, 162n20
capitalism, 3, 24, 84–85, 87, 117, 124
Carranza, Venustiano, 106, 160–161n11
Carrero, Jaime, 9, 155n1, 169n38, 182n20
Carrillo, Adolfo, 22
Casa del Obrero, 104
Casa Editorial Lozano, 41–43, 173n16
Castillo, Ana, 10, 155n8
Castillo, Debra A., 155n3, 171n8
Castillo, Rafael del, 44
Castro, J. C., 126
Cather, Willa, 12
Catholicism, 4, 25, 44, 174n17
Cervantes, Miguel de, 33
Chabram-Dernersesian, Angie, 163n2
Chalk, O. Roy, 160n10
Chávez, Denise, 155n8
Chicano literature, 22–34, 69, 71
Chicano movement, 18, 26, 164n33
Chicanos, 3, 4, 81–82
"Chicote," 48, 125
Christian, Karen, 155n5
científicos, 90
cigar workers, 44–47, 107–109, 141
Cisneros, Sandra, 10, 11, 13, 31, 32, 148,
    155n6, 156n8
civil rights, 19, 23, 24, 25
code switching, 27, 148, 159n12, 168n33,
    183n1
Cofer, Judith Ortiz, 155n5, 155–156n8
Colón, Jesús, 4–5, 9, 25, 48, 125, 141–
    144, 160n9, 174n19, 182n19, 184n7
Colonia, Sarita, 98

colonialism and post-colonialism,
    91–96, 100, 131, 146–147, 174n17
Colón López, Joaquín, 174n19
communism, 26, 93, 141, 147, 149
Corpi, Lucha, 148
corridos, 4, 5, 9, 26, 29, 51, 55, 80–81, 82,
    96, 164n1, 181n12
costumbristas, 124
Cotto-Thorner, Guillermo, 2, 15, 28,
    54, 69–71, 91–96, 100, 147, 157n10,
    163n27, 168n33, 174nn17,18,19,20
Cowart, David, 12, 13
crónicas and *cronistas*, 4, 15, 16, 30,
    48–49, 66, 111–113, 115, 122, 123–145,
    174n19, 182n18
Cruz, Nicky, 31, 32
Cruz, Sor Juana Inés de la, 114, 121,
    177n14
Cruz, Víctor Hernández, 10, 28
Cruz Blanca, 106
Cuban Revolution, 150–151, 157n2
culture conflict, 8, 9, 23, 29–30, 55, 96,
    125, 127, 144, 147

Danciger, Jack, 160n10
Davidson, Peter, 160n10
Dávila, Virgilio, 59–60
décimas, 8, 9, 26, 51, 59, 80–81
defense of the community, 36–40,
    160n5
DeLillo, Don, 13
DeVito, Lina, 176n3
diasporas, 18, 26, 63, 64, 77, 81, 89,
    109–110, 147, 156n10, 157n2, 169n40,
    183n4
Díaz, Junot, 12, 31
Díaz, Porfirio, 27, 40–41, 87–88, 90,
    100, 103, 110, 111, 171n8
Díaz Guerra, Alirio, 1–3, 5, 6, 9, 14, 31,
    50, 51, 55–57, 61, 81, 101, 159n16,
    164n12, 165n13
Diego Padró, José I. de, 50, 60–62,
    162n3, 163n4, 167nn26,27
discrimination, 3, 8, 24, 25, 33, 40,
    55, 70, 92–93, 95, 126, 147, 168n33,
    174n19

disillusionment, 5, 8, 9, 23, 29, 64, 75, 81
Don Quijote, 33, 81–82
Dorfman, Ariel, 26, 27
doubling, 111, 166n22. *See also* ambivalence

elite culture, 22, 27, 38, 39–44, 48, 73, 83, 86–89, 108, 111–122, 126–133, 162n21
Elizondo, Angelina, 110
Elizondo, Hortensia, 101, 110, 115–116, 177n17
Espinosa, Conrado, 2, 3, 8, 9, 33, 49, 66–68, 80, 81, 82–86, 101
Esteves, Pedro, 47
Esteves, Sandra María, 183n1
Estrada Cabrera, Manuel, 31
Ethnie, 93, 95
Eva (Eve) as a stereotype, 6, 9, 81
exile literature, 18–34, 38, 43–44, 50–51, 88, 110–119, 147–153, 156n10, 158nn6,9, 165n19, 169n40, 173n16, 183n4
exiles, 6, 16, 21, 54–55, 71, 73, 88, 103, 105, 110, 173n16

Falcón, Rafael, 167n26
Farrell, James, 10
Faymonville, Carmen, 11
feminism: anarcho-, 46–47, 106–109; conservative, 15, 102, 110–122, 177n11; militant, 103–109; and nation, 11, 15, 110, 116, 117, 137; radical, 113, 177n14
Fernández, Roberto, 148
Fernández de Lizardi, Joaquín, 124
flâneurs, 61, 124, 125, 137, 144
flappers, 6, 9, 25, 30, 48, 130–131, 133–141
Flores, Juan, 29
Flores Magón, Enrique, 105
Flores Magón, Ricardo, 105
folk literature, 4, 5, 15, 18, 26, 47–48, 55, 59, 79, 82, 96, 127, 155n1, 164n10
Fornet, Ambrosio, 161n18
foundational myths, 81

Franco, Francisco, 26
Franco, Jorge, 65–66, 81
free love, 47, 108, 120
Fuchs, Maura L., 171n8

Gabitofa. *See* O'Farril, Alberto
Galindo, Hermila, 115
Gálvez, Wenceslao, 9, 49–50
García, Cristina, 10, 12, 13, 31, 148, 156n10
García, Richard, 173n16
García Canclini, Nestor, 172n12
García Naranjo, Nemesio, 17, 40–42, 54, 111, 115, 157n2, 169n40, 171n8
Garza, María Luisa, 4, 111–113, 125
Gaspar de Alba, Alicia, 31, 177n14
Gazavic, Quezigno. *See* Vásquez, Ignacio
gender essay, 178n25
gender roles, 8, 15, 16, 31, 46–47, 50, 56, 64, 66, 70–72, 75, 77, 81, 101–145, 152, 153, 155–156n8, 165n13, 171n8, 180n7, 181n14, 182nn19,20
Glick, Nina, 17
globalization, 17, 23, 146
Golden Age, 81, 83–86, 90, 147
Gómez-Peña, Guillermo, 146–147
González, Jovita, 102
González, Leopoldo, 26
González Viaña, Eduardo, 2, 15, 28, 32, 33, 69, 77–79, 81, 96–100, 146, 147, 164n5
greenhorns. See *verdes*
Grossman, Sari, 10
Guadalupe Hidalgo Treaty, 40
Guzmán, Nuño de, 88

Hall, Stuart, 108–109
Hampa, El, 56, 61
Heras, Juan de, 40
Heredia, José María, 27, 29
Hernández, Eleuteria, 132
Hernández Cruz, Victor. *See* Cruz, Victor Hernández
Hernández Tovar, Inés, 176n6
Herrera-Sobek, María, 164n9

heteroglossia, 27
Hijuelos, Oscar, 3, 10, 13, 34, 150
Hinojosa, Rolando, 10, 22, 27, 30, 148, 183n1
homeland (patria), 5, 7–8, 15, 17, 21, 23, 25, 26, 30, 33, 34, 35, 50–51, 52–79, 80–89, 95, 111, 162n21, 166n22, 168nn33,34
hooks, bell, 109
Hostos, José María Eugenio de, 93
hybridity, 15, 23, 27–29, 31, 69–72, 76–77, 83–85, 88–95, 96, 146–153, 159n12, 168n33, 171n5

identity: Afro-, 174n19; American, 12–13, 53, 95; crisis, 23, 31; cultural, 1, 3, 24, 55–56, 63, 68, 70, 76–77, 95, 146–153; Hispanic, 3, 16, 19, 38–39, 48, 56, 149; national, 7, 15, 22, 34, 53–54, 68, 74, 76, 80, 82, 96, 124, 131; sexual, 130–131
imperialism, 146
indigenes, 81, 86–88, 171n7
indigenismo, 86–87, 89
Inferno metaphor, 56, 77–78, 147

Jaramillo, Cleofas, 102
jíbaros, 181n14
Jones Act, 2

Kalra, Virinder S., 157n2, 169n40
Kaskabel. See Padilla, Benjamín
Knippling, Alpana, 10
Kohn, Hans, 85
Kropotkin, Pëtr, 107

Labarthe, Pedro Juan, 175n22
labor and unions, 23, 25–26, 40, 44–47, 103–104, 105, 106–109, 141, 155n3, 161n17
language, 11–13, 18, 22, 27–29, 48, 51, 126–128, 156n9, 159nn11,12, 168n33, 180n7, 183n2, 184n5
"Latinos," 77, 163n4
Laviera, Tato, 27, 28, 30, 183n1
Lawson, Blanche. See Moncaleano, Blanca de

Lawson, John, 176n3
Lazarus, Emma, 56
League of United Latin American Citizens, 160n11
lectores, 45–47, 107, 161n18
León, Daniel De, 26
Librería de Quiroga, 43–44, 112
Liga de Mujeres Ibéricas e Hispanoamericanas, 116–117
Liga Protectora Mexicana de California, 40
Lionza, María, 98
Lirón, 26
Loisaida, 23, 28–29, 168n33
Lomas, Clara, 104, 106
Loreley. See Garza, María Luisa
Lozano, Ignacio E., 38, 41–43, 111, 161n14
Lund, Joshua, 87

Madero, Francisco I., 104, 126
Madrid, Arturo, 163n2
Magnón, Adolfo, 105
Malcriado, El. See Venegas, Daniel
Malinowski, Branislaw, 81
Malverde, San Jesús, 98
Marburg, Caesar, 40
Mariel generation, 32
Marín, Francisco Gonzalo "Pachín," 8, 50, 58
Marqués, René, 2, 3, 9, 24, 63–65, 80–81, 155n1, 163n26
Martí, José, 8, 20, 50, 57–58, 165n13
Martínez, Saturnino, 162n19
Martínez, Tomás Eloy, 26, 27, 32
Marxism, 108
melting pot, 7, 15, 17, 24, 35–36, 52, 72, 94, 96, 179n28
Mercer, Kobena, 159n14
Mesonero Romanos, Ramón de, 124
messianism, 84–86, 88, 173n14
mestizos, 82, 85, 86–87, 171nn6,7
Metropolis, as a theme, 1, 3, 7, 9, 15, 23, 24, 29, 31, 49, 50, 51, 55–79, 81, 84, 91–96, 155n1, 167n26
Mexía, Félix, 32
Mexican Liberal Party, 103–106

Mexican Revolution, 33, 34, 37, 40, 73–76, 88, 103–107, 110, 113, 115–119, 126, 157n2, 173n16
Mexican War, 19
México de Afuera, 22, 25, 28, 30, 40–42, 48, 54, 71, 74, 110–116, 125, 126–127, 137, 151, 158n9, 177nn11,16
minority literature, 100
Miquis Tiquis. *See* Colón, Jesús
modernity, 84, 117, 118, 164n12
Modern Language Association, 10
Mohr, Nicholasa, 13, 31, 33
Moncaleano, Blanca de, 103–104, 176n3
Moncaleano, Juan Francisco, 104, 176n3
Monsiváis, Carlos, 124–125
Morton, Carlos, 27
Moses, 97–98
Mujcinovic, Fatima, 156n10, 172n12
Mujer Mexicana, 111–116, 177n11
Mujer Moderna, 115–116
Mujer Nueva, 177n16
myths of origin, 96–100, 102. *See also* Golden Age

ñangotamiento, 64
nationalism, 4, 7, 8, 11, 12, 15, 16, 17–34, 35, 37, 38–42, 64–68, 70–71, 74, 77, 79, 80–104, 110–145, 146–153, 158n4, 166n22, 171n8, 172n12, 173n16, 181n14
native literature, 19–34, 69, 102, 168n33, 183n1
"new immigrants," 13
newspapers, 36–51
Noloesca, La Chata (Beatriz Escalona), 180n7
nostalgia, 59–60, 64, 71, 75, 78–79, 95, 114, 125, 151
Nuyorican movement, 22–34, 69, 71, 155n1, 168n33

Obregón, Alvaro, 41
Ofa. *See* O'Farrill, Alberto
O'Farrill, Alberto, 4, 25, 48, 125, 137–141, 144, 163n24, 184n7
Oliver-Rotger, María Antonia, 147
O'Neill, Gustavo, 181n14

Ong, Walter, 26
orality, 1, 4, 8, 26, 48
oral lore. *See* folk literature
Ortega y Gassett, José, 172n11

Pachucos, 23, 30, 163n2
Padilla, Benjamín, 4, 125
Padilla, Heberto, 26, 153
Pan American Conference on Women, 116
Pan American Round Table, 113
Pan-Hispanism, 18, 20, 38, 120, 137
Paradise Lost, 23, 29
Paredes, Américo, 29, 55, 163n2, 164n10
Park, Robert, 35–36, 124
Partido Liberal Mexicano. *See* Mexican Liberal Party
patria. See homeland
Payant, Katherine, 10–11, 12, 155n7
Paz, Octavio, 163n2
pelonas. See flappers
Pereda, Prudencio de, 33
Pérez, Emma, 103–104
Pérez, Héctor, 171n8
Pérez, Ramón "Tianguis," 68
Pérez Firmat, Gustavo, 16, 27, 29, 147–153, 155n3, 158n6, 183nn1,2,4, 184n5
Perón, Evita, 26
picaresque characters (*pícaros*), 23, 33, 48, 56, 61, 82, 144
Pietri, Pedro, 10
Pilar Sinués, María del, 44
Piña, Joaquín, 44
Pineda, Luziris, 112–113, 177n12
Pinochet, Augusto, 26
pitiyanquis, 4, 9, 23, 80, 125, 168n33
Plaza, Antonio, 44
pocho, 4, 23, 30, 53, 68, 72, 80, 163n2, 168n33
Poyo, Gerald, 158n5
Pratt, Mary Louise, 178n25
Protestant conversion narratives, 32
Protestants, 32, 48, 69, 93–95, 119, 125, 174n17
protest literature, 23, 24, 79, 82, 99
Publishers, 36–51, 101, 111–113, 124,

145, 157n2, 159n11, 160n10, 161n15, 162nn19,21
Puerto Ricans as immigrants, 2
Puherepechas, 86

Quesada, Roberto, 2, 32, 182n20
Quiroga, Vasco de, 86

racialization, 23, 53–54, 168n33, 171nn5,6
racism, 3, 5, 8, 23, 31, 35, 50, 67, 75, 82, 87, 120, 132, 174n19
Ramírez, Francisco, 10, 20, 22
Ramírez, Sara Estela, 103, 105, 110
Recovering U. S. Hispanic Literary Heritage, 18, 106, 156n1
refugees, 19–21, 37–40, 49–51, 72–74, 110–119, 126, 144–145, 156n10
religion, 24–25, 44, 104, 119, 121–122
renegado, 4, 9, 28, 30, 53, 111, 125, 136, 168n33
return to the homeland, 3, 8, 15, 21, 22, 23, 24, 30, 32, 40, 52–79, 80–89, 147, 150–152, 166n22
Riis, Jacob, 10
Ríos, Alberto, 10
Rivera, Edward, 148, 150
Rivera, Tomás, 10, 31
Rodríguez, José Policarpo, 32
Rodríguez, Netty and Jesús, 26, 180n7
Rodriguez, Richard, 10, 33, 148, 150, 153
Rose, Toby, 10–11, 12, 155n7
Roth, Henry, 10
Roth, Philip, 10
Ruiz, Viki, 181n12
Ruiz de Burton, María Amparo, 102

Sabina, María, 98
"Samurai," 48
Sánchez González, Lisa, 109
Sánchez Korrol, Virginia, 178n22
Santa Bárbara, 98
Santa Muerte, 98
Santiago, Esmeralda, 3
Schur, Joan, 10

segregation, 43
Seguín, Juan Nepomuceno, 32
Sellén, Francisco, 31
Sinclair, Upton, 12
slavery, 4, 24, 47, 61, 82, 84, 104, 121, 142–144
Smith, Anthony, 15, 87–88, 93, 173n16
social classes, 31, 47, 75–76, 82, 104, 107–108, 112, 128, 130–133, 173n16
socialism, 26, 107
Sodom and Gomorrah, 4, 9, 55–56, 91
Solano, Gustavo, 31
Souhuesera, 168n33
Spanish Black Legend, 32
Spanish Civil War, 33
Statue of Liberty, 6, 56, 159n16
Steele, Richard, 124
Stowe, Harriet Beecher, 44
Suárez, Virgil, 31

theater, 43, 47
Thomas, Piri, 10, 13, 31, 33, 148
Tiquis Miquis. See Colón, Jesús
Torres, Teodoro, 15, 28, 30, 41–42, 50, 69, 71–77, 81, 86–91, 96, 100, 101, 111, 147, 157n2, 169nn38,40, 171n8, 172nn11,14,15
Torres-Saillant, Silvio, 157n2, 158n6, 183n4
transmigrants, 17–34
transnationalism, 17–34, 146, 183n4
"tropics in Manhattan," 28

Ulica, Jorge. See Arce, Julio G.
Unión, Progreso y Caridad, 105
utopias, 15, 30, 50–51, 73–74, 76, 87–91, 96, 100, 108–109, 147, 173n16

Valdez, Luis, 10, 26, 27, 30, 183n1
Valle-Inclán, Ramón del, 182n18
Varela, Félix, 27, 32
Vasconcelos, José, 173n14
Vásquez, Ignacio G., 66, 134–137, 182n20
vaudeville, 4, 6, 8, 26, 27, 43, 48, 180n7
vendidos, 23, 30

Venegas, Daniel, 2, 4, 5, 6, 8, 9, 26–27,
    33, 39, 44, 50, 51, 52, 58, 64, 80, 81,
    101, 126, 133–135
Vera-Rojas, María Teresa, 119–122,
    178n25
verdes, 2, 3, 8, 23, 30–31, 48, 57–58, 82,
    127, 136–137
Vigil, Evangelina, 27
Villa, Pancho, 172n10
Villarreal, Andrea, 26, 103–104, 105, 119
Villarreal, José Antonio, 33
Villarreal, Teresa, 26, 103–104, 105, 119
Villarroel, Carolina, 117–118, 177n17
Villaseñor, Victor, 3, 48
Villegas de Magnón, Leonor, 103,
    105–106
Viola, P., 44
Viola Novelty Company, 43
Viramontes, Helena María, 155–156n8,
    156n10

Walker, Lara, 108
Warren, Nina Otero, 102
Wegner, Phillip, 90
White, Paul, 1, 52, 155n2, 166n22
Whitt Publishing, 43, 161n15
women's depiction, 4, 6, 9, 16, 64,
    123–145
women's liberation, 72, 104, 107, 115–
    122, 131, 137, 160n8, 177nn11,15
working-class culture, 3, 7, 8, 13, 23, 26,
    38–40, 44–51, 54, 58, 63, 64, 73–74,
    81, 102, 106–108, 127, 160n8, 162n16
Wright, Richard, 10

Young, Robert J. C., 87, 171n5, 173n14
Yuval-Davis, Nira, 131, 132, 180n6

Zieler, Wendy, 11

Ingram Content Group UK Ltd.
Milton Keynes UK
UKHW040439170723
425189UK00016B/231